改訂版

やっておきたい

英語長文

300

［問題編］

河合塾講師

杉山 俊一
塚越 友幸
山下 博子

［共著］

河合出版

河合塾
SERIES

改訂版

やっておきたい

英語長文

300

[問題編]

河合塾講師

杉山 俊一
塚越 友幸
山下 博子

［共著］

河合出版

15 min.
216 words

次の英文を読んで，設問に答えなさい。

An instinctive behavior is inherited: you're born with it. In (1), a learned behavior is developed from experience. Although humans and some animals (2a)do inherit an instinct to learn, the content of their learning is determined by their
5 experience.

Instinctive behavior does not change; it stays the same even when circumstances change. Birds migrate in the winter months even when the weather stays warm. But learned behavior is more (3). Humans don't *hibernate in winter, and most
10 humans don't change where they live seasonally. Instead, they have learned to dress warmly and heat their houses. Humans are very adaptable. Generally (4)we don't wait for evolution to change our responses to the environment; instead, learned behavior enables us to respond quickly to changing circumstances.
15 To learn from an experience, an organism must have a memory to store information to be used later. Memory helps an organism learn through trial and error. In trial-and-error learning, an organism tries to (2b)do a task again and again, sometimes making mistakes, but other times succeeding. (5)Eventually the
20 organism figures out what it did to succeed. A mouse will learn how to get through a maze to find food at the end by trying different routes again and again. The mouse eventually remembers which routes don't lead to food and which (2c)do.

（注）　hibernate：冬眠する，冬ごもりする

（東北学院大）

問1　空所(1)に入れるのに最も適当なものを，次のア～エから1つ選びなさい。

ア．fact　　　　イ．contrast　　　ウ．particular　　　エ．short

問2　下線部(2a)～(2c)と同じ用法の do を含む文を，次のア～エからそれぞれ1つずつ選びなさい。

ア．Do you ever go to the movies?

イ．I seldom eat sweets but my children often do.

ウ．I do talk a lot, but my wife talks even more.

エ．I have a lot of homework to do tonight.

問3　空所(3)に入れるのに最も適当なものを，次のア～エから1つ選びなさい。

ア．active　　　　イ．admirable　　　ウ．flexible　　　　エ．fundamental

問4　下線部(4)の内容として最も適当なものを，次のア～エから1つ選びなさい。

ア．状況の変化が速すぎて人間が対応できないため，人間は進化に取り残されている。

イ．進化を待っていても，進化が人間の環境への対応を変えさせることはない。

ウ．人間が進化を待たなくても，進化は人間の進化への対応を変えてしまうことがある。

エ．進化は時間がかかるので，人間は本能的な行動以外の方法で環境の変化に対応する必要がある。

問5　下線部(5)を日本語に訳しなさい。

2

15 min.
219 words

次の英文を読んで，設問に答えなさい。

The term "information overload," which refers to the problem of having too much information, is not new. These days, however, as more and more information is available thanks to new technologies, it is becoming more problematic than ever
5 before.

The first person to popularize the term was writer Alvin Toffler. (1)He mentioned it in a book published in 1970 and described that a person can have difficulty making a decision when there is too much information. One example can be seen
10 at supermarkets, where shoppers might have a hard time deciding which type of salad dressing or cereal to buy when there are (2) choices.

A bigger and more complex problem than choosing a product is the enormous amount of information available on the Internet.
15 Recent research points out that this flood of information — and its interruption of people's work — has (3)adverse effects on people's health and happiness as well as their decision-making abilities and their productivity. When people become too dependent on information, feelings of helplessness, confusion and
20 anger may increase.

Of course, having access to information is not a bad thing. The issue is rather our ability to select information and then to use it in effective ways. A key challenge for people in the 21st century is (4)[being controlled / by / controlling / information / it /
25 rather than].

(獨協大)

4

問1　下線部⑴を日本語に訳しなさい。

問2　空所(2)に入れるのに最も適当なものを，次のア～エから1つ選びなさい。

　　ア．dozens of 　　　　　　　　イ．a few

　　ウ．a small number of 　　　　エ．not any

問3　下線部⑶とほぼ同じ意味を表すものを，次のア～エから1つ選びなさい。

　　ア．beneficial 　　イ．powerful 　　ウ．negative 　　エ．various

問4　下線部⑷の語(句)を文意が通るように並べ換えなさい。

問5　本文の内容と一致するものを，次のア～エから1つ選びなさい。

　　ア．情報が多すぎると仕事の生産性が低下する場合がある。

　　イ．意思決定能力は情報を選別することによって高められる。

　　ウ．情報量を減らさなければ情報過多の問題は解決しない。

　　エ．できるだけ多くの人が情報を利用できるようにする必要がある。

3

20 min.
301 words

次の英文を読んで，設問に答えなさい。

While it is exciting to see new sights, to hear a different language and to eat different foods in a foreign country, sometimes the sudden change can make people uncomfortable. People may get homesick and (1) their families, friends and
5 the comfort of their home. This is known as culture shock.

When you first arrive in a new country, there is a lot to do and see, and it all seems very exciting. After a few weeks or months, however, people often begin to miss their old home. (2)There may be many difficulties that they don't know how to
10 deal with. As a result, they may start to spend time only with others from their own country, or refuse to eat the food from the new country. Sometimes, (3)[do / they / is / all / to / want] to complain about how bad things are, and they begin to dislike the country and the people there. This is a difficult time but such
15 feelings are a natural part of (4a)getting used to a new country.

Sometimes culture shock becomes serious and turns into a real sickness such as depression. A depressed person might have trouble sleeping or might sleep all the time and have no energy. They might stop eating and lose weight, or eat too much and
20 gain weight. People (4b)suffering from depression might even think about killing themselves. If this happens, it is time for them to see a doctor. (5)Feeling sad and homesick is very common but wishing to be dead is very serious. Most universities have international student offices and health centers on campus, with
25 trained staff who can help students to get over these "bad times". People shouldn't be afraid to go to talk to someone

6

about their problems. Sometimes a friendly chat is all that is needed to help.

（札幌学院大）

問1　空所（　1　）に入れるのに最も適当な1語を，本文中から探して答えなさい。

問2　下線部(2)を日本語に訳しなさい。

問3　下線部(3)の語を文意が通るように並べ換えなさい。

問4　下線部(4a)(4b)と同じ用法を含む文を，次のア～エからそれぞれ1つずつ選びなさい。

　　ア．He admitted telling a lie to her.

　　イ．I heard several people shouting on the street.

　　ウ．I talked to the man lying on the bench.

　　エ．It being Sunday, the park was crowded with people.

問5　下線部(5)を日本語に訳しなさい。

問6　次の質問について，答えとして最も適当なものを，次のア～エからそれぞれ1つずつ選びなさい。

　1．Why do people feel excited when they first arrive in a foreign country?

　　ア．A lot of things remind them of their home country.

　　イ．They can have new experiences.

　　ウ．They can talk about anything in a foreign language.

　　エ．They know a lot about the foreign country.

　2．Why do some people feel uncomfortable in a foreign country?

　　ア．They don't have any friends to talk with.

　　イ．They don't want to go out to eat the local dishes.

　　ウ．They'd like to go to another country.

　　エ．They cannot get used to the country.

　3．What happens when culture shock becomes serious?

　　ア．Some people would like to come out of the hospital.

　　イ．Some people find it difficult to sleep.

　　ウ．There are some people who don't want to go back to their own country.

エ. No one wants to meet people from their own country.

4

次の英文を読んで，設問に答えなさい。

Considerable attention has been paid to the size or relative size of the human brain. The first point of interest is that (1)the ratio of brain weight to body is at a maximum at birth and decreases with age, reaching a fairly steady level by maturity. In other words, newborn babies have very large brains, relatively speaking, 5 weighing some 300 grams. This is roughly the size of the brain of an adult male chimpanzee. Children and their brains continue to grow for many years, gradually increasing their ability to learn and remember. There have been suggestions that the growth of the brains of children is not steady, but occurs suddenly, each 10 period of rapid growth (2) associated with a particularly important developmental or intellectual stage. These stages could be the ability to reason abstractly, to talk, or even to do arithmetic. The idea of sudden brain growth is still around, but has not attracted much enthusiasm. 15

Some research has shown differences in the relative sizes of the brains of males and females of the same age, but so far no great differences have been found between people of the same age but of different ethnic groups. Obviously the brain of a small Japanese teenager is very much smaller than that of a 20 giant Russian boy. But when brain size is adjusted for size or weight of the body, there (3) great advantage for either with respect to intelligence. Moreover, in measuring intelligence one has, of course, to (4)take into account the effects of education and cultural background. 25

Individual brain sizes, particularly of famous people, have also attracted attention, but with very few real results. The brain of Albert Einstein, an intellectual giant of the twentieth century, has intrigued many people. (5)It is said to have been relatively large, and parts of it, lovingly preserved by an admirer, were recently discovered in the USA. It was suggested that his genius might have been due to the size or number of brain cells. However, on closer examination, there was actually very little difference between the brain cells of Einstein and those of other people.

(David Samuel, *Memory: How We Use It, Lose It and Can Improve it*, New York University Press)

(法政大)

問1　下線部(1)を日本語に訳しなさい。

問2　空所(　2　)に入れるのに最も適当なものを，次のア～エから1つ選びなさい。

　　　ア．is　　　　　　イ．has　　　　　ウ．being　　　　エ．having

問3　空所(　3　)に入れるのに最も適当なものを，次のア～エから1つ選びなさい。

　　　ア．seems to be　　　　　　　イ．does not seem to be

　　　ウ．seems to have　　　　　　エ．does not seem to have

問4　下線部(4)とほぼ同じ意味を表すものを，次のア～エから1つ選びなさい。

　　　ア．consider　　イ．ignore　　　ウ．exclude　　　エ．produce

問5　下線部(5)を日本語に訳しなさい。

問6　本文の内容と一致するものを，次のア～エから1つ選びなさい。

　　　ア．Many scientists are attracted by the fact that the growth of children's brains occurs irregularly.

　　　イ．A great deal of research has proved that intelligence has something to do with brain size.

　　　ウ．There is a general impression that the brains of Japanese people are comparatively large.

　　　エ．Some admirers of Einstein believed that his genius could be explained by the size or number of brain cells.

次の英文を読んで，設問に答えなさい。

Reading, like playing an instrument, is a complex skill that is not learned *all at once.* It ₍₁₎[achieve / takes / many years / to / most people] a skillful performance. And like piano playing there are wide variations among individuals exposed to the same amount of practice. ₍₂₎Some may achieve only in two or four years a level of proficiency that others may reach in eight or more, or perhaps never.

What do we mean by reading? More specifically, what is the essential reading skill?

The essential skill in reading is getting meaning from a printed or written message. Thus, reading and listening have much in common, (3) language being the common component of both. There are some differences between reading and understanding spoken messages. The written message does not have the intonation, stress, and emphasis of the spoken message. But the written message has punctuation and other conventions of print to tell the reader when to pause, and what to emphasize.

Of course, reading is much more than getting the literal meaning of the message itself — although even ₍₄₎this is quite an accomplishment, when we stop to think about it. For as John B. Carroll so aptly put it, to get the literal meaning of a verbal message means that we have not only recognized the words themselves, but have interpreted them "in their particular grammatical functions...." Moreover, each sentence has been interpreted ₍₅₎semantically; that is to say, we have given the proper meaning to each of the key words in the sentence.

And (6)<u>mature reading</u> implies even more than getting the literal meaning. It means evaluating the ideas for truth, validity, or importance. We do this by checking them against our own experience or knowledge. We think of the implications for future actions. And we may make inferences or draw conclusions that go far beyond what is explicitly stated in the text. When this is done, we are really engaging in "reasoning" or "thinking." And indeed, to read at the highest level of maturity means thinking and reasoning, and having an advanced command of language, concept, and experience.

(Used with permission of Hachette Books Group, from Learning to Read, Jeanne Chall, in *Communication, Language, and Meaning: Psychological Perspectives*, George A. Miller, ed., 1973; permission conveyed through Copyright Clearance Center, Inc.)

(徳島大)

問1　下線部(1)の語(句)を文意が通るように並べ換えなさい。

問2　下線部(2)を日本語に訳しなさい。

問3　空所(　3　)に入れるのに最も適当なものを，次のア～エから１つ選びなさい。

　　ア．by　　　　　イ．in　　　　　ウ．for　　　　　エ．with

問4　下線部(4)の内容として最も適当なものを，次のア～エから１つ選びなさい。

　　ア．reading is much more than getting the literal meaning of the message itself

　　イ．getting the literal meaning of the message itself

　　ウ．the literal meaning of the message itself

　　エ．the message itself

問5　下線部(5)の意味として最も適当なものを，次のア～エから１つ選びなさい。

　　ア．according to grammar

　　イ．in terms of meaning

ウ．in a different way

エ．in our favor

問 6　下線部(6)の説明として本文中に<u>述べられていない</u>ものを，次のア〜エから 1 つ選びなさい。

ア．It means getting the literal meaning.

イ．It means evaluating writer's ideas in light of ours.

ウ．It means reading between the lines.

エ．It means engaging in reasoning.

次の英文を読んで，設問に答えなさい。

One evening, hearing six-year-old Justin scream, I ran down the hall in the direction of the cry. I found my other son Julian — two years older and stronger — grinning outside the bathroom door while his brother continued to cry from within. Suddenly
5 angry, (1) that he must have done something awful to his brother, I shoved Julian away from the door so hard that he fell, his head grazing a nearby wall.

I flung open the bathroom door, expecting to see blood everywhere, but Justin seemed fine. He announced, "(2)"
10 I'm a psychologist, supposed to know how to handle people, especially little ones. Yet I had lost control of myself and nearly injured my child over a silly, harmless *prank, one that I had played a dozen times myself as a boy. I felt terrible about (3)it.

Our children make us angry sometimes. They get lazy, they
15 make mistakes, they do silly, mischievous or thoughtless things. But when we adults react without thinking, when we shout or strike, we usually accomplish little. And rightly so: we exhibit (4)the very behavior we're trying to discourage.

Children do need discipline, but how can we get them to do
20 the right thing without losing the calm, adult dignity that they need to witness in us?

(5)One of the most powerful ways children learn what to do and what not to do is by watching you. As you "model" various behaviors, sooner or later your children will imitate you. If you
25 shout to get your way, you can expect your children to do the same. If you watch television instead of doing the dishes, your

child will likely (　6　) a homework assignment.

And take a few deep breaths yourself! It's hard to think clearly when you're angry. You might forget every sensible thing you know about child-rearing. (7)<u>In the end, one of the best</u> ³⁰ <u>ways to become a better parent is to learn better ways of</u> <u>handling your own stress.</u>

（注）　prank：いたずら

（信州大）

問1　空所(　1　)に入れるのに最も適当なものを，次のア～エから1つ選び なさい。
　　ア．think　　　　イ．to think　　　ウ．thinking　　　エ．thought
問2　空所(　2　)に入れるのに最も適当なものを，次のア～エから1つ選び なさい。
　　ア．Oh, the lights went out!
　　イ．Daddy, Julian wounded me with a knife!
　　ウ．Ah, I cut my finger with a knife!
　　エ．Daddy, Julian turned the light off on me!
問3　下線部(3)の内容を50字以内の日本語で述べなさい。
問4　下線部(4)の意味として最も適当なものを，次のア～エから1つ選びなさ い。
　　ア．子供が大人にしてほしくないと思っている行動。
　　イ．子供が大人にしてほしいと思っている行動。
　　ウ．大人が自分の子供たちに見習ってほしくないと考えている行動。
　　エ．大人が自分の子供たちに見習ってほしいと考えている行動。
問5　下線部(5)を日本語に訳しなさい。
問6　空所(　6　)に入れるのに最も適当なものを，次のア～エから1つ選び なさい。
　　ア．deal with　　イ．put off　　　ウ．carry out　　エ．look into
問7　下線部(7)を日本語に訳しなさい。

7

次の英文を読んで，設問に答えなさい。

Waiting patiently is hard to do, even for grown-ups. (1)We develop patience, or at least learn to hide our impatience, because we know that it is socially unacceptable to do otherwise. For small children, waiting is especially difficult. They don't care yet about 5 what others think, so they express their impatience openly. (2)In addition, their limited comprehension of time makes it difficult for them to estimate how long they will have to wait for something. "How much longer?" "Can we go now?" "Are we there yet?" "When is it time?" These are questions that reveal how difficult 10 it is for small children not only to wait, but to understand the general framework of time passing.

Everyday life provides an abundance of opportunities to teach our children how to wait patiently. "(3)" a child cries impatiently. As we're preparing his food, we can explain to him 15 that the pasta needs to be cooked, the vegetables need to be cut, the orange must be peeled first. "I want an ice cube!" another child demands. By showing her the ice tray and explaining that it (4) time for the water to change into ice cubes, we help her understand why she has to wait, and give 20 her a science lesson at the same time. We can listen when our children express their impatience, and let them know we understand how hard it can be to wait, while explaining that some things take time, and that we need to learn to be (5) while the necessary steps are being taken.

25 Waiting in line at the grocery store or going on long car rides are particularly challenging situations for kids. But these times

too can provide them with valuable lessons in learning how to wait. We can help by showing them ways to make the time pass (6)agreeably: waiting in line may present an opportunity to chat about school or a recent activity that we haven't yet had a 30 chance to discuss. Car rides can be made much more pleasant when we bring or make up games to play along the way. Even very young children can pass the time more happily when they have something interesting to do: for example, counting all the trucks, red cars, or white houses they see. 35

(From *Children Learn What They Live* by Harris, Rachel, copyright © 1998. Reprinted by permission of Workman Adult, an imprint of Hachette Book Group, Inc.)

(東京学芸大)

問1　下線部(1)を日本語に訳しなさい。

問2　下線部(2)を日本語に訳しなさい。

問3　空所(　3　)に入れるのに最も適当なものを，次のア～エから1つ選びなさい。

　　ア．I'm tired out!

　　イ．I'm hungry!

　　ウ．I'd like to play video games!

　　エ．I want to watch the program!

問4　空所(　4　)に入れるのに最も適当なものを，次のア～エから1つ選びなさい。

　　ア．makes　　　イ．takes　　　ウ．gets　　　エ．saves

問5　空所(　5　)に入れるのに最も適当なものを，次のア～エから1つ選びなさい。

　　ア．imaginative　イ．honest　　ウ．patient　　エ．greedy

問6　下線部(6)とほぼ同じ意味を表すものを，次のア～エから1つ選びなさい。

　　ア．gently　　　イ．carelessly　ウ．thoughtfully　エ．pleasantly

次の英文を読んで，設問に答えなさい。

According to a recent study using computer simulations, another invasive *asteroid was identified. Unlike Oumuamua, the cigar-shaped rock (1a)that cruised through the inner solar system and right back out toward *interstellar space last winter, however, 5 this asteroid has taken up permanent residence among us.

The asteroid, known as 2015 BZ509 — "BZ" for short — was discovered in 2014 sharing orbital space with Jupiter and making a circuit of the sun about every 11.6 years. But it goes around the sun in the opposite direction of Jupiter and the other planets. 10 (2)The only reason why it can avoid crashing into Jupiter is that its orbit is egg-shaped, and so the rock slips inside and then outside of the giant planet's orbit as it goes around. Fathi Namouni, of the Observatoire de la Côte d'Azur in France, and his colleague Helena Morais, of the Universidade Estadual 15 Paulista in Brazil, were trying to figure out how the asteroid got (1b)that way.

Their curiosity was heightened by the additional discovery (1c)that the planet and asteroid are locked together in an orbital and gravitational *resonance: The asteroid completes an orbit in 20 the same time it takes Jupiter, and so the pair would regularly pull on each other. That meant the asteroid's orbit should be (3).

"But at the beginning of this investigation, we did not suspect BZ to be of interstellar origin," Dr. Namouni said. "(4)We 25 developed a new method that allows us to follow the asteroid back in time to see which part of the solar system it came from."

But as far back as they could trace the solar system — all the way to its birth, 4.5 billion years ago — BZ kept going around the same wrong way. That meant the asteroid could not have been part of the *swirling cloud of dust and gas from which the sun and planets originally condensed so long ago. In other words, it is (5) to our solar system. The results, they say, suggest (1d)<u>that</u> there are plenty more "extra-solar" immigrants out there.

(注) asteroid：小惑星　　interstellar：恒星間の　　resonance：共鳴
　　　 swirling：渦巻く

(© The New York Times. Distributed by The New York Times Licensing Group.)

（名古屋工業大）

問1　下線部(1a)～(1d)と同じ用法の that を含む文を，次のア～エからそれぞれ1つずつ選びなさい。

　ア．I can't find the letter that came yesterday.

　イ．We live in a beautiful city and we hope it stays that way.

　ウ．No one told me that he had been ill.

　エ．The fact that she lied made him angry.

問2　下線部(2)を日本語に訳しなさい。

問3　空所(3)に入れるのに最も適当なものを，次のア～エから1つ選びなさい。

　ア．circular　　イ．stable　　　ウ．widened　　エ．disturbed

問4　下線部(4)を日本語に訳しなさい。

問5　空所(5)に入れるのに最も適当なものを，次のア～エから1つ選びなさい。

　ア．a relative　　イ．a native　　ウ．an enemy　　エ．an outsider

問6　英文のタイトルとして最も適当なものを，次のア～エから1つ選びなさい。

　ア．Astronomers Discover New Asteroid Orbiting Jupiter

　イ．Research Shows Asteroid Came from Outside Our Solar System

ウ．Age of Solar System Now Estimated at 4.5 Billion Years

エ．Scientists Show That Solar System Is Older than Asteroid

次の英文を読んで，設問に答えなさい。

Lies are fascinating because there are so many possibilities for invention and elaboration. In a liar's mouth, facts are no longer boring and predictable, but interesting and surprising. (1)The sense of unlimited possibility is what lies have in common with another *vice that most people find irresistible: gossip. Gossip is 5 interesting because what we hear and pass on to others may be (2a), but it could also be a wild fantasy; we are captivated by the very uncertainty of what we hear.

In spite of the proverb, (2b) is seldom as strange or interesting as fiction. Most of us don't want to know (3)the 10 painful facts about other people's lives. I often feel burdened when friends confide in me about their marriage problems, childhood traumas, or job dissatisfactions. Even though I try my best to console and reassure, I can't help wishing my friends (4) someone else. 15

Gossip is entirely different. There is nothing virtuous about engaging in gossip, but we (5) it to the utmost. When someone tells us vague rumors about someone else's marriage problems, childhood secrets, or job scandals, our ears prick up. When the same information is told to us in confidence, we feel a 20 sinking sense of duty. We listen silently and carefully, trying to think of the few right words to say and maybe getting a headache in the process. When the information is passed on to us as gossip, we jump into the conversation with pleasure: nobody knows (2c) anyway, so we are free to offer our own 25 theories and interpretations. We can talk all we want.

（注）　vice：悪い行い

〈Kyoko Mori, *Polite Lies: On Being a Woman Caught between Cultures*, Henry Holt and Company〉

〔京都府立大〕

問1　下線部(1)を日本語に訳しなさい。

問2　空所（　2a　）～（　2c　）に共通して入るものを，次のア～エから1つ選びなさい。

　　ア．a lie　　　　　イ．the truth　　　ウ．gossip　　　　エ．a rumor

問3　下線部(3)の例として本文に述べられているものを3つ日本語で簡潔に答えなさい。

問4　空所（　4　）に入れるのに最も適当なものを，次のア～エから1つ選びなさい。

　　ア．tell　　　　　イ．told　　　　　ウ．had told　　　エ．will tell

問5　空所（　5　）に入れるのに最も適当なものを，次のア～エから1つ選びなさい。

　　ア．hate　　　　　イ．ignore　　　　ウ．believe　　　　エ．enjoy

次の英文を読んで，設問に答えなさい。

You may have heard that chimpanzees and dolphins are among the world's most intelligent creatures. (1)But recent discoveries have convinced scientists that many of the world's farm animals are smarter than we thought. Take sheep, for example. Scientists at the Babraham Institute in Cambridge, England, report that sheep are good at remembering faces. In a study of sheep's memories, they found that the woolly creatures can remember 10 human faces for more than two years. Of course, (2)[find / their own / memorable / sheep / even more / species]. They can remember 50 different sheep faces! Pigs are clever too, especially when food is involved. Researchers in Bristol, England, found that one pig would follow another to the food pan and then take his food! Pigs quickly learn to trick the clever pigs who are out to steal their dinner.

Other research has suggested that some animals even practice various forms of group decision making, as the following example illustrates: The African Buffaloes had agreed that it was time to head east. The decision was made quietly. Several members of the herd simply stared into the distance, and the whole group took off in that direction.

(3)The buffaloes' behavior has got the science-world talking. Last month, researchers announced in Nature magazine that they have learned how some animals make decisions — they vote! The study, by Larissa Conradt and Tim Roper of the University of Sussex in England, could change (4)the way people view animal behavior. "Most groups of animals have a dominant leader," says

23

Roper. People had assumed that the leader makes decisions and the group follows. This study suggests that the animal kingdom is more of a (5).

30 So, how do animals vote? It depends on the animal. Roper and Conradt observed *red deer in Scotland and surveyed other animal behavior studies to find other examples. Red deer move when more than 60% of the adults stand up. African buffaloes will travel in the direction that the adult females are looking. 35 *Whooper swans decide when to fly with head movements, and bees dance to get the other bees going. Does all of this sound simple? It is. As Roper says, "Democratic decision-making needn't be a complicated business."

(注) red deer：アカシカ　　whooper swan：オオハクチョウ

（西南学院大）

問1　下線部(1)を日本語に訳しなさい。

問2　下線部(2)の語（句）を文意が通るように並べ換えなさい。

問3　下線部(3)の内容を40字以内の日本語で説明しなさい。

問4　下線部(4)とほぼ同じ意味を表すものを，次のア～エから1つ選びなさい。

　　ア．the road where people watch animals move

　　イ．why people behave like animals

　　ウ．how people enjoy viewing animal behavior

　　エ．how people see the behavior of animals

問5　空所(5)に入れるのに最も適当なものを，次のア～エから1つ選びなさい。

　　ア．aristocracy　　イ．democracy　　ウ．monarchy　　エ．tyranny

問6　本文の内容と一致するものを，次のア～オから2つ選びなさい。

　　ア．Many farm animals have been discovered to be more intelligent than chimpanzees and dolphins.

　　イ．African buffaloes hold elections to choose their dominant leader.

24

ウ．Pigs have been observed stealing food from other pigs.

エ．Whooper swans shake their heads when they don't want to fly.

オ．If about two-thirds of the adults in a group of red deer stand up, the herd will begin to move.

11

次の英文を読んで，設問に答えなさい。

People have traveled ever since they first appeared on the earth.

In primitive times they did not travel for pleasure but to find new places (1a) their herds could feed, or to escape from
5 _(2a)hostile neighbors, or to find more favorable climates. They traveled on foot. Their journeys were long, tiring, and often dangerous. They protected themselves with simple weapons, such as wooden sticks or stone clubs, and by lighting fires at night and, above all, by keeping together.

10 Being intelligent and creative, they soon discovered easier ways of traveling. They rode on the backs of their _(2b)domesticated animals; they hollowed out tree trunks and, by using bits of wood as paddles, were able to travel across water.

₍₃₎Later they traveled, not from necessity, but for the joy and
15 excitement of seeing and experiencing new things. This is still the main reason (1b) we travel today.

Traveling, of course, has now become a highly organized business. There are cars and splendid highways, express trains, huge ships and jet airplanes, and all of them provide us with
20 comforts and security. This sounds wonderful. But there are difficulties. If you want to go abroad, you need a passport and visa, tickets, luggage, and a hundred and one other things. If you lose any of them, your journey may be ruined.

As for myself, I prefer doing my traveling from an armchair. I
25 like imagining ₍₄₎all those journeys that, despite human creativeness, one has never made and will never make. I like to think, for

example, that I have arrived in the world by *stork. I like to travel faster than time and have a look at the future, or go back into the past and talk to famous people. I also like to travel like a shell across ocean floors where I can explore the wrecks 30 of ships and see curious fish that people never have seen.

（注）　stork：コウノトリ

（聖心女子大）

問1　空所（　1a　）（　1b　）に入れるのに最も適当なものを，次のア～エから
　　それぞれ1つずつ選びなさい。
　　　ア．how　　　　　イ．when　　　　ウ．where　　　エ．why
問2　下線部(2a)(2b)とほぼ同じ意味を表すものを，それぞれア～エから1つ
　　ずつ選びなさい。
　　　(2a)　ア．aggressive　イ．friendly　ウ．sophisticated　エ．fundamental
　　　(2b)　ア．insecure　　イ．tamed　　ウ．threatening　　エ．wild
問3　下線部(3)を日本語に訳しなさい。
問4　下線部(4)の内容として本文中で<u>述べられていない</u>ものを，次のア～エか
　　ら1つ選びなさい。
　　　ア．時間より速く進んで，未来を見に行く旅。
　　　イ．宇宙に行って，宇宙人と出会う旅。
　　　ウ．過去にさかのぼって有名人と話をする旅。
　　　エ．貝になって海底をさまよう旅。
問5　本文の内容と一致するものを，次のア～エから1つ選びなさい。
　　　ア．In olden days when people traveled on foot, they carried wooden
　　　　sticks or stone clubs to play games with on the way.
　　　イ．Primitive people used hollowed-out tree trunks and bits of wood to
　　　　travel across water.
　　　ウ．The author prefers to travel by plane or car rather than to travel
　　　　by train or ship.
　　　エ．The author doesn't think it is a serious problem if you lose your
　　　　passport or visa when traveling abroad.

12

次の英文を読んで，設問に答えなさい。

There are many reasons for nations to declare an official language. Many developing nations have so (1)[spoken / that / within / their borders / many languages] they must pick one to be the official language to avoid dealing with five, ten, or more
5 languages on an official level. Some countries declare an *indigenous language to be official in order to (2) the language's heritage. A world language such as English or French is often chosen as the official language of a developing country, (3) it may not be the native language of any of
10 the people in that country. (4)Making a world language official in a country makes it easier for that country to participate in the world economy.

However, there are some people who fear that making a world language like English an official language can have serious
15 effects, both politically and socially. On the political side, they claim that making English the official language sets a *precedent of placing English above all other languages. This opens the door for laws abolishing bilingual *ballots, (5)which is likely to prevent citizens who are not comfortable with English from
20 participating in the political process. On the social side, opponents of official English argue that making English the official language *degrades all non-English languages and (6)gives people the feeling that their prejudices are justified.

（注）　indigenous：（ある土地に）固有の　　precedent：前例
　　　　ballot：投票用紙　　degrade：地位を下げる

28

(*Language Files*, Ohio State University Press)

問1　下線部⑴の語（句）を文意が通るように並べ換えなさい。

問2　空所(　2　)に入れるのに最も適当なものを，次のア～エから1つ選び
なさい。

　　ア．destroy　　　　イ．spoil　　　　ウ．preserve　　　エ．disregard

問3　空所(　3　)に入れるのに最も適当なものを，次のア～エから1つ選び
なさい。

　　ア．because　　　イ．even though　ウ．so　　　　　エ．unless

問4　下線部⑷を日本語に訳しなさい。

問5　下線部⑸を which の内容を明らかにして日本語に訳しなさい。

問6　下線部⑹の内容として最も適当なものを，次のア～エから1つ選びなさ
い。

　　ア．英語は他の言語より優れているという偏見が強まる。

　　イ．他の言語の方が英語より優れているという偏見が強まる。

　　ウ．英語は他の言語より優れているという偏見が正される。

　　エ．他の言語の方が英語より優れているという偏見が正される。

次の英文を読んで，設問に答えなさい。

As a British woman married to an American man, (1)I have found people here more well-mannered in many ways than in England. Whenever we phone my mother-in-law she thanks us: "You're so good to call." I found this charming, and decided I
5 should be more careful about thanking my family. So the next time my mother phoned I said, warmly, "It's so nice of you to call." (2)There was a surprised silence, and then she said, "Well, I'm your mother, aren't I?" My sister later told me that my mother had found my thanks very odd, as if she were an
10 acquaintance.

I have also found Americans (3) at giving and accepting compliments. Like most mothers, I receive a lot of compliments about my son. ("He's so tall!" "He's so cute!" "He's so bright!") I used to be embarrassed by these, but I have learned to smile
15 and say thank you. It seems ungracious to deny the compliment. (4)When my husband receives a compliment, he usually replies, "You're very kind to say so," which I think is a graceful response. It compliments the other person's good manners without seeming conceited.
20 Sometimes it is hard to change the way you speak, especially in the day-to-day exchanges we take for granted. When I buy something at a shop in England, the assistant and I thank each other excessively. I hand her the item I am buying, saying "thank you." She takes it and says "thank you." She tells me
25 the price, I hand her the money, and we both say "thank you." She hands me my change and the receipt; I say "thank you."

Finally she hands me the item in a bag and we both say a final "thank you." I know all these thanks are unnecessary, but (5)[us / both / they / comfortable / feel / make]. In New York this kind of exchange takes place in silence. The sales assistant may even 30 be talking to someone else. Sometimes when I say "thank you," the assistant will say "uh huh" as if she is doing me a favor! Of course New York is not typical of the U.S. Smaller communities still maintain the small rituals (6a) have become lost in the big city. And I have heard that in the South, (6b) they 35 pride themselves on their good manners, shoppers can have half-hour conversations about the items in a shopping basket.

(熊本県立大)

問1　下線部(1)を here の内容を明らかにして日本語に訳しなさい。

問2　下線部(2)の理由として最も適当なものを，次のア〜エから1つ選びなさい。

　　ア．筆者の娘が久しぶりに筆者に電話をしてきたから。

　　イ．筆者の娘が筆者の母とその知人を勘違いするとは，とても奇妙だと感じたから。

　　ウ．筆者の母は，筆者の感謝の言葉をとても感じがいいと思ったから。

　　エ．筆者の母は，筆者の感謝の言葉を知人に対する言葉のようで奇妙に感じたから。

問3　空所(3)に入れるのに最も適当なものを，次のア〜エから1つ選びなさい。

　　ア．more impolite　　　　　イ．more graceful

　　ウ．less sensitive　　　　　エ．less respectful

問4　下線部(4)を日本語に訳しなさい。

問5　下線部(5)の語を文意が通るように並べ換えなさい。

問6　空所(6a)(6b)に入れるのに最も適当なものを，次のア〜エからそれぞれ1つずつ選びなさい。

　　ア．what　　　　イ．where　　　　ウ．who　　　　エ．which

20 min.
330 words

次の英文を読んで，設問に答えなさい。

(1)The more we learn about how the brain functions, the more we come to realize that the brain is not a logical computer. In his book *How the Mind Works*, Steven Pinker relates human brains with computers, saying

5　　computers are *serial, doing one thing at a time; brains are parallel, doing millions of things at once. Computers are fast; brains are slow. Computer parts are reliable; brain parts are noisy. Computers have a limited number of connections; brains have *trillions. Computers are assembled according to
10　a blueprint; brains must assemble themselves.

This does not mean that computers are superior to the human brain. No. (2)There are things the human brain can do that computers cannot do. We humans are comfortable solving "ill-posed problems," while a computer will freeze when faced
15 with such a problem.

What is an "ill-posed problem?" To illustrate, let's use a mathematical example. If I were to ask you what the product of 4×6 was, you would say it is 24. This is a clearly posed problem. It gives you (3a) and asks you to solve for
20 (3b). You have enough information to solve the problem easily, and you would be very confident that there was only one right answer. Both you and a computer could solve this problem equally well. But what (4)[tell me / if / you / I / to / asked] that 24 is the product of what? You could answer that 24 is the product
25 of 4×6. That would be correct. But it would also be correct to

32

say that 24 is the product of 3×8, 2×12, 1×24, 0.5×48, and on and on. This is an example of an ill-posed problem, in which you are given only one number and asked to solve for two unknowns. (5) you find that there are many possible alternative answers, and you have no way of determining which of the many possible answers is the best.

〔注〕 serial：連続的な　　trillions：無数

（東京農工大）

問1　下線部(1)を日本語に訳しなさい。

問2　下線部(2)を日本語に訳しなさい。

問3　空所(3a)(3b)に入る最も適当な組み合わせを，次のア～エから1つ選びなさい。

　　ア．one number —— one unknown number

　　イ．one number —— two unknown numbers

　　ウ．two numbers —— one unknown number

　　エ．two numbers —— two unknown numbers

問4　下線部(4)の語(句)を文意が通るように並べ換えなさい。

問5　空所(5)に入れるのに最も適当なものを，次のア～エから1つ選びなさい。

　　ア．Moreover　　イ．Thus　　　ウ．However　　エ．Similarly

次の英文を読んで，設問に答えなさい。

If you were walking in the woods, and suddenly the path split into two different roads, which one would you choose: the one covered with grass that few people had taken or the cleared one that many others had already walked down? Anyone who has
5 read the poet, Robert Frost, probably recognizes this situation from one of his most famous poems, "The Road Not Taken." After carefully considering both roads, the speaker of the poem chooses the (1) one, or "the one less traveled by." Then he says that this choice "has made all the difference."
10 Most American school children are taught this poem, often with (2)a lesson that's actually simpler than the poem itself. The lesson goes something like this: we can have an ordinary life by making the same choices others make or we can have a rich, more satisfying life by taking risks and choosing to be different.
15 Or as the poem says, taking the less traveled road can make all the difference.

"To make the difference" is an expression that always has a positive meaning in English, (3) you're talking about something big or small. If a man tells his wife, for example,
20 that marrying her has made all the difference, he's saying that he's very happy he married her. Or in the case of something small, you might say that using honey instead of sugar in a cake recipe makes the difference. (4)In other words, the honey is what makes the cake taste so good. In Frost's poem, of course,
25 saying that the less traveled road has made all the difference suggests that the speaker has made the (5) choice.

I suppose this poem expresses part of the American Dream. That is, the idea that if you have the courage to be different and to follow your own path, life will be more (6). It's fairly common for teachers or parents to tell children, "If you believe 30 in yourself, you can do anything: become a doctor, a successful musician, or even the President of the United States. It's up to you."

〈Excerpt from *American Pie* by Kay Hetherly, NHK Publishing〉

（成蹊大）

問 1　空所(1)に入れるのに最も適当なものを，次のア～エから 1 つ選び なさい。

　　ア．crowded　　イ．ordinary　　ウ．cleared　　エ．grassy

問 2　下線部(2)の内容を日本語で説明しなさい。

問 3　空所(3)に入れるのに最も適当なものを，次のア～エから 1 つ選び なさい。

　　ア．what　　　　イ．whether　　ウ．although　　エ．unless

問 4　下線部(4)を日本語に訳しなさい。

問 5　空所(5)に入れるのに最も適当なものを，次のア～エから 1 つ選び なさい。

　　ア．different　　イ．similar　　ウ．wrong　　　エ．right

問 6　空所(6)に入れるのに最も適当なものを，次のア～エから 1 つ選び なさい。

　　ア．rewarding　　　　　　　　イ．disappointing

　　ウ．miserable　　　　　　　　エ．lonely

次の英文を読んで，設問に答えなさい。

One recent Halloween my five-year-old son entered a pumpkin-decorating contest at his school. He proudly took his entry to his school. It was a wild combination of carvings, paint and feathers he had constructed himself. We placed it among the
5 other creative pumpkins — witches, a snowman, and even a bubble-gum-blowing pumpkin wearing a baseball cap. I thought that the judges were going to have a tough time choosing a winner.

They must have thought (1)the same thing, because when we returned to the school that evening, we discovered all the
10 pumpkins were awarded the same black-and-gold ribbon. My son, eagerly looking to see (2) his entry had won, kept asking me, "Which pumpkin won? Where's the winner?"

What could I say? "Well, it looks like everyone won. Look. You got a ribbon, son!"

15 Kids are smart. "Yeah, but who won?" he asked. I could sense his disappointment — and my own. (3)Why should you have a contest if you're not going to pick a winner?

I understand that the school was trying to convey that everyone had done a great job, but I worry that (4)a different
20 message was sent: that losing is a hardship no one should face.

I've noticed this trend a lot lately. It's as if we adults believe (5)our children are too weak to handle defeat. But without a winner, a game or contest loses its excitement. It's part of human nature to be competitive. A competitive spirit is key to
25 our success as adults; why shouldn't we foster it in our children?

I'm not suggesting we make our children compete against each other in all aspects of life. (6)What I want to say is that healthy rivalries can teach our kids a lot about life.

Kids can endure failure. My son understood that he might not win the pumpkin-decorating contest. The disappointment for him was that nobody won. The following morning he asked, "Mummy, who really won the contest?"

"They didn't pick a winner," I explained again.

"Well, I think the snowman won," he said with a nod. And then he was satisfied.

(It's Not Just How We Play That Matters, Newsweek)

（和歌山大）

問1　下線部(1)の内容を20字以内の日本語で述べなさい。

問2　空所（　2　）に入れるのに最も適当なものを，次のア〜エから１つ選びなさい。

　　ア．if　　　　　　イ．because　　　ウ．unless　　　エ．though

問3　下線部(3)を日本語に訳しなさい。

問4　下線部(4)の内容を日本語で述べなさい。

問5　下線部(5)とほぼ同じ意味を表すものを，次のア〜エから１つ選びなさい。

　　ア．competitions are so difficult that our children can't handle them

　　イ．competitions aren't easy enough for our children to handle

　　ウ．our children are too strong to endure losing

　　エ．our children are not strong enough to endure losing

問6　下線部(6)を日本語に訳しなさい。

問7　本文の内容と一致するものを，次のア〜オから２つ選びなさい。

　　ア．The writer's son was not proud of his entry.

　　イ．The writer's son was very happy that everyone was given the same black-and-gold ribbon.

　　ウ．Recently adults have tried to take care not to make any child a loser in school competition.

　　エ．Human beings are competitive by nature.

　　オ．The child who had made a snowman won the pumpkin contest.

次の英文を読んで，設問に答えなさい。

(1)<u>Loneliness is a curious situation</u>. Almost everybody has experienced it at some time in their life. It can often overcome you when in fact you are not alone; at a party, in the theater, or in any group where you are surrounded by people who give
5 evidence of being supremely confident, friendly and capable of smooth, happy communication. What should you do? Lonely people are advised to go out and meet people. But is this the answer?

In a typical situation, such as your first day at a new school,
10 (2)<u>you get the impression that everybody else is confident and knows all the others, while you are helpless and alone</u>. But in reality most people put on a show of confidence to hide their true feelings. They may be as lonely as you. There is no reason at all to assume that, in a big city for example, all the
15 people around you are leading active, rich, fulfilling lives, while you alone are on the outside looking in. You may be less (3) of concealing your loneliness than others. You must try to put on a cheerful face; nobody will greet you at a party if you look utterly (4). Another point to remember is that you
20 should try to avoid joining groups where in fact you are a total stranger. For many reasons established groups do dislike intrusions and to accept you requires considerable effort. However, if you can offer something special any group may need, your entry may be quicker and less troublesome.
25 It is best to get to know other people who share a common interest with you. Even if you don't like all of them, at least the

shared experience is better than being alone.　This may all seem
rather *grim, but (5)we must face the fact that, no matter how
close we are to people around us, we are often alone.

（注）　grim：不快な

（福岡女子大）

問1　下線部(1)のように言えるのはなぜか，本文に即して30字以内の日本語で
　　　説明しなさい。

問2　下線部(2)を日本語に訳しなさい。

問3　空所（　3　）に入れるのに最も適当なものを，次のア〜エから1つ選び
　　　なさい。

　　　ア．able　　　　　イ．capable　　　ウ．possible　　　エ．impossible

問4　空所（　4　）に入れるのに最も適当なものを，次のア〜エから1つ選び
　　　なさい。

　　　ア．excited　　　イ．depressed　　ウ．happy　　　　エ．alone

問5　下線部(5)を日本語に訳しなさい。

18

次の英文を読んで，設問に答えなさい。

Did all the dinosaurs disappear 65 million years ago? It is sometimes tempting to seek the distant descendants of dinosaurs in some of the larger reptiles alive today, such as crocodiles or *Komodo dragons. In fact, these animals, although distant
5 relations of dinosaurs, are not their (　1　).

In order to find descendants of the dinosaurs in today's world, strange (　2　) it may seem, we need to turn to birds. In fact, the majority of today's scientists think that birds are descended from certain small meat-eating dinosaurs. If the skeleton of the
10 oldest known bird, which lived about 140 million years ago, is compared to that of the dinosaurs, (3)the resemblance is great. This has been confirmed by numerous recent finds of primitive birds that had dinosaur features, and of dinosaurs that were close to birds. Some Chinese remains from the beginning of *the
15 Cretaceous period, approximately 120 million years old, have even yielded the fossils of animals that may have been dinosaurs with feathers.

Fossils show us that at the time of the dinosaurs' disappearance, birds had already been in existence for a long time and had
20 developed into many different species. What happened to them when the disaster occurred? Experts have different opinions on this question, and (4)the known fossils are still too few in number to allow the question to be resolved. However, it is possible that a great extinction took place among birds as well and that the
25 group's evolution, when it started again at the beginning of *the Tertiary period, was based only on a few surviving species.

（注）　Komodo dragons：コモドドラゴン（世界最大のトカゲ）

　　　the Cretaceous period：白亜紀（1億4000万～6500万年前）

　　　the Tertiary period：第三紀（6500万～200万年前）

（九州大）

問1　空所（　1　）に入れるのに最も適当な1語を，本文中から探して答えなさい。

問2　空所（　2　）に入れるのに最も適当なものを，次のア～エから1つ選びなさい。

　　　ア．if　　　　　　　イ．as　　　　　　ウ．because　　　　エ．although

問3　下線部(3)の内容として最も適当なものを，次のア～エから1つ選びなさい。

　　　ア．最古の鳥が生息していた年代と恐竜が生息していた年代の類似。

　　　イ．最古の鳥の骨格と恐竜の骨格の類似。

　　　ウ．最古の鳥と小型肉食恐竜の類似。

　　　エ．最古の鳥と現代の鳥の類似。

問4　下線部(4)を日本語に訳しなさい。

問5　本文の内容と一致するものを，次のア～エから1つ選びなさい。

　　　ア．Fossil evidence indicates that only a few bird species existed in the dinosaur period.

　　　イ．The disaster which caused the dinosaurs to disappear affected only a few bird species.

　　　ウ．Experts have suggested that feathered dinosaurs existed in the Cretaceous period.

　　　エ．In the Tertiary period, all the dinosaurs became extinct and the first birds began to evolve.

次の英文を読んで，設問に答えなさい。

A study by Bent Flyvbjerg and his colleagues draws upon cost statistics for 245 large dams built between 1934 and 2007. It is by far the largest data set that any study of dam finances has collected. Without even taking into account social and
5 environmental impacts, which are almost invariably negative and frequently vast, the study finds that "the actual construction costs of large dams (1)[too / yield / to / are / a positive return / high]."

The researchers say planners are biased toward excessive optimism, which dam promoters exploit with deception or
10 *corruption. The study finds that actual dam expenses were on average nearly double pre-building estimates, and these additional costs were several times greater than those of other kinds of infrastructure construction, including roads, railroads, bridges and tunnels. In addition, dam construction on average took 8.6
15 years, more than a third longer than predicted — so much time, the researchers say, that large dams are "(2) in resolving urgent energy crises."

Dams typically consume large amounts of developing countries' financial resources. Many of the funds that support large dams
20 arrive as loans to the host countries and must eventually be paid off. But most dam revenue comes from electricity sales in local currencies. (3)When local currencies fall against the dollar, as almost invariably happens, the burden of those loans grows.

The economic impact on host countries was often destructive.
25 Dam projects are so huge that since the 1980s, dam expenses have become major components of debt crises in Turkey, Brazil,

and Mexico. "(4)For many countries, the national economy is so fragile that the debt from just one mega-dam can have a significant negative effect on it," stated Mr. Flyvbjerg.

Instead of building massive, one-of-a-kind *edifices like large 30 dams, the researchers recommend "*agile energy alternatives" like wind, solar and mini-hydro power. "We're stuck in a 1950s mode where everything was done in a very customized, manual way," Mr. Flyvbjerg added. "(5)We need things that are more easily standardized, things that fit inside a container and can be 35 easily transported."

(注) corruption：汚職，贈収賄   edifice：大建造物

　　　agile：動かしやすい，身軽な

(© The New York Times. Distributed by The New York Times Licensing Group.)

(横浜国立大)

問1　下線部(1)の語(句)を文意が通るように並べ換えなさい。

問2　空所(　2　)に入れるのに最も適当なものを，次のア〜エから1つ選び
　　なさい。

　　ア．effective　　　イ．ineffective　　　ウ．helpful　　　エ．helpless

問3　下線部(3)を日本語に訳しなさい。

問4　下線部(4)を日本語に訳しなさい。

問5　下線部(5)の内容として最も適当なものを，次のア〜エから1つ選びなさ
　　い。

　　ア．私たちは，もっと巨大ダムを造って，そこから電力を得るべきだ。

　　イ．私たちは，巨大ダムによる電力に頼るべきであり，他の形態のエネル
　　　ギーに頼るべきではない。

　　ウ．私たちは，巨大ダムによる電力ばかりでなく，他の形態のエネルギー
　　　も利用すべきだ。

　　エ．私たちは，巨大ダムによる電力に頼らずに，他の形態のエネルギーを
　　　利用すべきだ。

次の英文を読んで，設問に答えなさい。

Climate is sometimes mistaken for weather. But climate is different from weather because it is measured over a long period of time, (　1　) weather can change from day to day, or from year to year. The climate of an area includes seasonal
5 temperature, rainfall averages, and wind patterns. Different places have different climates. A desert, for example, has an *arid climate because little water falls, as rain or snow, during the year. Other types of climate include tropical climates, which are hot and humid, and temperate climates, which have warm
10 summers and cooler winters.

Climate change is the long-term alteration of temperature and typical weather patterns in a place. Climate change could refer to a particular location or the planet as a whole. Climate change may cause weather patterns to be less predictable.
15 (2)These unexpected weather patterns can make it difficult to maintain and grow crops in regions that rely on farming because expected temperature and rainfall levels can no longer be relied on. Climate change has also been connected with other damaging weather events, such as more frequent and more
20 intense hurricanes, floods, downpours, and winter storms.

In polar regions, the warming global temperatures associated with climate change have meant ice sheets are melting at an accelerated rate from season to season. (3)This contributes to sea levels rising in different regions of the planet, so that coastlines
25 retreat and low-lying islands are partially underwater.

The cause of the climate change we're experiencing now is

largely human activity, such as burning fossil fuels, like oil, coal, and natural gas. Burning these materials $_{(4)}$[called / what / releases / greenhouse gases / are] into Earth's atmosphere. There, these gases trap heat from the sun's rays inside the atmosphere, causing Earth's average temperature to rise. This rise in the planet's temperature, which is called global warming, impacts local and regional climates. Throughout Earth's history, the climate has continually changed. When occurring naturally, this is a slow process that has taken place over hundreds and thousands of years. The present (5) climate change is occurring at a much faster rate.

(注)　arid：乾燥した

(National Geographic Society, Climate Change, National Geographic)

(福島大)

問1　空所(1)に入れるのに最も適当なものを，次のア〜エから1つ選びなさい。

ア．once　　　　イ．since　　　　ウ．now that　　エ．while

問2　下線部(2)を日本語に訳しなさい。

問3　下線部(3)を This の内容を明らかにして日本語に訳しなさい。

問4　下線部(4)の語(句)を文意が通るように並べ換えなさい。

問5　空所(5)に入れるのに最も適当なものを，次のア〜エから1つ選びなさい。

ア．human-influenced　　　　イ．natural

ウ．regional　　　　　　　　エ．long-term

次の英文を読んで，設問に答えなさい。

Understandably, many workers today suffer from job anxiety. They fear losing their jobs to automation and having robots "steal" their livelihoods. (1)This worry is not only relevant to blue-collar employees, but many white-collar jobs are vulnerable,
5 too. Let's face it: AI and robots can do many routine jobs more efficiently and more cheaply than human workers. This makes massive layoffs a real possibility. No wonder so many workers are so uneasy.

But Martin Feldstein, an economics professor at Harvard, says,
10 "(2)." Why? "Simply put: history. For many years, we have been experiencing rapid technological change that substitutes machines and computers for individual workers." But this only means that new, more interesting "human" jobs are being created. At any rate, Feldstein believes that workers have
15 the flexibility it takes to "adjust positively to any changing technology."

Business experts don't expect large-scale unemployment to happen either. They predict that most workers won't actually be replaced by robots. Instead, more and more, they will be
20 teamed up with them. What will that be like? How will human workers get along with their machine partners? Dr. Steve Hunt, a business psychologist and systems designer, believes that "digitization" can, paradoxically, create a more human, more productive workplace. But this can only happen if digitization is
25 applied correctly. (3)Doing that depends mainly on companies changing their mindset. Most managers, Hunt says, tend to

expect workers to perform like machines. They judge employee performance by "concrete, immediate outcomes that measure the kind of output a machine would produce."

This must stop, says Hunt. "We are going to need more and 30 more workers to do the things robots can't do well. Humans excel at making emotional connections, scanning environments, and recognizing patterns. They can then adapt their behavior to fit the situation." (4)Hunt cites research that shows that human workers almost always treat the robots they work with as living 35 things. Companies must recognize this and incorporate this information into their management policies. They must prepare for the inevitable social and psychological interactions that will take place between man and machine.

(Jim Knudsen, *Mind Matters: The Psychology of Business and Work*, Nan'un-Do Co., Ltd.)

(摂南大)

問1　下線部(1)の This worry の内容を明らかにして，日本語に訳しなさい。

問2　空所(　2　)に入れるのに最も適当なものを，次のア～エから1つ選びなさい。

　　ア．No idea　　　　　　　　イ．Don't worry
　　ウ．Take action　　　　　　エ．Take care

問3　下線部(3)の内容として最も適当なものを，次のア～エから1つ選びなさい。

　　ア．よりよい職場を作ることは，主に企業が考え方を変えられるかどうかにかかっている。

　　イ．よりよい職場を作ることは，主に企業の変化していく考え方にかかっている。

　　ウ．デジタル化を適切に行うことは，主に企業が考え方を変えられるかどうかにかかっている。

　　エ．デジタル化を適切に行うことは，主に企業の変化していく考え方にかかっている。

問4　下線部(4)を日本語に訳しなさい。

問5　Martin Feldstein の見解を，次のア～エから1つ選びなさい。

ア．A lot of people might lose their jobs in the future.

イ．Companies should stop expecting workers to perform like machines.

ウ．History proves that humans can adapt to technological changes.

エ．Robots can adapt to situations well because they are not alive.

問6　英文のタイトルとして最も適当なものを，次のア～エから1つ選びなさい。

ア．The History of Robotics

イ．The Future of Work

ウ．Robots: The Best Workers

エ．Work Like a Machine

次の英文を読んで，設問に答えなさい。

One fast-food company is well known in Japan for (1)its extensive worker manual and the sales talk it covers. From the book, workers learn how to greet a customer, how to bow, how to take an order, pack a bag and give correct change. Customers find the same nice service in all the franchised 5 outlets, which contributes to both customer satisfaction and *corporate profits.

One day, a mother came into one of these restaurants, and while she was ordering at the counter, her baby grabbed an employee's hat and began to play with it. He was surprised and 10 embarrassed. (2)He could not concentrate on what the customer was saying and had to ask her to repeat her order twice. He knew he was losing his dignity as a company representative by having an infant tearing up part of his uniform, and he wanted to take it back, but at the same time he didn't know what to say 15 or do. He stood there (3) until the mother *retrieved the hat and gave it back to him. He put it on again, resumed his normal calm attitude, and took her order efficiently as if nothing had happened. But everyone in the restaurant could see that a one-year-old child had the power to bring the operation to a halt 20 and must have wondered about it.

What was the problem here? (4)Simply put, the manual, detailed as it may be, fails to cover what to do in a situation where a young child steals part of your uniform. And without the manual to guide his behavior, the employee was lost. This is a trivial 25 example of a very serious problem in Japan: the inability to

(5   ).

Training employees is important, especially employees who come into contact with customers on a regular basis. But in the
30 end (6a)it is a worker's own creativity and initiative that constitute true salesmanship. (7)A company must not only allow but actively encourage its employees to use their heads in order to deal with real-life situations. Corporate training is nothing more than a guide. When it comes to doing real business with real
35 customers, (6b)it is up to each individual employee to think on his or her feet and do what is best.

（注） corporate：企業の   retrieve：取り戻す

（Masami Atarashi, *A Primer for Japanese Business Success*, The Japan Times）

（新潟大）

問1　下線部(1)の manual に述べられていないものを，次のア～エから1つ選びなさい。

　　ア．客にあいさつの言葉をかけること。

　　イ．きちんとおじぎをすること。

　　ウ．帽子を脱いであいさつをすること。

　　エ．間違いなく釣り銭を渡すこと。

問2　下線部(2)のような状況になった理由を，30字程度の日本語で具体的に説明しなさい。

問3　空所(3   )に入れるのに最も適当なものを，次のア～エから1つ選びなさい。

　　ア．crying　　　　イ．helpless　　　　ウ．hopeful　　　　エ．relaxed

問4　下線部(4)を日本語に訳しなさい。

問5　空所(5   )に入れるのに最も適当なものを，次のア～エから1つ選びなさい。

　　ア．behave politely　　　　　　イ．stay calm

　　ウ．make a proper apology　　　エ．take personal initiative

50

問6　下線部(6a)(6b)と同じ用法の it を含む文を，次のア～エからそれぞれ1
つずつ選びなさい。

　　ア．I love the spring — it is the best season of the year.

　　イ．It is impossible to master a foreign language in a month.

　　ウ．It gets dark very early in the winter.

　　エ．It was in France that I first met Mr.Smith.

問7　下線部(7)を日本語に訳しなさい。

次の英文を読んで，設問に答えなさい。

A lot of people think cancer is the number one killer in the United States, but (1)it's not. The leading killer is heart disease. Cancer is number two. Heart disease is responsible for about one-quarter of the deaths in the U.S. each year.

5 Heart attacks (2a)account for over 500,000 deaths a year. One reason the number of deaths from heart attacks is so high is that when people experience chest pain, they don't realize they may be having a heart attack and wait too long before going to the hospital. (3a)Such a delay can be fatal. In fact, more than half 10 of all heart attack victims die before they reach the hospital.

What are the warning signs of a heart attack? According to the American Heart Association, the signs include uncomfortable pressure or pain in the middle of the chest for two minutes or longer; movement of pain to the shoulder, arm, neck, or jaw; 15 (3b)sweating may accompany the pain; *nausea and vomiting may also occur; and shortness of breath, dizziness, or fainting may be experienced with the other signs.

One of the factors that increase the risk of heart attack is high blood pressure. Today, with the stresses of everyday life, 20 nearly one out of every three adults suffers from high blood pressure. High blood pressure can be (2b)brought on by a fight with one's *spouse, problems at work, speaking in public, or even telling a lie. But it can also be brought on by something you enjoy, like the caffeine in a cup of coffee, cigarettes, or 25 alcohol.

(4)There are, fortunately, ways to lower blood pressure — ways that are just as varied as the behaviors that drive blood pressure up. They include maintaining a healthy diet, attaining one's recommended weight, and doing regular aerobic exercise. And there are unexpectedly simple ways of lowering blood pressure, 30 such as laughing or petting a dog or cat.

So while the bad news is that heart disease is the number one killer, the good news is that the death rate from heart disease has been (2c)declining since the 1950s as people adopt healthier lifestyles and the medical world develops improved drugs and 35 surgical techniques.

(注)　nausea and vomiting：吐き気と嘔吐　　spouse：配偶者

（近畿大）

問1　下線部(1)を it の内容を明らかにし，省略されたものを補って日本語に訳しなさい。

問2　下線部(2a)～(2c)とほぼ同じ意味を表すものを，次のア～エからそれぞれ1つずつ選びなさい。

- (2a)　ア．depend on　　イ．care for　　ウ．put off　　エ．result in
- (2b)　ア．raised　　　イ．lowered　　イ．caused　　エ．cured
- (2c)　ア．increasing　イ．decreasing　ウ．refusing　エ．accepting

問3　下線部(3a)(3b)の意味として最も適当なものを，ア～エからそれぞれ1つずつ選びなさい。

- (3a)　ア．胸に痛みを感じることもなく，心臓発作であることに気づくのが遅れれば，命に関わる事態になることもある。
  - イ．胸に痛みを感じることもなく，心臓発作の可能性に気づかなければ，病院に行くことが遅れることになるが，それも運命である。
  - ウ．胸に痛みを感じても，心臓発作かもしれないということに気づかず，病院に行くのが遅れるようなこともあるが，それも運命である。
  - エ．胸に痛みを感じても，心臓発作かもしれないということに気づ

かず，病院に行かずにぐずぐずしていると，命にかかわる事態と
なる場合もある。

(3b)　ア．痛みに伴って汗が出ることもある。

イ．汗をかくと痛みを誘発することもある。

ウ．汗をかくと痛みを和らげる場合もある。

エ．発汗と苦痛が交互に繰り返すこともある。

問4　下線部(4)を日本語に訳しなさい。

問5　本文の内容と<u>一致しない</u>ものを，次のア〜エから1つ選びなさい。

ア．Heart disease causes about 25% of the deaths in the U.S.
annually.

イ．The warning signs of a heart attack include pain in the middle of
the chest for two minutes or longer.

ウ．High blood pressure is one of the factors that increases the risk
of heart attack.

エ．It is possible to lower blood pressure by drinking a cup of coffee
or by touching a dog or cat softly.

次の英文を読んで，設問に答えなさい。

In our *hectic world, a good night's sleep is worth its weight in gold when it comes to improving physical and mental well-being. Much more than a basic method of energy conservation, sleep is a state during which muscle and bone are generated and repaired, and memories and learning systems are updated. 5 Sleep also allows the body and brain to clear out the toxic byproducts of the day's waking activity that might cause harm if we didn't sleep. (1), good sleep is a foundation of human health.

Sadly, (2) of us are blessed with the benefit of a good 10 night's sleep after a long and often tiring day. Around 30% of adults experience chronic insomnia at some point in their life — where sleep is disrupted for more than a month. Estimates are even higher in older populations and those who experience regular stress. 15

Insomnia can be devastating, and it has been linked to cognitive deficiencies. (3)Experiments reveal that when deprived of sleep, people are less sharp at mathematical and verbal tasks, and their attention span and memory decline. Severe cases of chronic insomnia can cause psychological problems, including 20 mood and anxiety disorders, and long-term health concerns, including obesity and *dementia.

The cost of insomnia goes well beyond just health. According to the National Sleep Foundation, insomniacs are two to four times more likely to have an accident — (4) over 72,000 25 traffic accidents a year in the US alone linked to sleep deprivation. Insomnia also costs US companies an estimated $150 billion in reduced productivity every year.

Research has shown that listening to self-selected music, or
30 music of your choice, can actually shorten stage two sleep cycles. This means people reach REM sleep, which is the restorative part of our sleep, more quickly.

In one study, students who listened to 45 minutes of music before bedtime for three weeks saw a positive effect on sleep
35 efficiency, and another study found a similar effect on older citizens. Following (5)this evidence, the *NHS now recommends listening to soft music before bedtime as a method to prevent insomnia.

(注) hectic：大変忙しい   dementia：認知症
      NHS：(イギリスの)国民保健サービス

(Victoria Williamson, How Listening to Music Could Help You Beat Insomnia, The Conversation)

(鹿児島大)

問1 空所(1)に入れるのに最も適当なものを，次のア～エから1つ選び なさい。
    ア．By contrast   イ．For example
    ウ．In short   エ．What's more
問2 空所(2)に入れるのに最も適当なものを，次のア～エから1つ選び なさい。
    ア．all   イ．not all   ウ．none   エ．most
問3 下線部(3)を日本語に訳しなさい。
問4 空所(4)に入れるのに最も適当なものを，次のア～エから1つ選び なさい。
    ア．by   イ．with   ウ．from   エ．of
問5 下線部(5)の内容を，日本語で述べなさい。

次の英文を読んで，設問に答えなさい。

Japanese people are usually characterized as polite. Although the Japanese language has a system of politeness that requires a pack of appropriate politeness levels, (1)this does not mean that the Japanese are always polite. As a casual look into a karaoke bar or a similar place for dining and drinking reveals, Japanese 5 people, given the right place and the right time, talk casually in a way that may seem to a foreigner quite impolite or even rude. (2)The myth that the Japanese are always polite has much to do with who is doing the observing; to an observer who is outside the *uchi* group, the impolite side of the Japanese is hardly ever 10 expressed. Only if participants are actually arguing (3)[drop / do / Japanese speakers / the expected level / of politeness] and formality toward the *soto* person.

Each individual is a member of several social groups — family, university, workplace, and so on. (4)Depending on the situation, 15 one of these groups is emphasized over the others. Within two contrasting and yet constantly changing social areas, *uchi* and *soto*, different social behaviors are observed. In *uchi* relations, where there is less psychological distance among the participants, politeness is usually avoided, and intimate and (5) formal 20 expressions are used. In *soto* relations, where the psychological and social distance is emphasized, appropriate levels of politeness must be maintained.

(Senko K.Maynard, *Japanese Communication: Language and Thought in Context*, University of Hawai'i Press)

問1　下線部(1)の内容を15字以内の日本語で述べなさい。

問2　下線部(2)を日本語に訳しなさい。

問3　下線部(3)の語（句）を文意が通るように並べ換えなさい。

問4　下線部(4)を the others の内容を明らかにして日本語に訳しなさい。

問5　空所（　5　）に入れるのに最も適当なものを，次のア〜エから1つ選び
なさい。

　　ア．highly　　　　イ．more　　　　ウ．less　　　　エ．quite

次の英文を読んで，設問に答えなさい。

My father had a special way with people. His warm smile and relaxed manner immediately made them feel comfortable. He always said the right word at the right moment. For years, I was convinced that his success with people was due to his speaking skills. 5

Before I went off to college, my father gave me (1)some advice that surprised me. "The key to success," he told me, "is being a good speaker and a better listener." Then he explained why. You learn more from listening than from talking. (2)If you are a good listener, people will feel at ease with you, and will open 10 their hearts. For me, these wise words have been (3).

In graduate school, I was given the same advice from a professor who was one of the world's most famous linguistic scholars. He defined listening as a social responsibility which promotes communication. When you listen, he told me, you 15 receive and then process the other person's spoken message. Your willingness to open a dialogue creates the miracle of communication.

At first, I was surprised by my professor's comment. I had always thought that in communication, (a) was more 20 important than (b). Perhaps I had reached this conclusion, because (c) is active while (d) is passive. Thanks to my professor's explanation, however, I learned that (e) is a powerful social tool which can create, distort, or destroy communication. Unfortunately most women and men do not 25 learn this skill. Only a few realize that (f) is a social responsibility.

Poor listeners are socially (4), because they stop or block communication. You probably know people who do not listen. They never stop talking. If you try to say a word, they do not listen, or they interrupt you in a loud voice. They are not interested in communication. They just want to be the center of attention. Quite simply, poor listeners are self-centered.

Many social problems stem from the behavior of women and men who are poor listeners. (5)If they stopped talking so much and started listening to each other, they could open a dialogue. It is amazing how many problems can be solved when people communicate.

I am (6) to both my father and my professor for teaching me why it is important to be a responsible listener. I hope that this lesson will help you too.

(Joan McConnell, *Lessons on Life*, 金星堂)

(宮崎大)

問1 下線部(1)の内容を50字以内の日本語で述べなさい。

問2 下線部(2)を日本語に訳しなさい。

問3 空所(3)(4)(6)に入れるのに最も適当な語を，次のア～エからそれぞれ1つずつ選びなさい。

　　ア．grateful　　イ．invaluable　　ウ．irresponsible　エ．unrealistic

問4 空所(a)～(f)には，listening か speaking かのいずれかが入る。listening が入る箇所の記号をすべて答えなさい。

問5 下線部(5)を日本語に訳しなさい。

問6 英文のタイトルとして最も適当なものを，次のア～エから1つ選びなさい。

　　ア．Becoming a Confident Speaker

　　イ．Being a Responsible Listener

　　ウ．Communication at Universitites

　　エ．Listening to Your Elders

次の英文を読んで，設問に答えなさい。

(1)The "global village" is an idealistic phrase meaning that all human beings are like members of one big village living peacefully on planet Earth. The fact is, however, that the surface of Earth is divided into some 200 nations by mostly unseen borders. Business activities between nations can be 5 either difficult or easy depending on these borders.

Only a few countries could survive without trading with other countries. Most countries depend on each other. (2)Japan, in particular, could not survive even one year were it isolated from the rest of the world. Japan's large economy is totally supported 10 by many other nations. To maintain their healthy economy, Japanese people should always be alert to what is going on in the world.

(3)News articles are sent from every corner of the world by worldwide news agencies. These big news agencies send 15 hundreds of reporters and photographers all over the world, and they send back reports and pictures day and night.

Japanese news crews are also active in many places, but quite often Japanese newspapers and TV stations buy reports and pictures from major news agencies abroad to put together their 20 news articles and programs. If you are able to read or listen to English news, you may be able to get news directly from international news sources. (4)Fresh news from abroad can affect the Japanese economy.

A piece of good political news from the United States may lift 25 the Japanese stock market. News of bad weather off the coast of Peru may have unfavorable effects on the Japanese fish market. News about Arab oil prices can have a particularly big impact on the Japanese economy.

30 The Internet, linked by satellites and parabolic antennas, enables us to keep in touch with the world. Raw news flies all over the world and breaks down national borders. No nation can hide its own domestic events from the rest of the world or keep unfavorable international news from its people. Therefore,

35 we should learn to adapt to the present (　5　) century.

（青木雅幸，Peter Williams, *The Globalized Business World*，成美堂）

（神戸学院大）

問1　下線部(1)の実情を最もよく表しているものを，次のア〜エから1つずつ選びなさい。

　　ア．The idea of the "global village" is accepted by all human beings on planet Earth.

　　イ．People all over the world live peacefully as members of one big community.

　　ウ．Planet Earth is separated into hundreds of countries by borders you cannot see.

　　エ．Business with other nations goes well along their borders.

問2　下線部(2)を日本語に訳しなさい。

問3　下線部(3)に関して，日本の新聞やテレビ局が頻繁に行っていることを，40字以内で述べなさい。

問4　下線部(4)の具体例を，日本語で3つ挙げなさい。

問5　空所(　5　)に入れるのに最も適当なものを，次のア〜エから1つ選びなさい。

　　ア．industrial　　イ．stable　　ウ．borderless　　エ．peaceful

次の英文を読んで，設問に答えなさい。

Reading and writing have long been thought of as skills supporting each other: (1)to read is to recognize and interpret language that has been written; to write is to plan and produce language so that it can be read. It is therefore assumed that being able to read implies being able to write — or, at least, 5 being able to spell. Often, children are taught to read but (2) no formal lessons in spelling; it is felt that spelling will be learned in a natural or spontaneous process. The attitude has (3)its counterpart in the methods of 200 years ago, when teachers carefully taught spelling, and assumed that reading would follow 10 automatically.

Recent research into spelling errors has begun to show that things are not so simple as you might think. There is no necessary link between reading and writing: good readers do not always make good writers. (4) is there any necessary link 15 between reading and spelling. (5)There are many people who have no difficulty in reading, but who have a major handicap in spelling — some researchers have estimated that this may be as many as 2 percent of the population.

With children, too, there is evidence that knowledge of reading 20 does not automatically transfer to spelling. If there (6) a close relationship, children would be able to read and spell the same words: but this is not so. It is common to find children who can read far better than they can spell. More surprisingly, the (7) happens with some children in the early stages of 25 reading. One study gave children the same list of words to read and to spell: several actually spelled more words correctly than they were able to read correctly.

〔From *How Language Works* by David Crystal published by Penguin. Copyright © 2005 David Crystal. Reprinted by permission of Penguin Books Limited.〕

（実践女子大）

問1　下線部(1)を日本語に訳しなさい。

問2　空所(　2　)に入れるのに最も適当なものを，下のア～エから1つ選びなさい。

　　ア．give　　　　　イ．given　　　　ウ．giving　　　　エ．to give

問3　下線部(3)の内容として最も適当なものを，次のア～エから1つ選びなさい。

　　ア．読むことができるようになれば，自然につづりも身につくという考え方。

　　イ．つづりを教えれば，自然に読めるようになるという考え方。

　　ウ．読み方とつづり方は同時に教えなければならないという考え方。

　　エ．読むことや書くことは自然に身につくものであるという考え方。

問4　空所(　4　)に入れるのに最も適当なものを，次のア～エから1つ選びなさい。

　　ア．As　　　　　イ．Either　　　　ウ．Nor　　　　エ．Or

問5　下線部(5)を日本語に訳しなさい。

問6　空所(　6　)に入れるのに最も適当なものを，次のア～エから1つ選びなさい。

　　ア．has been　　イ．had been　　ウ．were　　　　エ．will be

問7　空所(　7　)に入れるのに最も適当なものを，次のア～エから1つ選びなさい。

　　ア．reverse　　　イ．mistake　　　ウ．same　　　　エ．accident

次の英文を読んで，設問に答えなさい。

It is no secret that humans (1)<u>play favorites</u> when it comes to the life or death of a species. We rate animals and plants based on our use for them. If they are more valuable to us dead than alive, we kill them. We, as a species, see animals or plants as valuable if they give us food or medicine, or if they are beautiful 5 or cute. We often measure these values on the basis of money. Perhaps it is not right to put a price on animals or plants, but that is (2a) we do.

Humans also value species if they are (3) us. In terms of animals, we value mammals over birds, birds over fish, fish 10 over reptiles, and reptiles over insects. In addition, we value animals more than plants.

It is very difficult to find support to save a species of shark or a kind of grass. People do not like sharks, and grass does not walk around or show feelings, so we think it's okay to let them 15 become extinct.

(4)<u>The reality is, it's not okay to allow them to become extinct.</u> Although sharks are not really important to humans, they are important to other animals and plants. They are important to the ecosystem in (2b) they live. If they die out, the ecosystem 20 will become unbalanced. An unbalanced ecosystem puts other animals at risk. If we kill enough animals, it will eventually (5) humans as well.

The gorilla is a perfect example of how humans play favorites with popular animals. (6)<u>In the entire world there is no species 25 that is more like us than the gorilla</u>. For many years, however,

they were hunted for sport and for food. The gorilla was used for human entertainment, turned into a monster in movies like *King Kong*. People take their land away. Even today in
30 Cameroon, (2c) they are protected, people see gorillas as more valuable dead than alive.

（愛媛大）

問1　下線部(1)の意味として最も適当なものを，次のア～エから１つ選びなさい。
　　ア．好きなことをして遊ぶ。
　　イ．好き勝手に振る舞う。
　　ウ．えこひいきをする。
　　エ．人の頼みを聞いてやる。

問2　空所(2a)～(2c)に入れるのに最も適当なものを，次のア～エからそれぞれ１つずつ選びなさい。
　　ア．where　　　イ．why　　　ウ．what　　　エ．which

問3　空所(3)に入れるのに最も適当なものを，次のア～エから１つ選びなさい。
　　ア．superior to　　　　　　　イ．inferior to
　　ウ．different from　　　　　　エ．similar to

問4　下線部(4)を them の内容を明らかにして日本語に訳しなさい。

問5　空所(5)に入れるのに最も適当なものを，次のア～エから１つ選びなさい。
　　ア．satisfy　　　イ．benefit　　　ウ．damage　　　エ．affect

問6　下線部(6)を日本語に訳しなさい。

次の英文を読んで，設問に答えなさい。

There is a very close relationship between (1). One study showed that successful people in the United States of America always had one thing in common — a strong vocabulary. The study tested the vocabularies of thousands of people from all age groups and backgrounds. It was discovered that the people 5 who had the highest salaries also had the highest vocabularies.

When (2)[to / explain / of this study / asked / the results], the director of the study group said, "Words are the tools of thought. We think with words, we communicate our ideas to others with words and we understand the ideas of others with words. The 10 more words we know, the better we can explain and understand. (3)It is this ability to explain and understand that makes leaders."

Another example of the connection between a strong vocabulary and success can be seen in a study of university students. Half of the students were put into special classes 15 where they studied only to improve their vocabulary. The other students were put into regular classes. The group of students who studied only to improve their vocabulary got (4) grades in their 2nd, 3rd and 4th years at the university than did the students who had been placed in the regular classes. 20

The bigger your vocabulary is, (5)[your chances / better / success / for / the] are at school, in your profession or your business. And the best part is that you can increase your vocabulary quickly and easily, much more easily than you thought you could. (6)All you need to do is spend a few minutes each day 25 studying and reviewing. Within two or three months, you will notice a big improvement in your vocabulary power.

（宮崎大）

問1　空所(　1　)に入れるのに最も適当なものを，次のア〜エから1つ選び
　　なさい。

　　ア．vocabulary and career

　　イ．vocabulary and communication

　　ウ．vocabulary and success

　　エ．vocabulary and university study

問2　下線部(2)の語(句)を文意が通るように並べ換えなさい。

問3　下線部(3)を日本語に訳しなさい。

問4　空所(　4　)に入れるのに最も適当なものを，次のア〜エから1つ選び
　　なさい。

　　ア．lower　　　　イ．inferior　　　ウ．higher　　　エ．good

問5　下線部(5)の語(句)を文意が通るように並べ換えなさい。

問6　下線部(6)を日本語に訳しなさい。

改訂版

やっておきたい

英語長文

300

河合塾講師

杉山 俊一
塚越 友幸
山下 博子

［共著］

［解答・解説編］

河合出版

はじめに

　大学の入試問題では、読解問題が最も大きな割合を占めていますし，その割合はますます高くなっています。読解問題を解けるようにすることは，受験を突破するうえで避けては通ることができません。それでは，読解問題を解くためには，どのような力が必要なのでしょうか。語い力に加えて，一文一文の構造を正確に捉え，内容を把握する力が必要です。さらに，複数の文が集まって文章が構成されている以上，文と文のつながり，すなわち文脈を読み取る力も必要です。また，今日的な話題が出題されることが増えています。そうした話題について知っておくことも，内容を理解するためには大切です。

　こうした力をつけるためには，何よりも良い英文を読み，良い問題を解くことです。そこで，これまでに出題された問題の中から，英文の長さと難易度を基準に繰り返し読むに値する英文を選び，4冊の問題集にまとめました。設問は，ある文章に対して問うべきこと—内容の理解と英語の理解—という観点から，ほぼ全面的に作り変えてあります。

　やっておきたい英語長文300は，200語から400語の比較的短めで，やや易から標準レベルの英文30題で構成されています。**共通テストレベルの英文を読みこなせるようになることが目標です。**また，一文一文の構造を正確に捉え，内容を把握するために必須の表現を **Point** にまとめ，基礎的なものから順番に無理なく学習できるように問題が配列されています。

　やっておきたい英語長文300を終えた人は，**やっておきたい英語長文500**に挑戦してください。

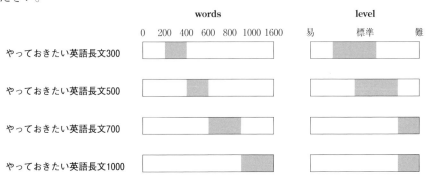

　本書が皆さんの想いの実現に向けて，役に立つことを願ってやみません。それでは，問題1にトライしてみましょう。

　最後に，本書を改訂するにあたり，Kathryn A. Craft 先生に英文校閲を行っていただきました。この場を借りて御礼申し上げます。

著者記す

本書の使い方

1　問題には語数と標準解答時間を示してあります。標準解答時間を目標に問題を解いてください。

2　解説には，解答と設問解説，構文・語句解説があります。設問解説を読み，解答を確認してください。設問解説中の第1・2段落第5文といった表記は，構文・語句解説の番号に対応しています。設問解説中の ➡ Point ⑤ は，対応する表現のポイント番号です。

3　構文・語句解説では，訳例と設問解説で触れなかった，構文および語句の解説があります。設問以外の箇所で理解できなかった部分を確認してください。

4　構文・語句解説では，問題文から下線を省き空所を埋めた形で英文を再録してあります。英文を繰り返し読んでもらいたいからです。こうすることが，速読の練習にもなりますし，語いの定着にもつながります。

5　英文を読む際には，音読とリスニングを組み合わせることで，リスニング力も強化できます。英語のネイティブ・スピーカーが読み上げた音声が用意されていますので，利用してください。

　音声は，パソコンやスマートフォンから下記の URL にアクセスして聴くことができます。QR コードからもアクセスできます。

https://www.kawai-publishing.jp/onsei/01/index.html

・ファイルは MP4形式の音声です。再生するには，最新版の OS をご利用ください。

また，パソコンから URL にアクセスしていただくことで，音声データのダウンロードも可能です。

※ホームページより直接スマートフォンへのダウンロードはできません。パソコンにダウンロードしていただいた上で，スマートフォンへお取り込みいただきますよう，お願いいたします。
・ファイルは ZIP 形式で圧縮されていますので，解凍ソフトが必要です。
・ファイルは MP3形式の音声です。再生するには，Windows Media Player や iTunes などの再生ソフトが必要です。
・Y301〜Y330の全30ファイル構成となっています。

＜音声データに関する注意＞
・当サイトに掲載されている音声ファイルのデータは著作権法で保護されています。本データあるいはそれを加工したものを複製・譲渡・配信・販売することはできません。また，データを使用できるのは，本教材の購入者がリスニングの学習を目的とする場合に限られます。
・お客様のパソコンやネット環境により音声を再生できない場合，当社は責任を負いかねます。ご理解とご了承をいただきますよう，お願いいたします。
・ダウンロードや配信サイトから聴くことができるのは，本書を改訂するまでの期間です。

本書で用いた記号

・（　）は省略可能な語句を表す。
・[ ]は直前の語句と書き換え可能な語句を表す。
・S は主語，O は目的語，C は補語を表す。
・A, B は名詞を表す。
・X, Y は文の中で同じ働きをするものを表す。
・*do* は動詞の原形を表す。
・to *do* は不定詞を表す。
・*doing* は動名詞または現在分詞を表す。
・*done* は過去分詞を表す。
・*one's* は主語と同じ所有格を表す。
・A's は主語と同じになるとは限らない所有格を表す。
・「自動詞＋前置詞」型の熟語は，account for A のように表す。
・「他動詞＋副詞」型の熟語は，put A off のように表す。
・他動詞は，solve「を解く」のように表す。

目　次

Point

①	do の用法	⑯	if
②	動名詞	⑰	no matter wh-節
③	分詞の形容詞用法	⑱	譲歩の as
④	分詞構文	⑲	程度を表す表現
⑤	付帯状況の with	⑳	目的・結果を表す表現
⑥	疑問詞 + to *do*	㉑	not only X but also Y
⑦	形式主語と形式目的語	㉒	強調構文
⑧	同格の that と関係代名詞の that	㉓	省略
⑨	関係代名詞 what	㉔	副詞節内の省略
⑩	the way S V	㉕	倒置
⑪	関係副詞	㉖	仮定法
⑫	非制限用法の関係詞	㉗	仮定法の条件節の倒置
⑬	連鎖関係詞節	㉘	共通関係
⑭	二重限定の関係詞節	㉙	最上級相当表現
⑮	whether	㉚	the + 比較級

本能と学習

▶▶▶ **設問解説** ◀◀◀

問1　直前の文では「本能的行動」について述べられていて，空所(1)の後ろでは「学習された行動」について述べられていることから，空所には前後に対照的な事柄を置くことができる表現が必要である。したがって，正解はイ。

　　それぞれの選択肢は，in と共に用いると以下の意味になる。

　　ア.「実際は」イ.「それとは対照的に」ウ.「特に」エ.「要するに」

問2　(2a) 動詞を強調するために用いられる助動詞。

　　(2b) 「をする」という意味の他動詞。

　　(2c) 前述の動詞句の代用として用いられる代動詞。 ➡ **Point ①**

　　ア.「映画に行くことがありますか」（疑問文を作る助動詞）

　　イ.「私は甘いものはめったに食べないが，子供たちはよく食べる」（代動詞）

　　ウ.「私は確かによく話しますが，妻はさらによく話します」（動詞強調の助動詞）

　　エ.「今夜はやるべき宿題がたくさんあります」（他動詞）

問3　直前の2文で「本能的行動は<u>変わらずに固定している</u>」ことが述べられている。空所(3)を含む文が逆接の接続詞 But で始まっていることと，また直後に述べられている学習による行動の具体例から，「学習による行動は<u>融通の利く，順応性が高いもの</u>である」ことがわかるので，正解はウ。

　　ア.「活動的な」イ.「立派な」ウ.「融通の利く，柔軟性のある」エ.「基本的な」

問4　下線部(4)は「私たちは，進化が環境に対する私たちの反応を変えるのを待ってはいない」というのが文字通りの意味。「人間には順応力があるので，長い時間のかかる生物学的な進化が人間の反応を変えるのを待つのではなく，環境の変化に自ら対応しようと行動する」というのがこの文の真意と考えられる。したがって，正解はエ。

□ wait for A to *do*「Aが…するのを待つ」　　□ evolution「進化」

□ response to A「Aに対する反応」　　□ environment「環境」

問5 figure A out で「Aを理解する」という意味。ここでは A が what it did to succeed「成功するために自分が何をしたのか」という疑問詞節となって out の後ろに移動している。なお，did は他動詞 do「をする」の過去形。

➡ **Point ①**

□ eventually「最終的に，やがては」　　□ organism「生物，有機体」

□ succeed「成功する」

Point ① do の用法

do には一般動詞，代動詞，助動詞の3つの用法がある。主な用法は以下の3つである。

1. 一般動詞の do は，「をする」という意味の他動詞として用いるのが通例。

例 You shouldn't try to **do** everything at a time.
「1度に何もかもしようとしてはいけない」

2. 代動詞の do は，前述の動詞句の代用として用いる。

例 Jane speaks French as well as you **do**.
「ジェーンはあなたと同じくらい上手にフランス語を話します」

3. 助動詞の do は，疑問文や否定文を作る場合に用いるだけでなく，動詞の意味を強調するためにも用いる。

例 You **do** look nice in that dress.
「そのドレス，ほんとうにお似合いですね」

▶▶▶ **構文・語句解説** ◀◀◀

第1段落

¹An instinctive behavior is inherited: you're born with it.　²In contrast, a learned behavior is developed from experience.　³Although humans and some animals do inherit an instinct to learn, the content of their learning is determined by their experience.

---

¹本能的な行動は遺伝的に受け継がれていく。つまり，人はそれを持って生まれるのである。²それに対して，学習による行動は経験から身につく。³人間と一部の動物が学習本能を遺伝的に受け継いでいるのは確かだが，学習の中身は経験によって決定されるのだ。

9

1 □ instinctive「本能的な」　　□ behavior「行動，振る舞い」　　□ inherit「を受け継ぐ」
　□ be born with A「生まれつきAを持っている」
2 □ learned「学習された，獲得された」　　□ develop「を身につける」
　□ experience「経験，体験」
3 □ humans「人間」　　□ instinct to learn「学習本能」　　□ content「内容，中身」
　□ learning「学習」　　□ determine「を決定する」

- -

―― 第 2 段落 ――

[1]Instinctive behavior does not change; it stays the same even when circumstances change. [2]Birds migrate in the winter months even when the weather stays warm. [3]But learned behavior is more flexible. [4]Humans don't hibernate in winter, and most humans don't change where they live seasonally. [5]Instead, they have learned to dress warmly and heat their houses. [6]Humans are very adaptable. [7]Generally we don't wait for evolution to change our responses to the environment; instead, learned behavior enables us to respond quickly to changing circumstances.

[1]本能的行動は変化しない。それは，たとえ環境が変化しても同じままである。[2]たとえ天気が暖かいままであっても，鳥は冬になると移動する。[3]しかし，学習による行動はもっと融通が利く。[4]人間は冬に冬眠することはなく，ほとんどの人は季節によって住む場所を変えることはない。[5]その代わりに，人間は温かい服装をしたり家を暖めたりすることができるようになったのである。[6]人間はとても順応性が高い。[7]概して私たちは，進化が環境に対する私たちの反応を変えてくれるのを待つことはしない。そうではなくて，学習された行動により，変化する環境に素早く反応することができるのである。

1 □ stay C「Cのままである」　　□ circumstances「状況，環境」
2 □ migrate「＜動物や鳥が＞移動する，渡る」　　□ weather「天気，天候」
4 where they live は change の目的語となる名詞節。　　□ seasonally「季節によって」
5 dress warmly と heat their houses が and で結ばれている。　　□ instead「その代わりに」
　□ learn to do「(努力や学習を通じて)…できるようになる」
　□ dress warmly「暖かい服装をする」　　□ heat「を暖める」
6 □ adaptable「順応性が高い，融通の利く」
7 □ generally「一般に，概して」　　□ enable O to do「Oが…するのを可能にする」
　□ respond to A「Aに反応する」

¹To learn from an experience, an organism must have a memory to store information to be used later. ²Memory helps an organism learn through trial and error. ³In trial-and-error learning, an organism tries to do a task again and again, sometimes making mistakes, but other times succeeding. ⁴Eventually the organism figures out what it did to succeed. ⁵A mouse will learn how to get through a maze to find food at the end by trying different routes again and again. ⁶The mouse eventually remembers which routes don't lead to food and which do.

¹経験から学ぶためには，生物は後で使えるように，情報を蓄える記憶力を持っていなければならない。²記憶は生物が試行錯誤を通じて学習を行うのを助けてくれる。³試行錯誤による学習においては，生物は，何度も繰り返して1つの作業を行おうとするが，時には失敗し，また時には成功をおさめる。⁴やがてその生物は，成功するために自分が何を行ったのかを理解する。⁵ハツカネズミは異なるルートを何度も試すことによって，終点にある食べ物を見つけるためには迷路をどのように通り抜ければよいかを学習する。⁶ハツカネズミは，どのルートが食べ物のところまで通じていないのか，どのルートが通じているのかを最終的に覚えるのである。

1 To learn from an experience は目的を表す副詞用法の不定詞句。a memory to store information to be used later の to store 以下は memory を修飾する形容詞用法の不定詞句。また，to be used later は store を修飾する，目的を表す副詞用法の不定詞句。

□ memory「記憶，記憶力」　　□ store「を蓄える」　　□ later「後で，後ほど」

2 □ help O do「Oが…するのを助ける」　　□ trial and error「試行錯誤」

3 sometimes making mistakes, but other times succeeding は2つの分詞構文が but で結ばれている形。また，sometimes ... , but (at) other times ... は「時には…であるが，またある時には」という相関表現になっている。

□ try to do「…しようと努める」　　□ again and again「何度も繰り返して」

5 how to ... the end は learn の目的語となっている。to find food at the end は目的を表す副詞用法の不定詞句。

□ how to do「どのように…すべきか，…する方法」　　□ get through A「Aを通り抜ける」

□ maze「迷路」　　□ route「ルート，経路」

6 which routes don't lead to food と which do が and で結ばれている。これらはいずれも疑問詞節で，remembers の目的語となっている。なお，ここの which do は which routes lead to food と同意。　　□ lead to A「＜道などが＞Aへとつながる，Aまで行く」

11

過剰な情報

解 答

問1　彼は，1970年に出版された本の中でそれに言及し，あまりに多くの情報があるとき，人は決定を下すことが困難になりうるのかを説明した。

問2　ア. dozens of

問3　ウ. negative

問4　controlling information rather than being controlled by it

問5　ア

▶▶▶　**設問解説**　◀◀◀

問1　and は mentioned ... 1970 と described ... information の2つの動詞句を結んでいる。published in 1970 は a book を修飾する過去分詞句。➡ **Point ③** that 節は described の目的語になっている。

　　　□ mention「に言及する」　　□ publish「を出版する」

　　　□ describe「を説明する，の特徴を述べる」

　　　□ have difficulty *doing*「…するのが困難である，…するのに苦労する」

　　　□ make a decision「決定する」

問2　空所(2)を含む文は，直前の第2段落第2文で述べられた「あまりに多くの情報があるとき決定を下すことが困難になる」具体例である。したがって，アが正解。

　　　ア.「多数ある」　イ.「少数ある」　ウ.「わずかな数ある」　エ.「まったくない」

問3　下線部(3)を含む文の次の文に「人々が情報に頼りすぎるようになると，無力や混乱，怒りといった感情が強くなるかもしれない」とあることから，adverse は「悪い，不利な」という意味であると考えられる。

　　　ア.「有益な」　イ.「力強い」　ウ.「否定的な」　エ.「様々な」

問4　直前の文に「問題は，むしろ我々が情報を選び出し，そして有効に利用できることである」とあることから，「21世紀の人々にとって重要な課題は，情報に管理されることではなく，情報を管理することなのだ」という意味になるように，A key challenge for people in the 21st century is [controlling information rather than being controlled by it]. とする。controlling information と being controlled by it はともに動名詞句であるが，動名詞で受動態の意味を表すとき

には being *done* という形になる。→ Point ②

問5　ア．第3段落第2文の内容に一致。

　　　イ．本文に記述なし。

　　　ウ．第4段落第2・3文の内容に不一致。

　　　エ．本文に記述なし。

Point ② 動名詞

　動詞の ing 形が名詞の働きをすることがあり，これを動名詞と呼ぶ。動名詞は動詞の性質も持っているので，その後には目的語や副詞(句)などを続けることができる。

例1　My father enjoys **playing** golf every Sunday.

　　　「私の父は，毎週日曜日にゴルフをするのを楽しんでいる」

例2　After **finishing** his work, Koji left without **saying** good-by.

　　　「仕事を終えて，コウジはさよならを言わないで帰ってしまった」

▶▶ 構文・語句解説 ◀◀

第1段落

[1]The term "information overload," which refers to the problem of having too much information, is not new. [2]These days, however, as more and more information is available thanks to new technologies, it is becoming more problematic than ever before.

[1]あまりに多くの情報があるという問題を指す「情報過多」という言葉は新しいものではない。[2]しかし，最近ではますます多くの情報が新しい科学技術のおかげで手に入るようになるにつれて，かつてないほど問題になってきている。

1 □ term「言葉，用語」　　□ overload「過多，積みすぎ」　　□ refer to A「Aを指す」

　 □ the problem of *doing*「…するという問題」

2 □ these days「最近，近頃」　　□ more and more A「ますます多くのA」

　 □ available「入手可能な」　　□ thanks to A「Aのおかげで」　　□ technology「科学技術」

　 □ problematic「問題のある」　　□ 比較級 ... than ever before「かつてないほど…」

第2段落

[1]The first person to popularize the term was writer Alvin Toffler. [2]He mentioned it in a book published in 1970 and described that a person can have difficulty making a decision

when there is too much information. ³One example can be seen at supermarkets, where shoppers might have a hard time deciding which type of salad dressing or cereal to buy when there are dozens of choices.

¹この言葉を最初に流行らせた人は，アルビン・トフラーという作家であった。²彼は，1970年に出版された本の中でそれに言及し，あまりに多くの情報があるとき，人は決定を下すことが困難になりうるのかを説明した。³一例がスーパーマーケットで見られるが，そこでは選択肢が多数あると，どの種類のサラダドレッシングやシリアルを買ったらよいのか買い物客が決めるのに苦労するかもしれない。

1 □ the first person to *do*「…する最初の人」　　□ popularize「を流行らせる，普及させる」
3 where 以下は supermarkets を修飾する関係副詞節。which type of salad dressing or cereal to buy は which A to *do*「どのAを…すべきか」の形で，deciding の目的語になっている。
　　□ example「例」　　□ shopper「買い物客」
　　□ have a hard time *doing*「…するのに苦労する」　　□ decide「を決める，決定する」
　　□ salad dressing「サラダドレッシング」　　□ cereal「シリアル，穀物加工食品」

── 第3段落 ──

¹A bigger and more complex problem than choosing a product is the enormous amount of information available on the Internet. ²Recent research points out that this flood of information — and its interruption of people's work — has adverse effects on people's health and happiness as well as their decision-making abilities and their productivity. ³When people become too dependent on information, feelings of helplessness, confusion and anger may increase.

¹製品を選択するよりも大きく複雑な問題は，インターネットで入手できる膨大な量の情報である。²最近の研究は，このような情報の洪水と，それが人々の仕事の邪魔になることが，彼らの意思決定能力と生産性だけではなく健康と幸福にも悪影響を与えることを指摘している。³人々が情報に頼りすぎるようになると，無力や混乱，怒りといった感情が強くなるかもしれない。

1 □ complex「複雑な」　　□ product「製品」　　□ enormous「膨大な」　　□ amount「量」
2 □ research「研究」　　□ point out that 節「…であることを指摘する」　　□ flood「洪水」

14

□ interruption「邪魔，中断」　　□ have a ... effect on A「Aに…な影響を与える」

□ X as well as Y「Yだけでなく X も／X も Y も」

□ decision-making ability「意思決定能力」　　□ productivity「生産性」

3 and は helplessness, confusion, anger の3つの名詞を結んでいる。

□ dependent on A「Aに頼って，依存して」　　□ helplessness「無力」

□ confusion「混乱」　　□ increase「増加する」

第4段落

¹Of course, having access to information is not a bad thing. ²The issue is rather our ability to select information and then to use it in effective ways. ³A key challenge for people in the 21st century is controlling information rather than being controlled by it.

---

¹もちろん情報にアクセスできることは悪いことではない。²問題は，むしろ我々が情報を選び出し，そして有効に利用できることである。³21世紀の人々にとって重要な課題は，情報に管理されることではなく，情報を管理することなのだ。

1 □ of course「もちろん」　　□ have access to A「Aにアクセスできる，Aを利用できる」

2 □ issue「問題点」　　□ rather「むしろ」

　□ A's ability to *do*「Aが…できること，Aが…する能力」

　□ select「を選び出す」　　□ in a ... way「…なやり方で」　　□ effective「有効な」

3 □ key「重要な，鍵となる」　　□ challenge「課題」

3 カルチャーショック

解　答

問1　miss

問2　彼らがどう対処すべきかわからない多くの困難があるのかもしれない。

問3　all they want to do is

問4　(4a) ア　　(4b) ウ

問5　悲しくてホームシックであると感じるのはごくありふれたことだが，死に
　　たいと思うことはとても深刻である。

問6　1.イ　　2.エ　　3.イ

▶▶▶　設問解説　◀◀◀

問1　第1段落第1文には「外国での突然の変化のために人は居心地が悪いと感じる」
　　とあり，空所の直前には「人はホームシックになる」と述べられている。その
　　結果，家族や友人などをどのように思うのかを考えればよい。「恋しく思う」と
　　いう意味の1語を探すことになる。したがって，第2段落第2文の miss が正
　　解。

問2　There be S「Sがある」の構文。that they don't know how to deal with は
　　many difficulties を修飾する関係代名詞節。
　　　□ how to *do*「どのように…すべきか，…する方法」　→　**Point** ⑥
　　　□ deal with A「Aを扱う」

問3　All S V ... is ～「Sが…するのは～だけである」を用いて，all they want to
　　do is とすれば意味が通じる。なお，they want to do は先行詞 all を修飾す
　　る関係代名詞節である。

問4　(4a) 前置詞 of の後ろに続く部分なので，名詞がこなければならない。したが
　　って，動名詞である。　→　**Point** ②
　　　(4b) People を修飾する形容詞用法の現在分詞。　→　**Point** ③
　　　ア.「彼は彼女にうそをついたことを認めた」（動名詞）
　　　イ.「何人かの人が通りで叫んでいるのが聞こえた」（補語となる現在分詞）
　　　ウ.「私はベンチで寝ている男に話しかけた」（形容詞用法の現在分詞）
　　　エ.「日曜日だったので，公園は人でいっぱいだった」（分詞構文）

問5　全体の文構造は Feeling sad and homesick(S) is(V) very common(C)　と

16

wishing to be dead(S) is(V) very serious(C) という 2 つの節が but で結ばれている。Feeling sad and homesick と wishing to be dead は共に動名詞句。

→ **Point** ②

□ common「ありふれた，並の」　　□ wish to *do*「…したいと思う」
□ serious「深刻な」

問 6　1.「人ははじめて外国に着いたときなぜわくわくするのか」
　　ア.「多くのことが彼らに母国を思い出させるから」
　　イ.「新しい体験ができるから」
　　ウ.「外国語で何でも話せるから」
　　エ.「その外国について多くのことを知っているから」
　　第 2 段落第 1 文から判断する。

　　2.「外国で居心地が悪いと感じる人がいるのはなぜか」
　　ア.「話をする友人がいないから」
　　イ.「その土地の食べ物を食べに出かけたくないから」
　　ウ.「別の国に行きたいから」
　　エ.「その国に慣れることができないから」
　　第 2 段落第 3 ～ 5 文から判断する。

　　3.「カルチャーショックが深刻になるとどうなるのか」
　　ア.「病院から出たいと思う人もいる」
　　イ.「眠るのが困難だと思う人もいる」
　　ウ.「母国に戻りたくない人もいる」
　　エ.「誰も自国出身の人には会いたいとは思わない」
　　第 3 段落第 2 文から判断する。

Point ③ 分詞の形容詞用法

　現在分詞と過去分詞には形容詞の働きがある。現在分詞が「…する，…している」と能動の意味を持つのに対して，過去分詞は「…される，…された」と受動の意味を持つ。また，単独で名詞を修飾するときには通例名詞の前に置かれ，他の語句を伴うときには名詞の後ろに置かれる。

例 1　**Spoken** language is different from **written** language.
　　　「話し言葉は書き言葉とは異なっている」

例 2　The average Japanese **working** in a big city lives in a small house often **called** a "rabbit hutch."
　　　「大都市で働く平均的な日本人はしばしば『ウサギ小屋』と呼ばれる小さな家で暮らしている」

── 第1段落 ──

[1]While it is exciting to see new sights, to hear a different language and to eat different foods in a foreign country, sometimes the sudden change can make people uncomfortable. [2]People may get homesick and miss their families, friends and the comfort of their home. [3]This is known as culture shock.

[1]外国で新しい景色を見たり，異なる言葉を耳にしたり，様々な食べ物を食べたりすることは，わくわくすることであるが，時には突然の変化のために人は居心地が悪いと感じることがある。[2]人はホームシックになり，家族や友人や自分の家の心地よさを恋しく思う。[3]これはカルチャーショックとして知られている。

1 it is exciting to see ... の it は形式主語で，真主語は to see ... 以下。

the sudden change can make ... の can は可能性を表す。また，make O *do* が無生物主語で用いられると，原因・理由の意味を表すことに注意。

□ uncomfortable「居心地の悪い」

2 □ comfort「心地よさ」

3 □ be known as A「Aとして知られている」

── 第2段落 ──

[1]When you first arrive in a new country, there is a lot to do and see, and it all seems very exciting. [2]After a few weeks or months, however, people often begin to miss their old home. [3]There may be many difficulties that they don't know how to deal with. [4]As a result, they may start to spend time only with others from their own country, or refuse to eat the food from the new country. [5]Sometimes, all they want to do is to complain about how bad things are, and they begin to dislike the country and the people there. [6]This is a difficult time but such feelings are a natural part of getting used to a new country.

[1]はじめて新しい国に着いたとき，したり見たりする多くのことがあり，すべてがとても楽しそうに思われる。[2]しかし，数週間か数ヶ月すると人は住み慣れた家を恋しく思い始めることが多い。[3]彼らがどう対処すべきかわからない多くの困難があるのかもしれない。[4]その結果，彼らは自国出身の人とだけ一緒に時間を過ごしたり，新しい国の食べ物を食べようとしないかもしれない。[5]時には彼らがやりたいことと言えば，状況がどれほど悪いか不平を言うだけで，そ

の国とそこの人を嫌いになり始める。⁶これは困難な時期であるが，そのように感じるのは新しい国に慣れる際に当然のことである。

1 a lot は名詞で「多くのこと」という意味。to do and see は a lot を修飾する形容詞用法の不定詞句。

2 □ miss「を恋しく思う」

4 □ as a result「その結果」　　□ refuse to *do*「どうしても…しようとしない」

5 how bad things are は about A の A の位置にきている名詞節。

　□ complain about A「Aについて文句を言う」　　□ dislike「を嫌う」

6 □ get used to A「Aに慣れる」

・・

── 第3段落 ──

¹Sometimes culture shock becomes serious and turns into a real sickness such as depression. ²A depressed person might have trouble sleeping or might sleep all the time and have no energy. ³They might stop eating and lose weight, or eat too much and gain weight. ⁴People suffering from depression might even think about killing themselves. ⁵If this happens, it is time for them to see a doctor. ⁶Feeling sad and homesick is very common but wishing to be dead is very serious. ⁷Most universities have international student offices and health centers on campus, with trained staff who can help students to get over these "bad times". ⁸People shouldn't be afraid to go to talk to someone about their problems. ⁹Sometimes a friendly chat is all that is needed to help.

¹時にはカルチャーショックは深刻なものになり，うつ病のような本当の病気になることもある。²気が滅入っている人は眠るのに苦労したり，眠ってばかりいて活力がないこともあるかもしれない。³食べることをやめ体重が減ることもあるかもしれないし，食べ過ぎて体重が増えることもあるかもしれない。⁴うつ病に悩んでいる人は自殺のことを考えることさえあるだろう。⁵こうなると彼らは医者に診てもらう時期である。⁶悲しくてホームシックであると感じるのはごくありふれたことだが，死にたいと思うことはとても深刻である。⁷ほとんどの大学にはキャンパスに留学生のための事務所と健康管理センターがあり，学生がこれらの「悪い時期」を乗り越えるのを手助けできる訓練を受けた職員がいる。⁸自分の問題を誰かに相談に行くのを恐れるべきではない。⁹手助けするのに必要なのは親しくおしゃべりするだけという場合もある。

1 □ turn into A「Aに変わる，なる」　　□ depression「うつ病」

2 might have trouble ... の might は「ひょっとしたら…だろう」という意味。第3・4文の might
　　も同じ用法。　　　□ depressed「気が滅入った，落ち込んだ」

　　　□ have trouble *doing*「…するのに苦労する」　　　□ all the time「いつも」

　　　□ energy「活力」

3 □ lose weight「体重が減る」　　　□ gain weight「体重が増える」

4 killing themselves は動名詞句。　　　□ suffer from A「Aに悩む，苦しむ」

　　　□ kill *oneself*「自殺する」

5 □ It is time for A to *do*「A は…する頃だ」　　　□ see a doctor「医者に診てもらう」

7 □ international「国際的な」　　　□ on campus「キャンパスに」　　　□ trained「訓練を受けた」

　　　□ staff「職員」　　　□ help O to *do*「Oが…するのを助ける」

　　　□ get over A「Aを克服する」

8 □ be afraid to *do*「…するのを恐れる」

9 all that is needed ... の that 以下は all を修飾する関係代名詞節。

　　　□ chat「おしゃべりをする」

4 脳の大きさ

▶▶▶ 設問解説 ◀◀◀

問1　the ratio of brain weight to body が主語。is at a maximum at birth と decreases with age という2つの動詞句が and で結ばれている。reaching 以下は連続・結果を表す分詞構文。➡ **Point** ④

　　□ the ratio of A to B「Bに対するAの比率」　　□ at a maximum「最大限である」

　　□ decrease「減少する」　　□ fairly「かなり」　　□ steady「一定の」　　□ level「水準」

　　□ maturity「成熟」

問2　空所(2)を含む文は，occurs suddenly までが完全な文であり，空所の直前の each period of rapid growth の前に接続詞がないので，ア．is とイ．has は入らない。したがって，分詞構文になると考えられるが，each period of rapid growth と associated ... の間には「急激な成長のそれぞれの段階が…と結びつけられる」という受動の意味関係があるのでウ．being が入る。

　　➡ **Point** ④

問3　直前に there があるので，there be S「Sがある」の構文であると考えられる。また，第2段落第1文では「同じ年齢でも異なる人種に属する人の間では脳の相対的な大きさに違いは見つかっていない」と述べられている。

問4　take A into account は「Aを考慮する」という意味の熟語。

　　ア．「を考慮する」イ．「を無視する」ウ．「を排除する」エ．「を作り出す」

問5　be said to *do* は「…すると言われている」という意味。主語の It は，直前の文の The brain of Albert Einstein を指す。lovingly preserved by an admirer

は and 以下の文の主語 parts of it の後ろに置かれ，補足説明をしている分詞構文。 → **Point** ④

☐ relatively「相対的に」　　☐ lovingly「大切に」　　☐ preserve「を保存する」

☐ admirer「崇拝者」　　☐ recently「最近」　　☐ discover「を発見する」

問6　ア.「子供の脳の成長は不規則に起きるという事実に興味を引かれている科学者が多い」第1段落第8文の内容に不一致。

イ.「知能は脳の大きさと何らかの関係があることを証明した研究がたくさんある」第2段落の内容に不一致。

ウ.「日本人の脳は比較的大きいという印象が一般にある」第2段落第2文の内容に不一致。

エ.「アインシュタインの才能は脳細胞の大きさや数によって説明できると考えるアインシュタインの崇拝者もいた」第3段落第4文の内容に一致。

Point ④ 分詞構文

　分詞が文の内容に対して付加的な説明をすることがある。これを分詞構文と呼ぶ。主語と能動の意味関係があるときには現在分詞を用い，受動の意味関係があるときは being *done* となるが，being は省略されることが多い。分詞の意味上の主語が文の主語と異なるときには，意味上の主語となる名詞をその直前に置く。

例1　**Seeing a policeman**, he ran away.
　　　「警官を見て，彼は逃げ出した」

例2　It **being Sunday**, the shops were all closed.
　　　「日曜日だったので，店はすべて閉まっていた」

　文頭に置かれると，前後関係から時「…するとき」，原因・理由「…するので」，条件「…すると」などの意味を表すと解釈できる場合がある。例1では「警官を見たとき［見たので］」と意味を取ることもできる。

例3　Her daughter, **persuaded to change her mind**, gave up her plan.
　　　「彼女の娘は，考えを変えるように説得され，計画をあきらめた」

　主語 Her daughter と「説得される」という受動の意味関係があるので，過去分詞が用いられている。また，主語の後ろに置かれたときは，主語に対する補足説明をしているものとして意味を取ればよい。

例4　The typhoon hit the island, **causing great damage**.
　　　「台風がその島を襲い，大きな被害をもたらした」

　文末に置かれたときは，同時動作・付帯状況「…しながら」，連続・結果「(～し，そして)…する」と意味を取る。

第1段落

¹Considerable attention has been paid to the size or relative size of the human brain. ²The first point of interest is that the ratio of brain weight to body is at a maximum at birth and decreases with age, reaching a fairly steady level by maturity. ³In other words, newborn babies have very large brains, relatively speaking, weighing some 300 grams. ⁴This is roughly the size of the brain of an adult male chimpanzee. ⁵Children and their brains continue to grow for many years, gradually increasing their ability to learn and remember. ⁶There have been suggestions that the growth of the brains of children is not steady, but occurs suddenly, each period of rapid growth being associated with a particularly important developmental or intellectual stage. ⁷These stages could be the ability to reason abstractly, to talk, or even to do arithmetic. ⁸The idea of sudden brain growth is still around, but has not attracted much enthusiasm.

¹人間の脳の大きさ，あるいは相対的な大きさがかなり注目されてきた。²興味深い第1の点は，身体に対する脳の重量の比率が出生時に最も大きく，年齢とともに減少し，成熟するまでにほぼ一定の水準に到達するということである。³言い換えれば，新生児は，およそ300グラムという，相対的に言えば，非常に大きな脳をしている。⁴これはおよそ，成長した雄のチンパンジーの脳の大きさである。⁵子供とその脳は何年もの間成長を続け，徐々に学習能力や記憶力を高めていく。⁶子供の脳の発達は一定ではなく，突発的に起き，急激な成長のそれぞれの段階が特に重要な発達や知的段階と結びついているという提言がたびたびなされてきた。⁷こうした段階とは，抽象的に考えたり，話をしたり，さらには計算したりする能力であるかもしれない。⁸突発的な脳の成長という考えは今でもあるが，あまり強い関心を集めてはいない。

1 □ considerable「かなりの，相当の」　　□ attention「注目，注意」　　□ relative「相対的な」
　　□ brain「脳」
2 that 以下は補語となる名詞節　　□ of interest「興味深い」
3 weighing some 300 grams は very large brains を修飾する現在分詞句。
　　□ in other words「言い換えれば」　　□ newborn baby「新生児」
　　□ relatively speaking「相対的に言えば」　　□ weigh ...「重さが…である」
4 □ roughly「およそ」　　□ male「雄(の)」
5 gradually increasing ... は同時動作・付帯状況を表す分詞構文。
　　□ continue to do「…し続ける」　　□ gradually「徐々に」　　□ ability to do「…する能力」
6 suggestions that ... の that 節は suggestions と同格の名詞節。　　□ suggestion「提言，提案」

23

□ growth「成長」　　□ occur「発生する」　　□ rapid「急な」

□ associate A with B「AをBと結びつける」　　□ particularly「特に」

□ developmental「発達の」　　□ intellectual「知的な」　　□ stage「段階」

7 □ could「…かもしれない」　　□ reason「論理的に考える，推論する」

□ abstractly「抽象的に」　　□ do arithmetic「計算する」

8 □ be around「出回っている」　　□ attract「を集める，引く」

□ enthusiasm「強い興味，熱狂」

・・

―― 第2段落 ――

[1]Some research has shown differences in the relative sizes of the brains of males and females of the same age, but so far no great differences have been found between people of the same age but of different ethnic groups. [2]Obviously the brain of a small Japanese teenager is very much smaller than that of a giant Russian boy. [3]But when brain size is adjusted for size or weight of the body, there does not seem to be great advantage for either with respect to intelligence. [4]Moreover, in measuring intelligence one has, of course, to take into account the effects of education and cultural background.

[1]同じ年齢の男性と女性の脳の相対的な大きさの違いを示した研究はあるが，これまでのところ同じ年齢でも異なる人種に属する人の間では大きな違いは見つかっていない。[2]言うまでもなく，小柄な日本人の10代の若者の脳は大柄なロシア人の少年の脳に比べるとはるかに小さい。[3]しかし，脳の大きさが身体の大きさや重さの点から調整されると，知能に関してはいずれにとっても大きく優位になることはないようである。[4]さらに知能を測るには，教育や文化的背景の影響を考慮しなければならないことは言うまでもない。

1 of the same age but of different ethnic groups の but は people を修飾する of the same age と of different ethnic groups を結んでいる。

□ research「研究」　　□ female「雌(の)」　　□ so far「これまでのところ」

□ ethnic group「人種集団」

2 that of a giant Russian boy の that は the brain の代用。

□ obviously「言うまでもなく，明らかに」　　□ much+比較級「ずっと…，はるかに…」

3 □ adjust「を調整する」　　□ advantage「優位」　　□ with respect to A「Aに関しては」

□ intelligence「知能」

4 □ moreover「さらに，そのうえ」　　□ measure「を測る」　　□ of course「もちろん」

□ effect「影響」　　□ education「教育」　　□ cultural「文化的な」　　□ background「背景」

24

¹Individual brain sizes, particularly of famous people, have also attracted attention, but with very few real results. ²The brain of Albert Einstein, an intellectual giant of the twentieth century, has intrigued many people. ³It is said to have been relatively large, and parts of it, lovingly preserved by an admirer, were recently discovered in the USA. ⁴It was suggested that his genius might have been due to the size or number of brain cells. ⁵However, on closer examination, there was actually very little difference between the brain cells of Einstein and those of other people.

¹また個人の脳の大きさが，特に有名人の場合，注目を集めてきたが，実質的に結果が出たことはほとんどない。²20世紀の知的巨人であるアルバート・アインシュタインの脳は，多くの人の興味をそそってきた。³それは比較的大きかったと言われているが，その一部が崇拝者によって大切に保存されており，最近アメリカで発見された。⁴彼の才能は，脳細胞の大きさや数によるものであったかもしれないと言われた。⁵しかし，さらによく調べてみると，アインシュタインの脳細胞と他の人の脳細胞の間には実際にはほとんど差はなかったのである。

1 but with very few real results は have also attracted attention を修飾する副詞句で，「実質的に結果が出たことはほとんどない」という意味。

□ result「結果」

2 □ intrigue「の興味をそそる」

4 It was suggested that ... の It は形式主語で，真主語は that 以下。

□ suggest「を示唆する」　　□ genius「才能／天才」

□ might have *done*「…だったかもしれない」　　□ be due to A「Aのためである」

□ cell「細胞」

5 those of other people の those は the brain cells の代用。

□ on examination「調べてみると」　　□ close「綿密な」　　□ actually「実際は」

5 読書

> ## 解 答
>
> 問1　takes most people many years to achieve
> 問2　他の人が 8 年かそれ以上かかって到達するか，あるいはまったく到達でき
> 　　　ないかもしれない水準の技量をわずか 2 年か 4 年で獲得する人もいるかもし
> 　　　れない。
> 問3　エ. with
> 問4　イ. getting the literal meaning of the message itself
> 問5　イ. in terms of meaning
> 問6　ア

▶▶▶ 設問解説 ◀◀◀

問1　It takes O_1 O_2 to *do* で「O_1が…するのにO_2を必要とする」という意味。直前
　　　の文に「読むということとは，1 度にすべて習得することができない複雑な技
　　　能である」とあるので，「たいていの人がうまく行えるようになるのに何年も要
　　　するのである」という意味になるように並べ換える。
　　　□ achieve「を達成する」

問2　主語の Some は名詞で Some people を表している。述語動詞 achieve の目的
　　　語が a level of proficiency である。that 以下は a level of proficiency を修飾
　　　する関係代名詞節。or perhaps never の後ろに reach が省略されている。in
　　　two or four years と in eight or more の in は期間を表す。
　　　□ proficiency「技量」

問3　空所の直後には，「言語が両者の共通の構成要素である」というように主語＋述
　　　語という意味関係が成立する名詞＋*doing* が続いているので，付帯状況の with
　　　が入る。 **→ Point ⑤**

問4　「あらためて考えてみると，大変な偉業である」ことが何かを考える。第 4 段落
　　　第 2・3 文には，get the literal meaning of a verbal message ということ
　　　が，「言葉自体の認識だけでなく，文法的機能の解釈やそれぞれの文における意
　　　味的解釈を伴うことである」と述べられている。したがって，正解はイ。

問5　直後にthat is to say「すなわち」とあるので，下線部⑸を含む部分と，we have
　　　以下が同じ内容になるはずである。we have 以下では，「文の鍵となる言葉それ

26

それに適切な意味を与えた」とある。

ア.「文法にしたがって」イ.「意味の点から」ウ.「異なるやり方で」エ.「自分の都合がいいように」

□ semantically「意味的に」

問6　ア.「文字通りの意味をとらえることである」第5段落第1文には「文字通りの意味をとらえるよりいっそう多くのことを伴う」とあるので，述べられていない。

イ.「筆者の考えを自分の考えと照らし合わせて評価することである」第5段落第3文の内容と一致。

ウ.「行間を読むことである」第5段落第5文の内容と一致。

エ.「論理的思考を行うことである」第5段落第6・7文の内容と一致。

□ mature「成熟した」

Point ⑤ 付帯状況の with

with A＋〜で「Aが〜である状態で」という意味を表す。〜には分詞，形容詞，副詞などがきて，直前の名詞 A との間に主語＋述語という意味関係が成立する。このような用法の with を付帯状況の with と呼ぶ。

例1 He was listening to music **with** his eyes closed, and tears running down his cheeks.

「彼は目を閉じて，涙で頬をぬらしながら音楽を聴いていた」

例2 She slept **with** the window open and the light on.

「彼女は窓を開け，灯りをつけたまま眠った」

▶▶▶ 構文・語句解説 ◀◀◀

― 第1段落 ―

¹Reading, like playing an instrument, is a complex skill that is not learned *all at once*. ²It takes most people many years to achieve a skillful performance. ³And like piano playing there are wide variations among individuals exposed to the same amount of practice. ⁴Some may achieve only in two or four years a level of proficiency that others may reach in eight or more, or perhaps never.

¹読むということとは，楽器を演奏することと同じように，１度にすべて習得することができない複雑な技能である。²たいていの人がうまく行えるようになるのに何年も要するのである。³それに，ピアノの演奏のように，同じだけの練習をした人の間でも大きな差がある。⁴他の人

が8年かそれ以上かかって到達するか，あるいはまったく到達できないかもしれない水準の技量をわずか2年か4年で獲得する人もいるかもしれない。

1 that is not learned *all at once* は a complex skill を修飾する関係代名詞節。
　□ instrument「楽器」　　□ complex「複雑な」　　□ skill「技能」
　□ all at once「1度にすべて／突然」
2 □ skillful「熟練した」　　□ performance「行うこと」
3 exposed to the same amount of practice は individuals を修飾する過去分詞句。
　□ variation「差，違い」　　□ expose A to B「AにBを受けさせる」
　□ the amount of A「Aの量」　　□ practice「練習」

- -

── 第2・3段落 ──

¹What do we mean by reading? ²More specifically, what is the essential reading skill?

³The essential skill in reading is getting meaning from a printed or written message. ⁴Thus, reading and listening have much in common, with language being the common component of both. ⁵There are some differences between reading and understanding spoken messages. ⁶The written message does not have the intonation, stress, and emphasis of the spoken message. ⁷But the written message has punctuation and other conventions of print to tell the reader when to pause, and what to emphasize.

¹読むということはどういうことなのだろうか。²もっと具体的に言えば，必須の読む技能とは何であろうか。

³読むことにおける必須の技能とは，印刷された，あるいは書かれたメッセージから意味をとらえることである。⁴したがって，読むことと聞くことは，言語が両者の共通の構成要素であり，共通点が多い。⁵読むことと話されるメッセージを理解することの間にはいくつか違いもある。⁶書かれたメッセージには，話されるメッセージにある抑揚や強勢や強調がない。⁷しかし，書かれたメッセージには句読法やその他の印刷の約束事があり，読み手にどこで区切ったり，何を強調するのかを伝える。

1 □ mean A by B「BでAのことを言う」
2 □ specifically「具体的には」　　□ essential「必須の，欠くことができない」
3 printed or written message の printed と written は message を修飾する過去分詞。
　□ meaning「意味」　　□ print「を印刷する」
4 □ have A in common「Aを共通して持つ」　　□ common「共通の」

□ component「構成要素」

5 spoken message の spoken は message を修飾する過去分詞。

6 □ intonation「抑揚，イントネーション」　　□ stress「強勢」　　□ emphasis「強調」

7 when to pause, and what to emphasize は tell の目的語。

□ punctuation「句読法」　　□ convention「約束事，慣例」　　□ pause「区切る，間を置く」

□ emphasize「を強調する」

---

[1]Of course, reading is much more than getting the literal meaning of the message itself — although even this is quite an accomplishment, when we stop to think about it. [2]For as John B. Carroll so aptly put it, to get the literal meaning of a verbal message means that we have not only recognized the words themselves, but have interpreted them "in their particular grammatical functions...." [3]Moreover, each sentence has been interpreted semantically; that is to say, we have given the proper meaning to each of the key words in the sentence.

---

[1]もちろん，読むということはメッセージそれ自体の文字通りの意味をとらえるだけのことではない。もっとも，このことさえも，あらためて考えてみると，大変な偉業ではあるが。[2]というのもジョン・B・キャロルが見事に言い表したように，言葉によるメッセージの文字通りの意味をとらえることは，言葉自体を認識しただけでなく，「特定の文法的機能において」解釈したということなのである。[3]さらに，それぞれの文が意味的に解釈されている。すなわち，文の鍵となる言葉それぞれに適切な意味を与えたということなのだ。

1 □ of course「もちろん」　　□ much＋比較級「ずっと…，はるかに…」

□ literal「文字通りの」　　□ accomplishment「偉業」　　□ stop to think「あらためて考える」

2 □ as S put it「S が言うように」　　□ aptly「適切に」　　□ verbal「言葉の」

□ not only X but (also) Y「X だけでなく Y も」　　□ recognize「を認識する」

□ interpret「を解釈する」　　□ particular「特定の」　　□ grammatical「文法的な」

□ function「機能」

3 □ moreover「さらに，そのうえ」　　□ sentence「文」

□ that is to say「すなわち，つまり」　　□ proper「適切な」　　□ key「鍵となる，主要な」

¹And mature reading implies even more than getting the literal meaning. ²It means evaluating the ideas for truth, validity, or importance. ³We do this by checking them against our own experience or knowledge. ⁴We think of the implications for future actions. ⁵And we may make inferences or draw conclusions that go far beyond what is explicitly stated in the text. ⁶When this is done, we are really engaging in "reasoning" or "thinking." ⁷And indeed, to read at the highest level of maturity means thinking and reasoning, and having an advanced command of language, concept, and experience.

¹そして，成熟した読み方は文字通りの意味をとらえるよりいっそう多くのことを伴う。²そこに述べられた考えを真実性，妥当性，重要性の点から評価することなのだ。³我々は，その考えを自らの経験や知識と照らし合わせることでこれを行う。⁴我々はこれからの行いに及ぼす影響について考える。⁵さらに我々は推測を行い，文章にはっきりと述べられていることをはるかにしのぐ結論を引き出すのかもしれない。⁶これが行われるとき，我々は本当に「論理的思考」あるいは「思索」を行っているのである。⁷そして実際に，最も成熟した水準で読むことは，思索し論理的に考えることなのであり，言語や概念，経験を高度に操ることができるということなのだ。

1 □ imply「を必然的に伴う」

2 □ evaluate「を評価する」　　□ validity「妥当性」

3 □ check A against B「AをBと照らし合わせる」　　□ experience「経験」
　□ knowledge「知識」

4 □ implication for A「Aに対する影響」　　□ action「行為，行い」

5 that go far beyond what is explicitly stated in the text は conclusions を修飾する関係代名詞節。what は関係代名詞。
　□ make inferences「推測する」　　□ conclusion「結論」　　□ go beyond A「Aにまさる」
　□ explicitly「はっきりと，明確に」　　□ state「を述べる」　　□ text「本文」

6 □ engage in A「Aに従事する」　　□ reasoning「論理的思考，推論」

7 □ maturity「成熟」　　□ advanced「高度な」　　□ have a command of A「Aを自由に操る」
　□ concept「概念」

よりよい親となるために

▶▶　**設問解説**　◀◀

問1　後ろに I shoved ... と完全な文がきているので，空所から his brother までが副詞的な働きになるように選ぶ。thinking を入れて分詞構文にすると，分詞句の意味上の主語も I となり，「私はジュリアンが弟に何かひどいことをしたに違いないと思って」と意味も通じる。したがって，正解はウ。なお，Suddenly angry は Suddenly being angry の being が省略された分詞構文。

→　**Point** ④

問2　第3段落第2文に述べられた a silly, harmless prank「ばかげた悪意のないいたずら」から判断する。

　　ア．「あっ，電気が消えた」

　　イ．「おとうさん，ジュリアンがナイフで僕を傷つけたよ」

　　ウ．「あっ，ナイフで指を切っちゃった」

　　エ．「おとうさん，ジュリアンは僕がいるのに明かりを消しちゃったんだよ」

問3　下線部(3)を含む文の意味は「そのことに私はひどい気分になった」である。したがって，ひどい気分になるような何を筆者がしたのかを答えればよい。第3段落第2文には「自制心を失って，自分も子供の頃に何度もやったばかげた悪意のないいたずらのことで，あやうく我が子を傷つけるところだった」と述べられているので，この部分を制限字数に留意してまとめる。

31

問4 we're trying to discourage は the very behavior を修飾する関係代名詞節
で，下線部は「我々がやめさせようとしているまさにその行動」という意味。
第4・5段落第3文に we adults とあるように we は「大人」のことである。
したがって，正解はウ。なお，ここでは誰にやめさせようとしているのか明示
されていないが，第4・5段落第1〜3文の文脈から，やめさせようとしてい
る相手が「子供」であることは明らかである。
　□ the very A「まさにそのA」　　　□ behavior「行動，振る舞い」
　□ discourage「を思いとどまらせる，妨げる」

問5 The way is by *doing* で「方法は…によってである」の表現。なお，children
learn ... to do は the most powerful ways を修飾する関係副詞節。
　➡ **Point ⑪** また，learn の目的語は and で結ばれた what to do と
what not to do である。➡ **Point ⑥**
　□ one of the A「A〈複数名詞〉のうちの1つ」
　□ powerful「効果的な／力強い」

問6 第6段落第3文から「あなたが食事の後片づけをしないでテレビを見れば」子
供が宿題をどうするのかを判断する。
　ア.「を扱う」イ.「を延期する」ウ.「を実行する」エ.「を調べる」

問7 全体の文構造は one(S) is(V) to learn ... stress(C) である。way to become
は，to become が形容詞用法の不定詞句で，「…になる方法」という意味。
　□ in the end「結局」　　　□ handle「を扱う，処理する」
　□ *one's* own A「自分自身のA」

Point ⑥ 疑問詞 + to *do*

　疑問詞 + to *do* は名詞句を作り，「疑問詞の意味 + すべきか[できるか]」と意
味を取る。

例1 The problem was **when to start**.
　　「問題はいつ出発すべきかであった」

例2 I taught him **how to swim**.
　　「私は彼に泳ぎ方を教えた」

▶▶▶ **構文・語句解説** ◀◀◀

── 第1・2段落 ──

　[1]One evening, hearing six-year-old Justin scream, I ran down the hall in the direction of
the cry. [2]I found my other son Julian — two years older and stronger — grinning outside
the bathroom door while his brother continued to cry from within. [3]Suddenly angry,

thinking that he must have done something awful to his brother, I shoved Julian away from the door so hard that he fell, his head grazing a nearby wall.

⁴I flung open the bathroom door, expecting to see blood everywhere, but Justin seemed fine. ⁵He announced, "Daddy, Julian turned the light off on me!"

¹ある晩，6歳になるジャスティンが叫ぶのを聞き，私は悲鳴のするほうに向かって廊下を走った。²するともう1人の息子のジュリアン—2歳年上で弟より強い—がバスルームのドアの外でにやにやして，弟は中から叫び続けていた。³私はジュリアンが弟に何かひどいことをしたに違いないと思って不意に怒りにかられ，ジュリアンをドアのところから強く押したので，彼は転び，頭が近くの壁をかすった。

⁴私はそこらじゅう血だらけだろうと思ってバスルームのドアをさっと開けたが，ジャスティンは元気そうに見えた。⁵ジャスティンは「おとうさん，ジュリアンは僕がいるのに明かりを消しちゃったんだよ」と言った。

1 hearing six-year-old Justin scream は分詞構文で，知覚動詞＋O *do* を用いた表現。
　□ scream「きゃっと悲鳴をあげる」　□ hall「廊下」　□ in the direction of A「Aの方向に」
2 □ grin「にやにやする」　□ continue to *do*「…し続ける」
3 so hard that ... は so ... that ～「非常に…なので～する」を用いた表現。his head grazing ... は分詞構文。　□ awful「恐ろしい」　□ shove「を押しのける」　□ graze「をかすめる」
4 expecting to see blood everywhere は分詞構文。　□ fling A open「Aをさっと開ける」
5 □ announce「を知らせる」

── 第3段落 ──

¹I'm a psychologist, supposed to know how to handle people, especially little ones. ²Yet I had lost control of myself and nearly injured my child over a silly, harmless prank, one that I had played a dozen times myself as a boy. ³I felt terrible about it.

¹私は心理学者で人々，特に幼い子供たちの扱いは心得ているはずである。²しかし，自制心を失って，自分も子供の頃に何度もやったばかげた悪意のないいたずらのことで，あやうく我が子を傷つけるところだった。³このことに私はひどい気分になった。

1 supposed to know ... は be supposed to *do*「…することになっている」を用いた表現で，ここでは being が省略された分詞構文になっている。little ones は「子供」のこと。

□ psychologist「心理学者」　　□ especially「特に」

2 one that I had ... の one は prank の代用。that 以下は one を修飾する関係代名詞節。as a boy は「子供の頃」という意味。

□ nearly「もう少しで…するところで，ほとんど」　　□ injure「を傷つける」

□ harmless「悪意のない」　　□ a dozen「かなりたくさんの」

— 第4・5段落 —

¹Our children make us angry sometimes. ²They get lazy, they make mistakes, they do silly, mischievous or thoughtless things. ³But when we adults react without thinking, when we shout or strike, we usually accomplish little. ⁴And rightly so: we exhibit the very behavior we're trying to discourage.

⁵Children do need discipline, but how can we get them to do the right thing without losing the calm, adult dignity that they need to witness in us?

¹子供はときに私たちを怒らせる。²怠けたり過ちを犯したり，ばかばかしいことやいたずら，無分別なことをする。³だが私たち大人が考えもなしに反応したり怒鳴ったりぶったりしても，たいていはほとんど効果がない。⁴それも当然だ。私たちは自分たちがやめさせようとしている行動そのものを見せているのだから。

⁵子供にしつけが必要なのは確かだが，子供たちが我々の中に見いだす必要のある冷静な大人らしい威厳を失うことなく，どのようにして彼らに正しいことをさせればよいのだろうか。

2 □ lazy「怠けた」　　□ mischievous「いたずら好きな」　　□ thoughtless「軽率な，考えのない」

3 accomplish little の little は名詞で「少ししかないもの」という意味。

□ react「反応する」　　□ accomplish「を成し遂げる」

4 □ rightly「当然のことだが」　　□ exhibit「を示す」

5 do need の do は動詞強調の助動詞 do。that 以下は the calm, adult dignity を修飾する関係代名詞節。　　□ discipline「規律，しつけ」　　□ get O to do「Oに…させる」

□ calm「落ち着いた」　　□ dignity「威厳」　　□ witness「を目撃する」

— 第6段落 —

¹One of the most powerful ways children learn what to do and what not to do is by watching you. ²As you "model" various behaviors, sooner or later your children will imitate you. ³If you shout to get your way, you can expect your children to do the same. ⁴If you watch television instead of doing the dishes, your child will likely put off a

homework assignment.

　¹子供がすべきこととすべきでないことを学ぶ最も効果的な方法の1つは，あなたを観察することによってである。²あなたがさまざまな行動の「モデル」を示すうちに，遅かれ早かれ子供はあなたをまねるようになる。³もしあなたが怒鳴って思い通りにするなら，子供もそうするようになると考えてよい。⁴あなたが食事の後片づけをしないでテレビを見れば，たぶん子供も宿題を後回しにするだろう。

2 □ model「の模範とする，を手本とする」　　□ sooner or later「遅かれ早かれ」
　 □ imitate「をまねる」
3 □ get *one's*（own）way「自分の思い通りにする」
　 □ expect O to *do*「Oが…するのを予期する」
4 □ instead of *doing*「…する代わりに，…しないで」　　□ do the dishes「皿洗いをする」
　 □ likely「たぶん」ここでは副詞。　　□ homework assignment「宿題」

────── 第7段落 ──────

　¹And take a few deep breaths yourself! ²It's hard to think clearly when you're angry. ³You might forget every sensible thing you know about child-rearing. ⁴In the end, one of the best ways to become a better parent is to learn better ways of handling your own stress.

　¹行動を起こす前に心を落ち着かせなさい。²怒っているときに明瞭に考えるのは難しい。³子育てについてあなたが知っている賢明な事柄をすっかり忘れてしまうかもしれない。⁴結局，よりよい親になる最善の方法の1つは，自分自身のストレスに対処するためのよりよい方法を学ぶことである。

1 take a few deep breaths は文字通りの意味は「数回深呼吸する」だが，「行動を起こす前に心を落ち着かせる」という意味で用いられる慣用表現。
2 It's hard to think ... の It は形式主語で，真主語は to think 以下。
3 you know about child-rearing は every sensible thing を修飾する関係代名詞節。
　 □ might「ひょっとすると…かもしれないだろう」　　□ sensible「分別のある」
　 □ child-rearing「子育て」

7 辛抱強く待つこと

解 答

問1 我々は忍耐力を養うか，少なくともじれったい気持ちを隠すことを学ぶ。なぜならそのようにしないことは社会的に容認されないということを知っているからである。

問2 そのうえ，時間に関する理解が限られているため，何かを得るのにどれくらい待たなければならないかを推測するのは幼い子供には困難である。

問3 イ

問4 イ. takes

問5 ウ. patient

問6 エ. pleasantly

▶▶▶ 設問解説 ◀◀◀

問1 or が結んでいるのは，develop patience と learn to hide our impatience である。また，その理由を表す because 節は，we(S) know(V) that ...(O)という構造。it は形式主語で，to do otherwise が真主語である。 **➡ Point ⑦**

なお，ここでの otherwise は「別のやり方で，違ったふうに」という意味で，「さもなければ」ではないことに注意。

> **例1** He left home three minutes earlier; otherwise he would have missed the train.
> 「彼は3分早めに家を出た。さもなければその電車に乗り遅れていたであろう」

> **例2** If you think otherwise, then what is your alternative?
> 「もしそう考えないのだったら他にどうお考えですか」

□ develop「を発達させる」　　□ patience「忍耐力」　　□ at least「少なくとも」

□ hide「を隠す」　　□ impatience「じれったさ，気短」

□ unacceptable「容認できない」

問2 全体の文構造は，形式目的語を用いた S make it C for A to *do*「SはAが…するのをCにする」という形である。 **➡ Point ⑦** estimate の目的語は how long ... の疑問詞節である。なお，their / them / they はすべて第1段落第3文の small children を指している。

□ in addition「そのうえ」　　□ limited「限られた」　　□ comprehension「理解」

□ estimate「を見積もる」　　□ how long S V ...「どのくらい…」

□ will have to *do*「…しなければならないだろう」

問3 次の文の「彼の食べるものを用意しているとき」という内容から判断する。

　ア.「疲れ切っている」

　イ.「お腹がすいた」

　ウ.「テレビゲームがしたい」

　エ.「その番組が見たい」

問4 It takes O for A to *do* ...「…するのにAにはO〈時間〉かかる」の表現。

問5 第2段落は，第2段落第1文に述べられた「忍耐強く待つことを教える多くの機会」の具体例として，お腹をすかせた子供と氷を要求する子供の例を挙げている。したがって，子供が学ばなければならないことは「忍耐強く待つこと」である。

　ア.「想像力豊かな」イ.「正直な」ウ.「忍耐強い」エ.「どん欲な」

問6 agreeably は「楽しく」という意味。たとえ意味を知らなくても，コロン（：）以下の内容，特に第3段落第4文 Car rides can be made much more pleasant および第5文 pass the time more happily の部分から推測すること。

　ア.「優しく」イ.「不注意に」ウ.「思慮深く」エ.「楽しく」

Point ⑦ 形式主語と形式目的語

　不定詞句や名詞節が主語になるときには，it を形式主語として用いて，本来の主語を後ろに置くことがある。

例　**It** is a pity that Takashi can't come.

　「タカシが来られないのは残念です」

　不定詞句や名詞節が SVOC の目的語になるときには，it を形式目的語として用いて，本来の目的語を後ろに置くことがある。

例　She found **it** easy to solve the problem.

　「彼女はその問題を解くのは簡単だとわかった」

--- 第 1 段落 ---

¹Waiting patiently is hard to do, even for grown-ups. ²We develop patience, or at least learn to hide our impatience, because we know that it is socially unacceptable to do otherwise. ³For small children, waiting is especially difficult. ⁴They don't care yet about what others think, so they express their impatience openly. ⁵In addition, their limited comprehension of time makes it difficult for them to estimate how long they will have to wait for something. ⁶"How much longer?" ⁷"Can we go now?" ⁸"Are we there yet?" ⁹"When is it time?" ¹⁰These are questions that reveal how difficult it is for small children not only to wait, but to understand the general framework of time passing.

¹忍耐強く待つことは大人にとってさえも難しいことである。²我々は忍耐力を養うか，少なくともじれったい気持ちを隠すことを学ぶ。なぜならそのようにしないことは社会的に容認されないということを知っているからである。³幼い子供にとって待つことは特に難しい。⁴彼らは他人が考えていることをまだ気にしないので，あからさまにじれったい気持ちを表す。⁵そのうえ，時間に関する理解が限られているため，何かを得るのにどれくらい待たなければならないかを推測するのは幼い子供には困難である。⁶「あとどれくらいかかるの？」⁷「もう行けるの？」⁸「もう着いた？」⁹「それはいつ？」¹⁰これらの質問は，幼い子供が待つことだけでなく時間の経過の大まかな枠組みを理解することもいかに難しいかを示すものである。

1 □ patiently「忍耐強く」　　□ grown-up「大人」

3 □ especially「特に」

4 what others think の what は関係代名詞で「他人が考えること」という意味。

　□ care about A「Aを気にかける」　　□ express「を表す，表現する」

10 that reveal ... time passing は questions を修飾する関係代名詞節。

　how difficult it is for ... は形式主語構文 It is＋形容詞＋for A to do「Aが…するのは～である」を用いたもので，全体は reveal の目的語となる名詞節である。ここでは to do の部分に not only X but（also）Y「XだけでなくYも」の表現が用いられている。

　□ reveal「を示す」　　□ general「全般的な」　　□ framework「枠組み」

--- 第 2 段落 ---

¹Everyday life provides an abundance of opportunities to teach our children how to wait patiently. ²"I'm hungry!" a child cries impatiently. ³As we're preparing his food, we can explain to him that the pasta needs to be cooked, the vegetables need to be cut, the

orange must be peeled first. ⁴"I want an ice cube!" another child demands. ⁵By showing her the ice tray and explaining that it takes time for the water to change into ice cubes, we help her understand why she has to wait, and give her a science lesson at the same time. ⁶We can listen when our children express their impatience, and let them know we understand how hard it can be to wait, while explaining that some things take time, and that we need to learn to be patient while the necessary steps are being taken.

¹毎日の生活が子供にどうすれば忍耐強く待つことができるかを教える多くの機会を与える。²「お腹がすいた」と子供はじれったく大声で言う。³子供の食べるものを用意しているとき，パスタは調理する必要があること，野菜は切る必要があること，オレンジはまず皮をむかなければならないことを子供に説明することができる。⁴「氷が１つほしい」と別の子供が要求する。⁵その子に製氷皿を見せて水が氷になるには時間がかかることを説明することによって，子供がなぜ待たなければならないかを理解するのを助け，同時に理科の勉強もさせてやることができる。⁶子供がじれったい気持ちを表すとき，我々は耳を傾け，待つことがどれほど大変かがわかっていることを子供に知らせてやることができる。その一方で時間を必要とすることもあること，また必要な手段が講じられている間，忍耐強く待つことができるようにならなければならないことを説明できるのだ。

1 how to wait patiently は teach の目的語。　　□ provide「を与える」

　　□ an abundance of A「豊富なA」　　□ opportunity to *do*「…する機会」

2 □ impatiently「じれったそうに，気短に」

3 that the pasta ... peeled first は explain の目的語となる名詞節。

　　□ prepare「を準備する」　　□ explain (to A) that 節「(A〈人〉に)…だと説明する」

　　□ vegetable「野菜」　　□ peel「の皮をむく」

4 □ ice cube「角氷」　　□ demand「要求する」

5 and give her ... の and が結んでいるのは，help her ... と give her ... である。

　　□ ice tray「製氷皿」　　□ change into A「Aに変わる，変化する」

　　□ help O *do*「Oが…するのを助ける」

6 how hard ... to wait は understand の目的語となる名詞節であり，it は形式主語で，真主語は to wait。while explaining that ... は while の後に S＋be が省略された形。the necessary steps are being taken は take steps「手段を講じる」が進行形の受動態で用いられている。

　　□ let O *do*「Oに…させる」

¹Waiting in line at the grocery store or going on long car rides are particularly challenging situations for kids. ²But these times too can provide them with valuable lessons in learning how to wait. ³We can help by showing them ways to make the time pass agreeably: waiting in line may present an opportunity to chat about school or a recent activity that we haven't yet had a chance to discuss. ⁴Car rides can be made much more pleasant when we bring or make up games to play along the way. ⁵Even very young children can pass the time more happily when they have something interesting to do: for example, counting all the trucks, red cars, or white houses they see.

¹食料雑貨店で並んで待つことや長時間車で出かけることは，子供にとって特に忍耐力を試すような状況である。²しかし，このようなときも，どのように待つべきかを学ぶ価値ある教訓を子供に与えることができる。³我々は子供に時間が楽しく過ぎるような方法を示すことによって子供を助けてやることができる。並んで待てば，学校のことや我々がまだ話し合う機会のなかった最近の活動についておしゃべりをする機会が与えられるかもしれない。⁴ドライブは道中で遊べるゲームを持っていったり作ったりすると，ずっと楽しくなることもある。⁵とても幼い子供でさえ，たとえば，目に入るトラックや赤い車，白い家をみんな数えるような，おもしろくやれることがあるとより楽しく時間を過ごせるのだ。

1 Waiting in ... rides は動名詞句で are の主語。
　　□ in line「一列に並んで」　　□ grocery store「食料雑貨店」
　　□ challenging「(人の)技能や能力を試すような」ここでは忍耐強く待つことができるかどうか，子供にとって大変な状況という意味。　　□ situation「状況」　　□ kid「子供」
2 □ provide A with B「A〈人〉にBを与える」　　□ valuable「価値のある」
　　□ lesson「教訓，教え」
3 make the time pass は使役動詞 make O do「Oに…させる」を用いた表現。
　chat about A「Aについておしゃべりする」Aに相当するのは，school or a recent activity。that we haven't ... to discuss は a recent activity を修飾する関係代名詞節。
　　□ recent「最近の」　　□ activity「活動」　　□ discuss「について話し合う」
4 Car rides can be made much more pleasant は make O C「OをCにする」を受動態にした形。なお，much は比較級を強調している。　　□ make A up「Aを作る」
　　□ along the way「途中で，道中で」
5 they see は all the trucks, red cars, or white houses を修飾する関係代名詞節。
　　□ count「を数える」　　□ truck「トラック」

新発見された小惑星

解 答

問1 (1a) ア　　(1b) イ　　(1c) エ　　(1d) ウ

問2 それが木星に衝突することを避けられる唯一の理由は，その軌道が卵形であるということであり，そのためこの岩が公転するとき，巨大惑星の軌道の内側に入り，次にその外側に出ていくのである。

問3 イ. stable

問4 その小惑星が太陽系のどの部分から来たのかを知るために過去にさかのぼってそれをたどって行けるようにする新しい方法を私たちは開発しました。

問5 エ. an outsider

問6 イ. Research Shows Asteroid Came from Outside Our Solar System

▶▶▶ 設問解説 ◀◀◀

問1 (1a) 主格の関係代名詞。(1b) 指示形容詞。(1c) 同格の名詞節を導く接続詞。(1d) 目的語となる名詞節を導く接続詞。 **➡ Point ⑧**

ア.「昨日来た手紙が見つかりません」(主格の関係代名詞)

イ.「私たちは美しい街に暮らしていて，街がそうあり続けることを望んでいます」(指示形容詞)

ウ.「誰も私に彼が病気だったと言わなかった」(目的語となる名詞節を導く接続詞)

エ.「彼女がうそをついたという事実は彼を怒らせた」(同格の名詞節を導く接続詞)

問2 前半の構造は The only reason ...(S) is(V) that 〜(C) であり，「…の唯一の理由は，〜ということ」である。why it can avoid crashing into Jupiter は The only reason を修飾する関係副詞節。and then の and が結んでいるのは inside と outside であり，共通して of the giant planet's orbit が続いている。as は接続詞で，「…するとき」という意味。

□ avoid *doing*「…することを避ける」　　□ crash into A「Aに衝突する」

□ Jupiter「木星」　　□ orbit「軌道」　　□ egg-shaped「卵形の」

□ slip「(滑るように)進む」　　□ inside of A「Aの内側に」

□ outside of A「Aの外側に」　　□ planet「惑星」　　□ go around「周りを回る」

問3 空所(3)を含む文の前の第3段落第1文の that 以下に「木星と小惑星が重力に
よって軌道共鳴状態に固定されている，つまり，その小惑星が木星と同じ時間
で軌道を一周するため，2つの天体が規則正しくお互いを引きつけ合っている」
とあることから，「その小惑星の軌道は<u>安定している</u>」と考えられるので，正解
はイ。
　　ア.「円形の」イ.「安定した」ウ.「拡大された」エ.「乱された」

問4 that 以下は a new method を修飾する関係代名詞節。➡ **Point ⑧** 節内
では allow O to *do*「Oが〜することを可能にする」が用いられており，follow
O back in time は「過去にさかのぼってOをたどって行く」という意味。to
see 以下は目的を表す副詞用法の不定詞句であるが，訳出の際には，この部分
を最初に訳すことになるので，ここで it が指す内容 the asteroid を明らかに
するとよい。
　　□ develop「を開発する」　　□ method「方法」　　□ see wh-節「…かを知る，確かめる」
　　□ the solar system「太陽系」

問5 空所(5)を含む文は，前に述べたことを言い換えるときに用いられる In other
words「言い換えれば」から始まっており，直前の文には「この小惑星は，は
るか昔最初に太陽と惑星が濃縮してできる元になったチリとガスから成る渦巻
く雲の一部であったはずがない」とあるので，エが正解。
　　ア.「親戚」イ.「先住者」ウ.「敵」エ.「部外者」

問6 本文では，「BZ と呼ばれる，他の惑星とは逆向きに太陽の周りを回っている小
惑星が，太陽系外から飛来し，太陽系誕生以前から存在してきた可能性を示し
た研究」が紹介されている。したがって，正解はイ。
　　ア.「天文学者が木星を回る新たな小惑星を発見」
　　イ.「小惑星が太陽系の外から来たことを研究が証明」
　　ウ.「太陽系の年齢は現在45億歳と推定」
　　エ.「太陽系は小惑星よりも古くからあることを科学者が証明」

Point ⑧ 同格の that と関係代名詞の that

1．同格の that

　先行する名詞の内容を that 節で表すことがある。この that は名詞節を導
き，that の後ろは主語や目的語が欠けていない完全な文になる。なお，同格の
that 節を従える名詞には次のようなものがある。

fact that ...「…という事実」/ idea that ...「…という考え」/ possibility that ...
「…という可能性」/ rumor that ...「…といううわさ」/ feeling that ...「…とい
う感じ」

例 There is no hope **that** he will recover.
「彼が回復する見込みはない」

2．関係代名詞の that

　that が主格の関係代名詞(who / which)と目的格の関係代名詞(whom / which)の代わりに用いられることがある。関係代名詞 that の後ろは主語や目的語が欠けている不完全な文になる。また，目的格の関係代名詞は省略されることが多い。

例1 The street **that** leads to the station is very wide.
「駅に通じている通りはとても広い」

例2 The steak (**that**) I ate yesterday was not so good.
「私が昨日食べたステーキはあまりおいしくなかった」

▶▶ 構文・語句解説 ◀◀

— 第1段落 —

[1]According to a recent study using computer simulations, another invasive asteroid was identified. [2]Unlike Oumuamua, the cigar-shaped rock that cruised through the inner solar system and right back out toward interstellar space last winter, however, this asteroid has taken up permanent residence among us.

[1]コンピュータシミュレーションを用いた最近の研究によると，別の外来小惑星が確認された。[2]もっとも，昨冬に内太陽系を通過し，恒星間宇宙空間へと戻って行った葉巻形の岩であるオウムアムアとは異なり，この小惑星は私たちの間に恒久的に留まっている。

1 using computer simulations は a recent study を修飾する現在分詞句。

　□ according to A「Aによると」　　□ recent「最近の」　　□ study「研究」
　□ computer simulation「コンピュータシミュレーション」　　□ invasive「外来の，侵入する」
　□ identify「を確認する」

2 □ unlike A「Aと異なり」　　□ cigar-shaped「葉巻形の」　　□ cruise「巡航する」
　□ the inner solar system「内太陽系」太陽系でも地球型惑星である火星を含めたそれより内側の領域のこと。　　□ right back out toward A「外に戻ってAの方へ」
　□ take A up「Aを占める」　　□ permanent「恒久的な」　　□ residence「滞在，居住」

¹The asteroid, known as 2015 BZ509 — "BZ" for short — was discovered in 2014 sharing orbital space with Jupiter and making a circuit of the sun about every 11.6 years. ²But it goes around the sun in the opposite direction of Jupiter and the other planets. ³The only reason why it can avoid crashing into Jupiter is that its orbit is egg-shaped, and so the rock slips inside and then outside of the giant planet's orbit as it goes around. ⁴Fathi Namouni, of the Observatoire de la Côte d'Azur in France, and his colleague Helena Morais, of the Universidade Estadual Paulista in Brazil, were trying to figure out how the asteroid got that way.

¹2015 BZ509, 略して BZ として知られる小惑星が木星と軌道空間を共有しており, およそ11.6年かけて太陽を1周していることが2014年に発見された。²しかし, それは木星や他の惑星とは反対の方向に太陽の周りを回っている。³それが木星に衝突することを避けられる唯一の理由は, その軌道が卵形であるということであり, そのためこの岩が公転するとき, 巨大惑星の軌道の内側に入り, 次にその外側に出ていくのである。⁴フランス, コートダジュール天文台のファティ・ナムニと彼の共同研究者であるブラジルのサンパウロ州立パウリスタ大学のエレナ・モライスは, どのようにその小惑星がそのようなところにたどり着いたのかを理解しようとしていた。

1 □ known as A「Aとして知られ」　　□ for short「略して」
　 □ discover O *doing*「Oが…しているのを発見する」　　□ share A with B「AをBと共有する」
　 □ orbital「軌道の」　　□ make a circuit of A「Aを1周する」
　 □ every + 数詞 + 複数名詞「…ごとに」
2 □ go around A「Aのまわりを回る」
　 □ in the opposite direction of A「Aとは反対の方向に」
4 □ figure out wh-節「…を理解する」

¹Their curiosity was heightened by the additional discovery that the planet and asteroid are locked together in an orbital and gravitational resonance: The asteroid completes an orbit in the same time it takes Jupiter, and so the pair would regularly pull on each other. ²That meant the asteroid's orbit should be stable.

¹木星と小惑星が重力によって軌道共鳴状態に固定されている，つまり，その小惑星が木星と同じ時間で軌道を一周するため，2つの天体が規則正しくお互いを引きつけ合っている，というさらなる発見によって，彼らの好奇心が高まった。²これが意味することは，その小惑星の軌道は安定しているはずであるということであった。

1 it takes Jupiter は the same time を修飾する関係代名詞節。the planet とはここでは木星のこと。

☐ curiosity「好奇心」　　☐ heighten「を高める」　　☐ additional「さらなる，追加の」
☐ discovery「発見」　　☐ be locked together in A「一緒にAに固定されている」
☐ gravitational「重力の」　　☐ complete「を終える」　　☐ regularly「規則正しく」
☐ pull on A「Aを引っ張る」　　☐ each other「お互い」

─── 第4段落 ───

¹"But at the beginning of this investigation, we did not suspect BZ to be of interstellar origin," Dr. Namouni said. ²"We developed a new method that allows us to follow the asteroid back in time to see which part of the solar system it came from."

¹「しかし，この調査を始めたころは，BZ が恒星間に起源を持つとは思ってもいませんでした」と，ナムニ博士は述べた。²「その小惑星が太陽系のどの部分から来たのかを知るために過去にさかのぼってそれをたどって行けるようにする新しい方法を私たちは開発しました」

1 ☐ investigation「調査」　　☐ suspect O to be C「OがCでないかと思う」
☐ of ... origin「…に起源がある」

─── 第5段落 ───

¹But as far back as they could trace the solar system — all the way to its birth, 4.5 billion years ago — BZ kept going around the same wrong way. ²That meant the asteroid could not have been part of the swirling cloud of dust and gas from which the sun and planets originally condensed so long ago. ³In other words, it is an outsider to our solar system. ⁴The results, they say, suggest that there are plenty more "extra-solar" immigrants out there.

¹しかし，太陽系をはるばるその誕生まで，すなわち45億年前までさかのぼってみる限り，BZ は同じように逆向きに回り続けていた。²これが意味することは，この小惑星は，はるか昔最初に太陽と惑星が濃縮してできる元になったチリとガスから成る渦巻く雲の一部であったはずがないということである。³言い換えれば，その小惑星は太陽系にとって部外者であるということなのだ。⁴この結果からすると，宇宙にはずっと多くの「太陽系外」からやってきたものが存在しているということになると，博士たちは言っている。

1 the same wrong way ここでは，「現在と同様に惑星とは逆向きに」ということ。

  □ as far back as S can *do* ... 「過去にさかのぼって…できる限り」

  □ trace 「の跡をたどる」   □ all the way to A 「はるばるAまで」

  □ keep *doing* 「…し続ける」

2 from which 以下は the swirling cloud of dust and gas を修飾する関係代名詞節。

  □ could not have been 「…だったはずがない」   □ cloud 「雲」   □ dust 「チリ」

  □ gas 「ガス，気体」   □ originally 「最初に，もともと」

  □ condense A from B 「BからAを濃縮する」

4 The results, they say, suggest ... の they say は，本来は主節に相当する節が挿入された形。

  (＝They say that the results suggest ...)

  □ plenty more A 「ずっと多くのA」   □ extra-solar 「太陽系外の」

  □ immigrant 「移住者」   □ out there 「向こうに」ここでは「宇宙に」ということ。

うそとゴシップ

解 答

問1 無限の可能性という感覚は，うそがほとんどの人にとって抵抗し難いもう
　　1つの悪い行いと共通に持っているものである。

問2 イ. the truth

問3 結婚問題，子供の頃の心の傷，仕事上の不満

問4 ウ. had told

問5 エ. enjoy

▶▶▶ **設問解説** ◀◀◀

問1 全体の文構造は The sense of unlimited possibility(S) is(V) what ...
irresistible(C) である。what は「…するもの，…すること」という意味の名詞
節を導く関係代名詞。**➡ Point ⑨** なお，that 以下は another vice を修
飾する関係代名詞節。

　　□ sense「感覚」　　□ unlimited「無限の，制限のない」　　□ possibility「可能性」

　　□ have A in common with B「BとAを共通して持つ，BとAを共有する」

　　□ find O C「OをCだと思う」

　　□ irresistible「（欲求・誘惑などに）抵抗できない，打ち勝てない」

問2 空所(2a)の直後の but it could also be a wild <u>fantasy</u> から，空所(2a)には
fantasy と対照的な意味の語句が入ることが推測できるので，the truth を入れ
るのが自然。また，空所(2b)と(2c)に the truth を入れても，それぞれの文意
が自然になることから，正解はイ。

　　ア.「うそ」イ.「真実」ウ.「ゴシップ」エ.「うわさ」

問3 第2段落第3文に筆者の友人が their marriage problems, childhood traumas,
or job dissatisfactions を筆者に打ち明ける例が挙げられている。

　　□ painful「痛ましい，悲惨な」

問4 wish S *did* は「現在の事実に反する願望」を表し，wish S had *done* は「過
去の事実に反する願望」を表す。ここでは，すでに友人が悩みを自分に打ち明
けたことに対して「そうでなければよかったのに」と願っているので，had
told を選ぶ。

問5 第2段落で「真実や事実が楽しいことはめったにない」という内容を述べたの

を受けて，第3段落第1文で「ゴシップはまったく違う」と述べているので，エが正解。

ア.「を嫌う」 イ.「を無視する」 ウ.「を信じる」 エ.「を楽しむ」

Point ⑨ 関係代名詞 what

what が関係代名詞として用いられ，名詞節を導くことがある。「…するもの，…すること」という意味で，what = the thing(s) which と考えてよい。

例 **What** you have to do is to study English harder.

「君がやらなければならないのは，英語をもっと一生懸命に勉強することだ」

▶▶ 構文・語句解説 ◀◀

第1段落

[1]Lies are fascinating because there are so many possibilities for invention and elaboration. [2]In a liar's mouth, facts are no longer boring and predictable, but interesting and surprising. [3]The sense of unlimited possibility is what lies have in common with another vice that most people find irresistible: gossip. [4]Gossip is interesting because what we hear and pass on to others may be the truth, but it could also be a wild fantasy; we are captivated by the very uncertainty of what we hear.

[1]うそは，でっちあげたり入念に仕上げたりする可能性がとても多いので魅力的である。[2]うそつきにとっては，事実はもはや退屈で目新しいところのないものではなく，興味深く驚くべきものなのである。[3]無限の可能性という感覚は，うそがほとんどの人にとって抵抗し難いもう1つの悪い行いであるゴシップと共通に持っているものである。[4]ゴシップは，私たちが耳にしたり他人に伝えたりする事柄が本当かもしれないので面白いのだが，また途方もない空想でもあり得るのである。私たちは自分たちが耳にする事柄のまさにその不確かさに夢中になってしまうのである。

1 □ lie「うそ」 □ fascinating「魅力的な」 □ possibility for A「Aの可能性」
  □ invention「でっちあげ」 □ elaboration「念入りな仕上げ，細工」

2 □ liar「うそつき」 □ no longer「もはや…ない」 □ boring「退屈な」
  □ predictable「予測可能な」 □ interesting「面白い」 □ surprising「驚くべき」

4 because 節内の主語は，関係代名詞 what で導かれた名詞節 what we hear and pass on to others である。and は hear と pass on to others を結んでいる。
  □ pass A on to B「BにAを伝える」 □ wild fantasy「途方もない空想」

□ captivate「を魅惑する，うっとりさせる」　　□ the very A「まさにそのA」
□ uncertainty「不確かさ」

¹In spite of the proverb, the truth is seldom as strange or interesting as fiction.　²Most of us don't want to know the painful facts about other people's lives.　³I often feel burdened when friends confide in me about their marriage problems, childhood traumas, or job dissatisfactions.　⁴Even though I try my best to console and reassure, I can't help wishing my friends had told someone else.

¹ことわざがあるにもかかわらず，事実はめったに虚構ほど奇妙でもなく面白くもないのである。²私たちのほとんどが，他人の人生に関する痛ましい事実など知りたいとは思っていない。³友人から結婚問題や子どもの頃に受けた心の傷や仕事の不満などを打ち明けられると，私は気が重くなることが多い。⁴私は最善を尽くして慰めたり力づけたりしようとするのだが，友人が他の誰かに打ち明けてくれていればと願わざるを得ない。

1 seldom as＋原級＋as A で「Aほど…なことはめったにない」という意味。なお，ここでの the proverb は Truth is stranger than fiction.「事実は小説よりも奇なり」のこと。
　□ in spite of A「Aにもかかわらず」　　□ proverb「ことわざ」
　□ seldom「めったに…ない」　　□ strange「奇妙な」　　□ fiction「虚構，フィクション」
2 □ most of A「Aのほとんど」　　□ lives＜life「人生，生活」の複数形。
3 □ burdened「重荷を課せられた」　　□ confide in A about B「AにBのことを打ち明ける」
　□ marriage「結婚」　　□ childhood trauma「子どもの頃に受けた心の傷」
　□ dissatisfaction「不満」
4 □ even though S V ...「…だけれども／たとえ…でも」
　□ try one's best to do「…しようと最善を尽くす」　　□ console「(を)慰める，元気づける」
　□ reassure「(を)安心させる」　　□ can't help doing「…せずにはいられない」

¹Gossip is entirely different.　²There is nothing virtuous about engaging in gossip, but we enjoy it to the utmost.　³When someone tells us vague rumors about someone else's marriage problems, childhood secrets, or job scandals, our ears prick up.　⁴When the same information is told to us in confidence, we feel a sinking sense of duty.　⁵We listen silently

and carefully, trying to think of the few right words to say and maybe getting a headache in the process. ⁶When the information is passed on to us as gossip, we jump into the conversation with pleasure: nobody knows the truth anyway, so we are free to offer our own theories and interpretations. ⁷We can talk all we want.

---

¹ゴシップはまったく違う。²ゴシップに関わることに高潔なところなど何もないが，私たちは最大限にそれを楽しむ。³誰かに他の誰かの結婚問題や子どもの秘密や仕事上のスキャンダルに関するはっきりしないうわさを教えてもらうとき，私たちの耳はそば立つのである。⁴同じ情報が私たちだけに内緒で伝えられると，私たちは気の滅入るような義務感を感じる。⁵言うべきぴったりした言葉をいくつか考え出そうと努めながら，そしてその過程で頭痛を感じたりもしながら，無言のまま注意して耳を傾けるのである。⁶その情報がゴシップとして伝えられる時は，私たちは喜んでその会話の中に飛び込んで行く。とにかく誰も真実を知らないのだから，私たちは自分の説と解釈を自由に述べることができる。⁷話したいだけ話をすることができるのだ。

1 □ entirely「まったく，完全に」 □ different「違っている，異なっている」

2 There is nothing + 形容詞 + about A は「A には…なところはない」という意味。

  □ virtuous「高潔な，徳の高い」 □ engage in A「A に携わる，従事する」

  □ enjoy「を楽しむ」 □ to the utmost「できる限り，最大限に」

3 □ vague「あいまいな」 □ rumor「うわさ」 □ secret「秘密」

  □ scandal「スキャンダル，醜聞」 □ prick up「(耳が)そば立つ」

4 □ information「情報」 □ in confidence「秘密裏に，内緒で」

  □ a sinking sense of duty「気の滅入るような義務感」

5 trying 以下は同時動作・付帯状況を表す分詞構文。また，and は trying ... to say と (maybe) getting ... the process の2つの現在分詞句を結んでいる。to say は the few right words を修飾する形容詞用法の不定詞。

  □ silently「黙って，無言で」 □ carefully「注意深く」 □ try to *do*「…しようと努める」

  □ think of A「A を思いつく，考え出す」 □ right「ぴったりした」

  □ get a headache「頭痛がする」 □ process「過程」

6 □ jump into A「A に飛び込む」 □ conversation「会話」 □ with pleasure「喜んで」

  □ anyway「とにかく，いずれにせよ」 □ be free to *do*「自由に…できる」

  □ offer「を提供する，差し出す」 □ theory「説，理論」 □ interpretation「解釈」

7 talk all we want の we want は all を修飾する関係代名詞節。なお，ここでは talk が他動詞として用いられている。

動物の知能

問1　しかし，最近の発見によって，科学者は，世界の農場にいる動物の多くは私たちが思っていたよりも頭がいい，と確信するようになった。

問2　sheep find their own species even more memorable

問3　群れの中の何頭かが遠くを見つめると，群れ全体がその方向に動き始めたこと。（36字）

問4　エ. how people see the behavior of animals

問5　イ. democracy

問6　ウ，オ

▶▶ **設問解説** ◀◀

問1　S convince O that 節で「SはOに…ということを確信させる」という意味。「Sにより，Oは…を確信している」と訳出することもできる。

　　☐ recent「最近の」　　☐ discovery「発見」

　　☐ farm animals「農場にいる動物」　　☐ smart「頭がいい」

　　☐ 比較級 + than S thought「Sが思っていたよりも…」

問2　直前に「10人の人間の顔を覚えることができる」とあり，直後に「50匹のヒツジの顔を覚えることができる」とあることから，「同じ種の方が覚えやすい」ことがわかる。動詞は find しか与えられていないことに注目し，find O C「OがCだとわかる，気づく」の形を用いて O = their own species，C = even more memorable とする。memorable even more としないことに注意。

　　☐ even + 比較級「さらに…，いっそう…」

　　☐ memorable「覚えやすい，記憶しやすい」

問3　アフリカスイギュウについては第2段落で述べられており，その第3文 Several members of the herd simply stared into the distance, and the whole group took off in that direction.の内容をまとめる。

問4　下線部は「動物の行動に対する人々の見方」という意味。the way S V ... は「SがV…する方法」という意味なので how S V ... と同意であり，また他動詞 view は「を見る」という意味なので see と同意であることに注目する。

→ **Point ⑩**

ア．「人々が動物が動くのを見守る道路」

イ．「人々が動物と同じように振る舞う理由」

ウ．「人々が動物の行動を眺めるのを楽しんでいる方法」

エ．「人々が動物の行動を見る方法」

問5　空所(5)を含む文の主語 This study は第3段落第3文で述べられている Larissa Conradt と Tim Roper による研究を指し，その内容は「動物が意思決定を行う際に投票を行う」というものである。したがって，空所には「投票を行って意思決定を行うような体制」に当たる単語を入れることがわかり，イが正解。

ア．「貴族社会」イ．「民主主義社会」ウ．「君主制国家」エ．「専制国家」

問6　ア．「たくさんの農場の動物がチンパンジーやイルカより知能が高いことが発見されている」第1段落第2文に「農場の動物の多くは私たちが思っていたより頭がいい」と述べられてはいるが，「チンパンジーやイルカより知能が高い」とは述べられていない。

イ．「アフリカスイギュウは支配的なリーダーを選ぶために選挙を行っている」第2段落の内容に不一致。

ウ．「ブタは他のブタから食べ物を盗むのを観察されている」第1段落第9文の内容に一致。

エ．「オオハクチョウは飛びたくないときに頭を横に振る」第4段落第6文の内容に関連するが「飛びたくないときに頭を横に振る」とは書かれていないので不一致。

オ．「アカシカの集団の成長したシカの約3分の2が立ち上がると，群れは動き始める」第4段落第4文の内容に一致。

Point ⑩ the way S V

the way S V ... は「…する方法，様子，点」という意味であり，how S V ... と同意である。

例1　I don't like **the way** he talks.

=I don't like **how** he talks.

「彼の話し方が気に入らない」

例2　I was satisfied with **the way** she was enjoying herself.

=I was satisfied with **how** she was enjoying herself.

「彼女が楽しんでいる様子に満足した」

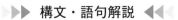

--- 第1段落 ---

[1]You may have heard that chimpanzees and dolphins are among the world's most intelligent creatures. [2]But recent discoveries have convinced scientists that many of the world's farm animals are smarter than we thought. [3]Take sheep, for example. [4]Scientists at the Babraham Institute in Cambridge, England, report that sheep are good at remembering faces. [5]In a study of sheep's memories, they found that the woolly creatures can remember 10 human faces for more than two years. [6]Of course, sheep find their own species even more memorable. [7]They can remember 50 different sheep faces! [8]Pigs are clever too, especially when food is involved. [9]Researchers in Bristol, England, found that one pig would follow another to the food pan and then take his food! [10]Pigs quickly learn to trick the clever pigs who are out to steal their dinner.

[1]みなさんは，チンパンジーとイルカが世界で最も知能の高い生き物の仲間であると聞いたことがあるかもしれない。[2]しかし，最近の発見によって，科学者は，世界の農場にいる動物の多くは私たちが思っていたよりも頭がいい，と確信するようになった。[3]ヒツジを例にとってみよう。[4]イギリスのケンブリッジにあるバブラハム研究所の科学者の報告によれば，ヒツジは顔を覚えるのがうまいようである。[5]ヒツジの記憶力の研究で，科学者は，この毛むくじゃらの生き物が10人の人間の顔を2年以上にわたって覚えていることができる，とわかった。[6]もちろん，ヒツジには自分の種の方がさらに覚えやすい。[7]なんと50匹もの違うヒツジの顔を覚えることができるのである！[8]ブタも，特に食べ物が関わるときには頭がいい。[9]イギリスのブリストルの研究者は，あるブタが別のブタの跡をつけてエサ入れの所まで行き，そのブタのエサをとってしまうことを発見した。[10]ブタは自分の食事を盗もうとする頭のいいブタをすぐにだませるようになる。

1 □ may have *done*「…したかもしれない」　　□ dolphin「イルカ」

　 □ be among A「Aの中にいる」　　□ intelligent「知能の高い」　　□ creature「生物」

3 □ take A for example「Aを例に挙げる」

4 □ institute「研究所」　　□ report that 節「…だと報告する」

　 □ be good at *doing*「…するのが得意だ」

5 the woolly creatures はヒツジのこと。

　 □ memory「記憶，記憶力」　　□ the woolly creatures「その毛むくじゃらの生き物たち」

8 □ clever「利口な，頭のいい」　　□ especially「特に」　　□ involve「に関わる」

9 □ researcher「研究者」　　□ follow A to B「Aの後を追ってBに行く」

☐ food pan「エサ入れ」

10 who 以下は the clever pigs を修飾する関係代名詞節。

☐ learn to *do*「…することを覚える，…できるようになる」　　☐ trick「をだます」

☐ be out to *do*「…しようとしている」　　☐ steal「を盗む」

---

[1]Other research has suggested that some animals even practice various forms of group decision making, as the following example illustrates: The African Buffaloes had agreed that it was time to head east.　[2]The decision was made quietly.　[3]Several members of the herd simply stared into the distance, and the whole group took off in that direction.

---

[1]他の研究によると，動物の中には，以下の例が示すように，様々な種類の集団による意思決定を行っているものさえある。アフリカスイギュウたちは東に向かうべきときだと意見が一致した。[2]決定は静かに行われた。[3]群れの中の何頭かが単に遠くを眺めると，集団全体でその方向へと出発したのである。

---

1 as the following example illustrates は，直前の Other research ... decision making の節の内容を補足説明する関係代名詞節。

☐ research「研究，調査」　　☐ suggest that 節「…だと示唆する」

☐ practice「を行う，実行する」　　☐ various「いろいろな，様々な」

☐ form「形式，種類」　　☐ group decision making「集団の意思決定」

☐ following「次の，以下の」　　☐ illustrate「を説明する，例示する」

☐ African Buffalo「アフリカスイギュウ」　　☐ agree that 節「…だと意見が一致する」

☐ it is time to *do* ...「…すべき時である」

2 ☐ quietly「静かに」

3 ☐ herd「〈ウシ・ヒツジなどの〉群れ」　　☐ simply「単に，ただ」

☐ stare into A「Aをじっと見つめる」　　☐ the distance「遠方，遠景」

☐ whole「全体の，すべての」　　☐ take off「出発する」　　☐ direction「方向」

---

[1]The buffaloes' behavior has got the science-world talking.　[2]Last month, researchers announced in Nature magazine that they have learned how some animals make decisions — they vote!　[3]The study, by Larissa Conradt and Tim Roper of the University of Sussex in England, could change the way people view animal behavior.　[4]"Most groups of animals

---

have a dominant leader," says Roper. [5]People had assumed that the leader makes decisions and the group follows. [6]This study suggests that the animal kingdom is more of a democracy.

---

[1]このスイギュウの行動によって科学界に議論が巻き起こった。[2]動物がどのように意思決定を行うかを発見したが，なんと投票をしているのだ，と先月ネイチャー誌に発表した研究者がいる。[3]その研究はイギリスのサセックス大学のラリッサ・コンラッドとティム・ローパーによるもので，動物の行動に対する人間の見方を変えるかもしれない。[4]「ほとんどの動物の集団には支配的なリーダーがいる」とローパーは言う。[5]そのリーダーが決定を行い集団がそれに従う，と人々は思い込んでいた。[6]動物界はもっと民主的な社会であることをこの研究は示唆している。

1 □ behavior「行動，振る舞い」　　□ get O *doing*「Oを…している状態にする，Oに…させる」
2 □ announce that 節「…ということを発表する」　　□ vote「投票する」
3 by Larissa Conradt ... in England は直前の The study を補足説明する前置詞句。
　 □ study「研究」
4 □ most A「ほとんどのA」　　□ dominant「支配的な」
5 □ assume that 節「(証拠もないのに)…だと思い込む」　　□ follow「後について行く」
6 □ the animal kingdom「動物界」自然界を the animal kingdom「動物界」，the vegetable kingdom「植物界」，the mineral kingdom「鉱物界」の3つに区分することがある。

- -

┌─ 第4段落 ─
[1]So, how do animals vote? [2]It depends on the animal. [3]Roper and Conradt observed red deer in Scotland and surveyed other animal behavior studies to find other examples. [4]Red deer move when more than 60% of the adults stand up. [5]African buffaloes will travel in the direction that the adult females are looking. [6]Whooper swans decide when to fly with head movements, and bees dance to get the other bees going. [7]Does all of this sound simple? [8]It is. [9]As Roper says, "Democratic decision-making needn't be a complicated business."

---

[1]では，動物はどのように投票をしているのだろう? [2]それは動物による。[3]ローパーとコンラッドはスコットランドでアカシカを観察し，他の動物の行動の研究を調べて，他の例を見つけた。[4]アカシカは成長したシカの60パーセント以上が立ち上がると動く。[5]アフリカスイギュ

ウは成長した雌が眺める方向に移動する。⁶オオハクチョウは頭の動きでいつ飛ぶべきかを決め，ハチはダンスをして他のハチを動かす。⁷これらはすべて単純なことのように聞こえるであろうか？⁸そう，単純なのである。⁹ローパーが言うように，「民主的な意思決定は複雑なことである必要はない」

2 □ depend on A「Aによる，A次第である」

3 to find other examples は目的を表す副詞用法の不定詞句。　　□ observe「を観察する」

　　□ survey「を調査する」

4 □ adult「成長した(動物)」

5 that 以下は the direction を修飾する関係詞節。

6 decide when to fly with head movements は decide A with B「AをBで決定する」の形。

　　□ when to fly「いつ飛ぶべきか」　　□ head movement「頭の動き」

7 all of this は，前文までに挙げられている動物の行動を指している。

　　□ sound C「Cのように聞こえる」

8 It is. = All of this is simple.

9 As Roper says の as は，第2段落第1文の as と同様，関係代名詞として使われている。

　　□ democratic「民主的な」　　□ needn't do「…する必要はない」　　□ complicated「複雑な」

　　□ business「事柄」

解　答

問1　(1a)　ウ. where　　(1b)　エ. why

問2　(2a)　ア. aggressive　　(2b)　イ. tamed

問3　その後人々は，必要からではなく，新しいものを見たり経験したりする喜びと興奮を求めて旅をするようになった。

問4　イ

問5　イ

▶▶▶　設問解説　◀◀◀

問1　(1a)　直前に場所を表す名詞 new place があり，空所以下 feed までが完全な文であることから，正解はウ。

(1b)　直前に reason があり，空所の後ろに完全な文が続いていることから，正解はエ。➡ **Point** ⑪

問2　(2a)　hostile は「敵意のある」という意味。

ア.「攻撃的な，侵略的な」イ.「友好的な」ウ.「洗練された」エ.「基本的な」

(2b)　domesticated は「飼い慣らされた，家畜化した」という意味。

ア.「不安定な」イ.「飼い慣らされた」ウ.「脅威的な」エ.「野性の」

問3　not from necessity, but for ... new things は not X but Y「X ではなく Y」の表現。➡ **Point** ㉑ of 以下は the joy and excitement を修飾する形容詞句。また，seeing と experiencing に共通する目的語が new things であることに注意。

□ later「後になって」　　□ necessity「必要，必要性」　　□ joy「喜び」

□ excitement「興奮」　　□ experience「を経験する，体験する」

問4　ア，ウ，エの内容は第6段落第4・5文に述べられているが，イは本文には述べられていない。

問5　ア.「昔，人々が徒歩で旅をしていた頃は，途中で遊ぶために木の棒や石のこん棒を持ち歩いていた」第1・2段落第5文の内容に不一致。

イ.「原始人は，水路を旅するために，くり抜いた木の幹と木切れを使った」第3・4段落第2文の内容に一致。

ウ.「筆者は列車や船で旅をするより，飛行機や車で旅をする方が好きだ」第6

段落第1文の内容に不一致。

エ.「筆者は海外旅行中にパスポートやビザをなくしても深刻な問題にはならないと思っている」第5段落第5・6文の内容に不一致。

Point ⑪ 関係副詞

関係副詞 where/when/why に導かれる節が名詞を修飾することがあり，関係副詞の後ろには，主語や目的語が欠けていない完全な文がくる。

1．関係副詞 where で導かれた節は場所を表す名詞を修飾する。

例 Would you tell me the name of the hotel **where** your sister is staying?
「お姉さんが滞在しているホテルの名前を教えていただけませんか」

2．関係副詞 when で導かれた節は時を表す名詞を修飾する。

例 I remember the day **when** I first met Susan.
「私は初めてスーザンに会った日を覚えている」

3．関係副詞 why で導かれた節は理由を表す名詞 reason を修飾する。

例 The reason **why** the president resigned suddenly is unknown.
「社長が急に辞めた理由はわかっていない」

▶▶ **構文・語句解説** ◀◀

—— 第1・2段落 ——

[1]People have traveled ever since they first appeared on the earth.

[2]In primitive times they did not travel for pleasure but to find new places where their herds could feed, or to escape from hostile neighbors, or to find more favorable climates. [3]They traveled on foot. [4]Their journeys were long, tiring, and often dangerous. [5]They protected themselves with simple weapons, such as wooden sticks or stone clubs, and by lighting fires at night and, above all, by keeping together.

[1]人は初めて地上に姿を現して以来ずっと旅をしてきた。
[2]原始時代には，人は楽しみのためでなく，自分たちの飼っている動物の群れがエサにありつくことができる新しい場所を見つけるために，または敵意に満ちた隣人から逃れるために，あるいはより好ましい気候を求めて旅をした。[3]彼らは徒歩で旅をした。[4]彼らの旅は長くて疲れるものであり，しばしば危険であった。[5]彼らは木の棒や石のこん棒などの単純な武器を使って，また夜は火をおこすことにより，そして何よりも一緒にいることで自分を守った。

1 □ ever since S V ...「…して以来ずっと」　　□ appear「現れる，姿を現す」

2 they did not travel for pleasure but to find ... は not X but Y「Xではなくて Y」の表現。ここ
では X＝for pleasure，Y＝to find 以下となっている。なお，to find 以下では to find ... could
feed と to escape ... neighbors と to find more favorable climates の3つの不定詞句が or で結
ばれている。　　□ primitive times「原始時代」

□ for pleasure「楽しみのために」　　□ herd「〈ウシ・ヒツジなどの〉群れ」

□ feed「物を食べて生きていく」　　□ escape from A「Aから逃れる」

□ neighbor「隣人，近所の人」　　□ favorable「好都合な，有利な」

□ climate「気候，風土」

3 □ on foot「徒歩で，歩いて」

4 □ tiring「疲れさせる，骨の折れる」　　□ dangerous「危険な」

5 with simple ... stone clubs と by lighting fires at night と by keeping together の3つの前置
詞句が and で結ばれて protect themselves を修飾している。

□ protect「を守る，保護する」　　□ weapon「武器」

□ A, such as B「たとえば B のような A」　　□ wooden「木製の」　　□ stick「棒」

□ club「こん棒」　　□ light a fire「火をおこす」　　□ above all「特に，とりわけ」

□ keep together「一緒にいる」

── 第3・4段落 ──

[1]Being intelligent and creative, they soon discovered easier ways of traveling. [2]They
rode on the backs of their domesticated animals; they hollowed out tree trunks and, by
using bits of wood as paddles, were able to travel across water.

[3]Later they traveled, not from necessity, but for the joy and excitement of seeing and
experiencing new things. [4]This is still the main reason why we travel today.

---

[1]知能が高く創造力に富んでいたので，彼らはまもなく旅をするもっと楽な方法を発見し
た。[2]彼らは自分たちが飼い慣らした動物の背中に乗った。彼らは木の幹をくり抜き，そして木
切れを櫂（かい）として使うことで，水路を旅することができた。

[3]その後人々は，必要からではなく，新しいものを見たり経験したりする喜びと興奮を求めて
旅をするようになった。[4]これは依然として今日私たちが旅をする主な理由である。

---

1 Being intelligent and creative は理由を表す分詞構文。　　□ intelligent「知能の高い」

□ creative「創造力のある，独創的な」　　□ discover「を発見する」

□ way of *doing*「…する方法」

2 hollowed out tree trunks と were able to travel across water の2つの動詞句が and で結ばれている。　□ ride on A「Aに乗る」　□ back「背中」
　□ hollow A out「Aをくり抜く」　□ trunk「(木の)幹」　□ bits of wood「木切れ」
　□ as A「Aとして」　□ paddle「櫂，パドル」　□ across A「Aを横切って」
4 □ still「今でも，いまだに」　□ main「主な」

─ 第5段落 ─

¹Traveling, of course, has now become a highly organized business. ²There are cars and splendid highways, express trains, huge ships and jet airplanes, and all of them provide us with comforts and security. ³This sounds wonderful. ⁴But there are difficulties. ⁵If you want to go abroad, you need a passport and visa, tickets, luggage, and a hundred and one other things. ⁶If you lose any of them, your journey may be ruined.

¹もちろん，旅は今ではきちんと計画して行われるようになっている。²自動車と立派な自動車専用道路，特急列車，巨大な船，そしてジェット機があり，そのすべてが快適さと安全を提供してくれる。³これは素晴らしい話である。⁴しかし，やっかいな点もある。⁵外国へ行きたい場合，パスポートとビザ，チケット，荷物，そしてその他たくさんの物が必要なのだ。⁶そのどれ1つを失っても，旅行は台無しになるかもしれない。

1 □ of course「もちろん，確かに」　□ highly「高度に，大いに」
　□ organized「組織化された，組織的な」　□ business「事柄」
2 cars and splendid highways と express trains と huge ships と jet airplanes の4つの名詞(句)が There be 構文の主語となっている。　□ splendid「立派な，素晴らしい」
　□ highway「自動車専用道路，幹線道路」　□ express trains「特急列車」
　□ huge「巨大な」　□ provide A with B「AにBを与える，提供する」
　□ comfort「＜通例複数形で＞生活を快適にするもの」　□ security「安全，安心」
3 □ sound C「Cのように聞こえる」
4 □ difficulty「難点，やっかいな事柄」
5 a passport and visa と tickets と luggage と a hundred and one other things の4つが and で結ばれている。　□ visa「ビザ，旅行査証」　□ luggage「(旅行者の)手荷物」
　□ a hundred and one「たくさんの」
6 □ journey「旅行」　□ ruin「を台無しにする」

¹As for myself, I prefer doing my traveling from an armchair. ²I like imagining all those journeys that, despite human creativeness, one has never made and will never make. ³I like to think, for example, that I have arrived in the world by stork. ⁴I like to travel faster than time and have a look at the future, or go back into the past and talk to famous people. ⁵I also like to travel like a shell across ocean floors where I can explore the wrecks of ships and see curious fish that people never have seen.

¹私はと言えば，ひじ掛け椅子に座って旅行をする方が好きだ。²私は，人間に創造性が備わっているにもかかわらず，誰も今までにしたこともないし，これからも決してしないような旅を想像するのが好きなのだ。³たとえば，自分がコウノトリに運ばれてこの世に現れた，と考えることが好きだ。⁴私は時間より速く旅をして未来を見たり，過去に戻って有名人と話をしたりするのが好きだ。⁵私はまた，船の残骸を探検したり，人々が今までに見たこともないような奇妙な魚が見られる海底を貝のように旅をするのも好きだ。

1 □ as for A「Aに関して言えば」　□ prefer *doing*「…する方を好む」
　□ armchair「ひじ掛け椅子」

2 all those ... never make の that 以下は all those journeys を修飾する関係代名詞節。and は has never made と will never make の2つの動詞句を結んでいる。
　□ imagine「を想像する」　□ despite A「Aにもかかわらず」（＝in spite of A）
　□ human「人間の」　□ creativeness「創造性，創造力」

4 travel faster ... the future と go back ... famous people の2つの動詞句が or で結ばれている。それぞれの動詞句の中では，さらに2つの動詞句が and で結ばれている。
　□ have a look at A「Aを見る，一見する」　□ the past「過去」

5 where 以下は ocean floors を修飾する関係副詞節。explore the ... of ships と see curious ... have seen の2つの動詞句が and で結ばれている。なお，that 以下は curious fish を修飾する関係代名詞節。　□ like A「Aのように」　□ shell「貝」　□ ocean floor「海底」
　□ explore「を探検する」　□ wreck「残骸」　□ curious「好奇心をそそる，奇妙な」

公用語

▶▶▶ **設問解説** ◀◀◀

問 1 下線部(1)の後ろの「公式の場で5，10，あるいはそれ以上の言語を扱うのを避けるために，1つの言語を公用語として選ばなければならない」という内容から，「多くの発展途上国ではたくさんの言語が話されている」ことが推測できる。したがって，so many languages「とてもたくさんの言語」に spoken within their borders「国境の内部で話されている」という形容詞用法の過去分詞句を続ける。➡ **Point ③** 最後に that を置いて，so ... that ～構文「とても…なので～」を完成する。➡ **Point ⑲**
□ border「国境」

問 2 ウ以外の選択肢はいずれも否定的な内容の動詞であることに注目する。土着の言語を公用語に選ぶのは「その言語の伝統を守るため」という肯定的な内容が自然である。
ア.「を破壊する」 イ.「を台無しにする」 ウ.「を守る」 エ.「を無視する」

問 3 空所(3)を含む文の前半は「英語やフランス語などの世界的言語が公用語として選ばれる」という内容であり，空所の後ろは「それはその国の誰にとっても母語ではないかもしれない」という内容なので，「たとえ…でも」という意味の接続表現が最も自然。
ア.「なぜなら…」 イ.「たとえ…でも」 ウ.「だから…」 エ.「…しない限り」

問 4 S make it＋形容詞＋for A to *do*「Aが…するのを～にする」の形式目的語構文。➡ **Point ⑦** S が動名詞句になっているので，「Sをすれば，Aは…

するのが～になる」と訳出してもよい。なお，Making a world language official in a country は，a world language が O，official 以下が C となっている。

 □ make O C「OをCにする」 □ participate in A「Aに参加する」

 □ economy「経済」

問5 which の直後に is が続くので，which は複数形の名詞 ballots や laws ではなく，前の節全体またはその一部の内容を補足的に説明する非制限用法の関係代名詞であると考えられる。➡ Point ⑫ which が prevent 以下の「市民が政治に参加するのを妨げる」という内容に対する主語となっていることから which は「二カ国語投票を廃止することは」と訳出できる。➡ Point ② 全体の構造は S prevent O from *doing*「SはOが…するのを妨げる」の形。「SのせいでOは…できない」と訳出してもよい。また，who are not comfortable with English は citizens を修飾する関係代名詞節。

 □ be likely to *do*「…する可能性が高い，たぶん…するだろう」 □ citizen「国民，市民」

 □ be comfortable with A「A<言語など>を楽に操れる」

 □ political「政治の，政治的な」 □ process「過程，プロセス」

問6 下線部(6)の文字通りの意味は「人々が持っている偏見が正当化されたのだという気持ちを人々に与えてしまう」である。この「偏見」は「英語が公用語になることによって英語以外のすべての言語の地位を下げる」ことの結果として正当化されるものなので，正解はア。

 □ feeling「考え，感じ」 □ prejudice「偏見，先入観」 □ justify「を正当化する」

Point ⑫ 非制限用法の関係詞

 関係詞には，関係詞の直前にコンマを打ち，名詞を補足的に説明する用法があり，これを非制限用法と呼ぶ。非制限用法の which は前の節全体またはその一部の内容を補足的に説明することもある。

例1 She sent him an e-mail, **which** he didn't answer.
  「彼女は彼にEメールを送ったのだが，彼は返事を出さなかった」

例2 She says she sent him an e-mail, **which** is not true.
  「彼女は彼にEメールを送ったと言っているが，それは本当ではない」

― 第1段落 ―

[1]There are many reasons for nations to declare an official language. [2]Many developing nations have so many languages spoken within their borders that they must pick one to be the official language to avoid dealing with five, ten, or more languages on an official level. [3]Some countries declare an indigenous language to be official in order to preserve the language's heritage. [4]A world language such as English or French is often chosen as the official language of a developing country, even though it may not be the native language of any of the people in that country. [5]Making a world language official in a country makes it easier for that country to participate in the world economy.

[1]国が公用語を宣言する理由はたくさんある。[2]発展途上国の多くは，その国境の内部でとても多くの言語が話されているので，公式の場で5，10，あるいはそれ以上の言語を扱うのを避けるために，1つの言語を公用語として選ばなければならない。[3]土着の言語を公用語として宣言して，その言語の伝統を守ろうとしている国もある。[4]英語やフランス語のような世界的な言語は，たとえそれがその国のどの国民の母語でなくても，発展途上国の公用語として選ばれることが多い。[5]世界的言語をある国の公用語にすれば，その国が世界経済に参加しやすくなるのである。

1 □ reason for A to *do*「Aが…する理由」　□ nation「国，国家」
　□ declare O (to be C)「Oを(Cであると)宣言する」　□ official language「公用語」
2 to avoid 以下は目的を表す副詞用法の不定詞句。　□ developing nation「発展途上国」
　□ pick O to *do*「Oを選んで…させる」　□ avoid *doing*「…するのを避ける」
　□ deal with A「A を扱う，処理する」　□ level「レベル，段階」
3 □ in order to *do*「…するために」　□ heritage「遺産，伝統」
4 □ world language「世界的言語」　□ A such as B「たとえばBのようなA」
　□ choose A as B「AをBとして選ぶ」　□ native language「母語」

― 第2段落 ―

[1]However, there are some people who fear that making a world language like English an official language can have serious effects, both politically and socially. [2]On the political side, they claim that making English the official language sets a precedent of placing English above all other languages. [3]This opens the door for laws abolishing bilingual ballots, which is likely to prevent citizens who are not comfortable with English from

participating in the political process. ⁴On the social side, opponents of official English argue that making English the official language degrades all non-English languages and gives people the feeling that their prejudices are justified.

¹しかし，英語のような世界的言語を公用語にすることは，政治的にも社会的にも深刻な影響を及ぼしかねない，と危惧する人々もいる。²政治的な面では，英語を公用語にすることは，英語を他のすべての言語より重要と考えるという先例を作ることになるとその人たちは主張する。³このことはニカ国語投票を廃止する法律を作る道を開くことになり，その結果，英語を楽に操ることができない国民が政治的過程に参加できない可能性が高くなる。⁴社会的な面では，公用語としての英語に反対する人は，英語を公用語にすることは英語以外のすべての言語の地位を下げ，人々が持っている偏見が正当化されたのだという気持ちを人々に与えてしまう，と論じている。

1 who fear that ... は some people を修飾する関係代名詞節。that 節内は making a ... official language が主語となっている。

　□ however「ところが」　　□ fear that 節「…だと心配する」

　□ have a ... effect「…な影響を与える」　　□ politically「政治的に」　　□ socially「社会的に」

2 that 節内は making English ... official language が主語。

　□ on a ... side「…な面で」　　□ claim that 節「…だと主張する」

　□ set「＜例・模範＞を示す，作る」　　□ place A above B「A を B よりも重要と考える」

3 abolishing bilingual ballots は laws を修飾する現在分詞句。

　□ open the door for A「A への道を開く」　　□ law「法律」　　□ abolish「を廃止する」

4 argue の目的語である that 節内は making English the official language が主語で，degrades all non-English languages と gives people ... are justified の 2 つの動詞句が and で結ばれている。the feeling that ... の that 節は the feeling と同格の名詞節。

　□ opponent「反対論者」　　□ argue that 節「…だと論じる，主張する」

　□ non-English「英語以外の」

13 イギリス人とアメリカ人

▶▶▶ 設問解説 ◀◀◀

問1 全体の文構造は I(S) have found(V) people here(O) more well-mannered(C) で，find O C は「OがCだとわかる，気づく」という意味。here は直前の「アメリカ人男性と結婚したイギリス人女性として」という内容と than in England から，アメリカのことだとわかる。

□ well-mannered「礼儀正しい」　　□ in many ways「多くの点で」

問2 第1段落第6文の「母は私の感謝の言葉をまるで自分が知人みたいでとても奇妙だと思ったそうだ」という内容から判断する。

問3 空所(3)を含む文の意味は「アメリカ人は褒め言葉を言ったり言われたりするのが(　3　)ということもわかった」である。この段落に述べられている具体例から判断する。

ア.「より無礼な」イ.「より上品な」ウ.「敏感でない」エ.「敬意を表さない」

問4 which は前の節全体の内容を補足説明する非制限用法の関係代名詞。

➡ **Point** ⑫　また，連鎖関係詞節の形であることにも注意。

➡ **Point** ⑬

□ receive「を受け取る」　　□ compliment「褒め言葉」　　□ reply「と答える」

□ S is kind to *do*「…するとはS〈人〉は親切だ」　　□ response「返答」

問5 下線部(5)の直前にある but に着目すると，下線部の文意はその直前の内容と逆接の内容にならなければならない。S になる they は all these thanks を指しているので，動詞 make を make O *do*「Oに…させる」の形で用いて「それ

らは私たち2人を気持ちよくする」という英文を作ればよい。なお，both の位置に注意。both は代名詞 us と同格として用いて us both の語順とする。

　　□ feel C「Cの感じがする」　　□ comfortable「心地よい」

問6　(6a) 直前に人以外のものを表す名詞 the small rituals があり，直後に主語のない不完全な文が続いていることから主格の関係代名詞 which が入る。

　　(6b) 直前に場所を表す名詞 the South があり，直後に完全な文が続いていることから関係副詞 where が入る。 ➡ **Point ⑪**

Point ⑬ 連鎖関係詞節

　後ろに that 節を取る動詞の，that 節内の要素（主語／目的語など）が関係詞になっている関係詞節を連鎖関係詞節という。連鎖関係詞節を構成する動詞は，believe / imagine / know / suppose / think などである。なお，この形では that は原則として省略される。また，連鎖関係詞節の場合，関係詞は主格でも省略可能。

例1　The man **(who) I thought** was my cousin turned out to be a stranger.
　　「いとこだと思った男性は他人だとわかった」

例2　Don't hesitate to do **what you think** is right.
　　「自分が正しいと思うことをためらわずにしなさい」

▶▶▶ **構文・語句解説** ◀◀◀

─ 第1段落 ─

¹As a British woman married to an American man, I have found people here more well-mannered in many ways than in England. ²Whenever we phone my mother-in-law she thanks us: "You're so good to call." ³I found this charming, and decided I should be more careful about thanking my family. ⁴So the next time my mother phoned I said, warmly, "It's so nice of you to call." ⁵There was a surprised silence, and then she said, "Well, I'm your mother, aren't I?" ⁶My sister later told me that my mother had found my thanks very odd, as if she were an acquaintance.

¹アメリカ人男性と結婚したイギリス人女性として，私はここの人たちはイギリスよりも多くの点で礼儀正しいのがわかった。²義母に電話するといつも彼女は「電話してくれてありがとう」とお礼を言う。³私はこれは感じがいいと思い，もっと気をつけて自分の家族にも感謝しなくてはと決心した。⁴それで母が次に電話してきたとき，私は優しく「電話してくれて親切ね」と言った。⁵びっくりした沈黙があり，それから彼女は言った。「ええと，私はあなたの母親よ

ね？」⁶後で妹から聞いたのだが，母は私の感謝の言葉をまるで自分が知人みたいでとても奇妙
だと思ったそうだ。

1 married to an American man は an English woman を修飾する分詞句。　　□ as A「Aとして」
2 □ phone「(に)電話をする」　　□ mother-in-law「義理の母親」　　□ thank「に感謝する」
3 □ charming「感じがよい」
4 □ the next time S V ...「次に…するとき」
　□ It's nice of A to *do*「…するとはA〈人〉は親切だ」
5 I'm your mother, aren't I? は付加疑問文。
6 □ thanks「感謝(の言葉)」　　□ odd「奇妙な」　　□ as if S V ...「まるで…のように」
　□ acquaintance「知り合い」

── 第2段落 ──

¹I have also found Americans more graceful at giving and accepting compliments. ²Like most mothers, I receive a lot of compliments about my son. (³"He's so tall!" ⁴"He's so cute!" ⁵"He's so bright!") ⁶I used to be embarrassed by these, but I have learned to smile and say thank you. ⁷It seems ungracious to deny the compliment. ⁸When my husband receives a compliment, he usually replies, "You're very kind to say so," which I think is a graceful response. ⁹It compliments the other person's good manners without seeming conceited.

¹またアメリカ人の方が褒め言葉を言ったり言われたりするのが上手だということもわかった。²ほとんどの母親と同様，私も息子について褒め言葉をたくさん言われる。(³「本当に背が高いのね」⁴「とっても可愛いわ」⁵「頭がいいのね」) ⁶こうした褒め言葉には気恥ずかしい思いをしたものだったが，笑顔を浮かべてありがとうと言えるようになった。⁷褒め言葉を否定するのは無愛想なことに思われる。⁸夫は褒め言葉を言われると，たいてい「そう言っていただいてありがとう」と答えるのだが，私はこれを上品な返答だと思う。⁹うぬぼれていると思われずに相手の礼儀正しさを褒めている。

2 □ a lot of A「多くのA」
4 □ cute「可愛い」
5 □ bright「利口な」
6 □ used to *do*「以前は…した」　　□ be embarrassed by A「Aに気恥ずかしい思いをする」
7 It seems ... の It は形式主語で，真主語は to deny 以下。

□ ungracious「不作法な，無礼な」　　□ deny「を打ち消す」

9 □ compliment「をほめる」　　□ manners「マナー，礼儀作法」

□ conceited「うぬぼれの強い」

＝＝

── 第3段落 ──

¹Sometimes it is hard to change the way you speak, especially in the day-to-day exchanges we take for granted. ²When I buy something at a shop in England, the assistant and I thank each other excessively. ³I hand her the item I am buying, saying "thank you." ⁴She takes it and says "thank you." ⁵She tells me the price, I hand her the money, and we both say "thank you." ⁶She hands me my change and the receipt; I say "thank you." ⁷Finally she hands me the item in a bag and we both say a final "thank you." ⁸I know all these thanks are unnecessary, but they make us both feel comfortable. ⁹In New York this kind of exchange takes place in silence. ¹⁰The sales assistant may even be talking to someone else. ¹¹Sometimes when I say "thank you," the assistant will say "uh huh" as if she is doing me a favor! ¹²Of course New York is not typical of the U.S. ¹³Smaller communities still maintain the small rituals which have become lost in the big city. ¹⁴And I have heard that in the South, where they pride themselves on their good manners, shoppers can have half-hour conversations about the items in a shopping basket.

¹話し方を変えるのが難しいこともある。特に当然のことと思っている日常のやりとりにおいては。²イギリスの店で何かを買うときは，店員と私はお互いにありがとうと必要以上に言う。³「ありがとう」と言いながら私が彼女に買う物を渡す。⁴彼女はそれを取って「ありがとう」と言う。⁵彼女が私に値段を伝え，私は彼女にお金を渡し，2人で「ありがとう」と言い合う。⁶彼女は私にお釣りとレシートを渡す。私は「ありがとう」と言う。⁷最後に彼女は私に袋に入れた品物を渡し，それから私たち2人は最後の「ありがとう」を言う。⁸このような感謝の言葉はすべて不必要とは思うが，それで2人とも気持ちがいいのだ。⁹ニューヨークではこの種のやりとりは黙って行われる。¹⁰店員は誰か他の人と話していることすらある。¹¹私が「ありがとう」と言うと，店員は私の頼みを聞いてくれているかのように「うん，うん」と言うこともあるのだ。¹²もちろんニューヨークはアメリカを代表しているのではない。¹³より小さな地域社会では，大都市で失われたちょっとした慣習をまだ守っている。¹⁴そして作法がよいのが自慢の南部では，買い物客同士が買い物かごの中の品物のことで30分も話ができるそうである。

1 it is hard ... の it は形式主語で，真主語は to change 以下。we take for granted は the day-to-day exchanges を修飾する関係代名詞節。　□ the way S V ...「…する方法」

　□ especially「特に」　　□ day-to-day「日常の」　　□ exchange「やり取り／会話」

　□ take A for granted「Aを当然のことと思う」

2 □ assistant「店員」　　□ excessively「過度に」

3 I am buying は the item を修飾する関係代名詞節。saying "thank you" は分詞構文。

　□ hand O₁ O₂「O₁〈人〉に O₂〈物〉を手渡す」　　□ item「品目」

6 □ change「釣り銭」　　□ receipt「レシート」

9 □ take place「起こる，行われる」　　□ in silence「黙って」

11 □ do A a favor「A〈人〉の頼み事を聞く」

12 □ be typical of A「Aを代表している，Aの特徴を示している」

13 □ community「地域社会」　　□ maintain「を維持する」　　□ ritual「慣習，儀式」

14 □ the South「(アメリカの)南部」　　□ pride *oneself* on A「Aを誇りに思う」

脳とコンピュータ

問1 脳がどのように機能するのか知れば知るほど，脳が論理的なコンピュータではないことがわかるようになる。

問2 人間の脳にはできてコンピュータにはできないことがある。

問3 ウ. two numbers – one unknown number

問4 if I asked you to tell me

問5 イ. Thus

▶▶▶ **設問解説** ◀◀◀

問1 the＋比較級 ... , the＋比較級～「…すればするほど，ますます～」の構文が用いられている。 ➡ **Point ㉚** 前半部の about A「Aについて」のAの位置に疑問詞節 how the brain functions がきている。

☐ function「機能する」　　☐ come to *do*「…するようになる」

☐ realize that 節「…だと気づく，はっきり理解する」　　☐ logical「論理的な」

問2 二重限定の関係詞節に注意。the human brain can do と that computers cannot do という2つの関係代名詞節が things を修飾している。

➡ **Point ⑭**

問3 第3段落第3文に述べられた例から「2つの数字」と「1つの未知の数字」であることがわかる。

問4 次の文の「24は4×6の積だと答える」という内容から「24は何の積かを私に言うようにあなたに求めたとしたらどうだろうか」という意味の英文を作る。What if S V ... ? は「…したらどうなるだろうか」という表現で if 節内で過去形を用いると控えめな意味合いになる。

例　What if you moved this table a little?
　　「このテーブルをちょっと動かしたらどうなるだろう」

☐ ask O to *do*「Oに…するように頼む」

問5 空所の後ろの「あなたは他にも答えとなるものが多くあることに気づき，可能性のある多くの答えのどれが最適なのかあなたは決定のしようがないのである」という内容は，空所の前の内容から引き出される結果である。したがって，イが正解。

ア.「そのうえ」イ.「したがって」ウ.「しかし」エ.「同様に」

Point ⑭ 二重限定の関係詞節

名詞が2つの関係詞節によって修飾されることがある。これを二重限定の関係詞節と呼ぶ。1つめの関係詞節によって修飾された名詞を，さらに2つめの関係詞節が修飾している。1つめの関係詞節を訳出したうえで次に2つめの関係詞節を訳出すればよい。なお，1つめの関係詞は省略されることが多い。

例 There is nothing **I have which you'll like**.

「私が持っているものであなたが気に入るようなものは何もないですよ」

▶▶ **構文・語句解説** ◀◀

― 第1・2段落 ―

[1]The more we learn about how the brain functions, the more we come to realize that the brain is not a logical computer. [2]In his book *How the Mind Works*, Steven Pinker relates human brains with computers, saying

computers are serial, doing one thing at a time; brains are parallel, doing millions of things at once. [3]Computers are fast; brains are slow. [4]Computer parts are reliable; brain parts are noisy. [5]Computers have a limited number of connections; brains have trillions. [6]Computers are assembled according to a blueprint; brains must assemble themselves.

[7]This does not mean that computers are superior to the human brain. [8]No. [9]There are things the human brain can do that computers cannot do. [10]We humans are comfortable solving "ill-posed problems," while a computer will freeze when faced with such a problem.

---

[1]脳がどのように機能するのか知れば知るほど，脳が論理的なコンピュータではないことがわかるようになる。[2]*How the Mind Works* という著書の中でスティーブン・ピンカーは人間の脳とコンピュータを対比して述べている。

コンピュータは連続的で一度に1つのことをするが，脳は並列的で一度に無数のことをする。[3]コンピュータは速いが脳は遅い。[4]コンピュータの部品は信頼できるが，脳の部位は乱れることがある。[5]コンピュータの接続は数に限りがあるが，脳の場合は無数にある。[6]コンピュータは青写真に従って組み立てられるが，脳は自分で自分を組み立てなくてはならない。

[7]これはコンピュータの方が人間の脳より優秀だという意味ではない。[8]そうではない。[9]人間

の脳にはできてコンピュータにはできないことがある。¹⁰我々人間は「不良設定問題」をたやすく解くのに対して，コンピュータはそのような問題にぶつかると動かなくなってしまう。

2 saying ... は分詞構文。doing one ... a time と doing millions ... at once も分詞構文。
　□ relate A with B「AをBと関連づける」　　□ at a time「一度に」
　□ parallel「並列的な」　　□ millions of A「何百万ものA，無数のA」　　□ at once「一度に」
4 noisy「騒がしい，雑音の入る」ここでは reliable と対比的に用いられているので，「乱れる」ぐらいの意味合い。　　□ reliable「信頼できる」
5 □ limited「限られた」
6 □ assemble「を組み立てる」　　□ according to A「Aに従って」　　□ blueprint「青写真」
7 □ be superior to A「Aより優れている」
10 when faced with ... = when it is faced with ...　　□ comfortable *doing*「楽に…できる」
　□ freeze「(コンピュータが)フリーズする，動かなくなる」
　□ be faced with A「Aに直面する」

───── 第3段落 ─────

¹What is an "ill-posed problem?" ²To illustrate, let's use a mathematical example. ³If I were to ask you what the product of 4×6 was, you would say it is 24. ⁴This is a clearly posed problem. ⁵It gives you two numbers and asks you to solve for one unknown number. ⁶You have enough information to solve the problem easily, and you would be very confident that there was only one right answer. ⁷Both you and a computer could solve this problem equally well. ⁸But what if I asked you to tell me that 24 is the product of what? ⁹You could answer that 24 is the product of 4×6. ¹⁰That would be correct. ¹¹But it would also be correct to say that 24 is the product of 3×8, 2×12, 1×24, 0.5×48, and on and on. ¹²This is an example of an ill-posed problem, in which you are given only one number and asked to solve for two unknowns. ¹³Thus you find that there are many possible alternative answers, and you have no way of determining which of the many possible answers is the best.

　¹「不良設定問題」とは何だろう。²説明のために数学の例を挙げてみよう。³私が 4×6 の積はいくらかと尋ねたら，あなたは24だと答えるだろう。⁴これは明確に設定された問題である。⁵この問題は2つの数字を与えて1つの未知の数字を求めさせる。⁶あなたには問題を簡単に解くだけの情報があり，正しい答えは1つだけだということに大いに自信があるだろう。⁷あなたもコンピュータもこの問題を同じようにうまく解くことができるだろう。⁸しかし，24は何

の積か答えるようにあなたに求めたとしたらどうだろうか。⁹あなたは24とは 4 × 6 の積だと答えられるだろう。¹⁰それは正しい。¹¹だが24は 3 ×8, 2 × 12, 1 × 24, 0.5 × 48などの積だと答えることもできる。¹²これが不良設定問題の一例であり，1 つの数字だけを与えられて 2 つの未知の数字を求めることを要求されている。¹³したがって，あなたは他にも答えとなるものが多くあることに気づき，可能性のある多くの答えのどれが最適なのかあなたは決定のしようがないのである。

2 □ illustrate「例を挙げて説明する」   □ mathematical「数学の」

3 □ If S were to *do* ... , S' would *do* ～「仮に S が…するなら，S' は～するだろう」

　 □ product「積」

4 □ clearly「明確に」

5 □ unknown「未知の」

6 would be の would は仮定法の助動詞。第 7 ～11文の助動詞もすべて同様。

　 □ enough A to *do*「…するのに十分な A」

　 □ information「情報」   □ be confident that 節「…に自信を持っている」

7 □ equally「等しく」

10 □ correct「正しい」

11 it would also be ... の it は形式主語で，真主語は to say 以下。

　 □ on and on「引き続き，どんどん」

12 in which ... は an example を修飾する関係代名詞節。given only one number と asked to solve for two unknowns を and が結んでいる。

　 □ ask O to *do*「O〈人〉に…するように頼む」

13 which 以下は determining の目的語となる名詞節。

　 □ alternative「代わりの，あれかこれかの」   □ way of *doing*「…する方法」

　 □ determine「を決定する」

人と違う道を選択すること

解 答

問1　エ. grassy
問2　他人と同じ選択をして平凡な生活を送ることもできるし，危険を冒して人と異なることに決めることで，豊かで満足のいく生活を送ることもできるということ。
問3　イ. whether
問4　すなわち，蜂蜜こそが，そのケーキをとてもおいしくするものなのである。
問5　エ. right
問6　ア. rewarding

▶▶ 設問解説 ◀◀

問1　空所(1)を含む文の both roads とは第1段落第1文の the one covered with grass that few people had taken と the cleared one that many others had already walked down のことである。空所の後ろの or 以下で"the one less traveled by"「あまり人の通っていない道」と言い換えているので，正解はエ。ア.「混みあった」イ.「普通の」ウ.「邪魔なものが取り除かれた」エ.「草に覆われた」

問2　次の文に The lesson goes something like this とあるので，これに続く we can have 以下を抜き出してまとめればよい。
　　　□ lesson「教訓」

問3　前後に完全な文があるので，空所(3)には前後の文内容が適切なつながりになる接続詞が入る。また，後ろに or があることから，whether ... or ～「…であろうと～であろうと」とすると，「『違いを生む』とは，話題にしていることが大きなことでも，小さなことでも，英語では常に積極的な意味を持つ表現である」となり，文意が成立する。➡ Point ⑮

問4　関係代名詞 what で導かれた名詞節が補語になっている。➡ Point ⑨
　　　makes the cake taste ... は make O do「Oに…させる」の形。
　　　□ in other words「すなわち，言い換えれば」　　□ taste C「Cの味がする」

問5　空所(5)を含む文は saying that ... the difference が主語。この that 節内にあ

る，make the difference とは，第3段落第1文で「常に積極的な意味を持つ
表現である」と述べられており，さらに第2〜4文で具体例を挙げて「違いを
生む，重要である」という意味であることを説明している。よって，「あまり人
の通っていない道が大きな違いを生むということ」が，どのような選択を話し
手がしたことを示唆するのかを考えればよい。

ア.「異なる」 イ.「同じ」 ウ.「間違った」 エ.「正しい」

問6 本文は全体として，ロバート・フロストの詩を紹介する中で，「人と違う道を選
ぶことが大切である」ということを言っている。

ア.「報いのある」 イ.「がっかりするような」 ウ.「惨めな」 エ.「孤独な」

Point ⑮ whether

　whether で導かれる節は，「…であろうと〜であろうと」という意味の譲歩の
副詞節になる場合と，「…かどうか（ということ）」という意味の名詞節になる場
合がある。また，名詞節の whether が動詞の目的語になっている場合には if
を用いることもできる。

例1 **Whether** he works hard or not, the result will be the same.
「彼が一生懸命がんばってもがんばらなくても，結果は同じだろう」

例2 **Whether** he works hard or not is of no interest to me.
「彼が一生懸命がんばっているかどうかは私には興味がない」

例3 I don't know **whether [if]** he works hard or not.
「彼が一生懸命がんばっているかどうかはわからない」

▶▶▶ 構文・語句解説 ◀◀◀

── 第1段落 ──

　[1]If you were walking in the woods, and suddenly the path split into two different roads,
which one would you choose: the one covered with grass that few people had taken or the
cleared one that many others had already walked down? [2]Anyone who has read the poet,
Robert Frost, probably recognizes this situation from one of his most famous poems, "The
Road Not Taken." [3]After carefully considering both roads, the speaker of the poem
chooses the grassy one, or "the one less traveled by." [4]Then he says that this choice
"has made all the difference."

¹もしも森の中を歩いていて，思いもよらず道が２つに分かれているとすれば，どちらの道を選ぶであろうか。通った人のほとんどいない草に覆われた道か，それまでに歩いた人が他にもたくさんいる草の生えていない道か。²詩人，ロバート・フロストの作品を読んだことのある人であれば，彼の最も有名な詩の１つ『選ばれざる道』からこのような状況に覚えがあるだろう。³両方の道を慎重に検討したうえで，この詩の語り手は草に覆われた道，つまり「あまり人の通っていない道」を選ぶ。⁴そして，この選択が「大きな違いを生んだ」と言う。

1 If you were walking … , which one would you choose は仮定法過去の文。

the one covered with grass that few people had taken の one は road の代用。covered with grass は the one を修飾する過去分詞句。that 以下は the one を修飾する関係代名詞節。

the cleared one that many others had already walked down の one は road の代用。that 以下は the cleared one を修飾する関係代名詞節。

□ path「道」　　□ split into A「Aに分かれる」　　□ cover A with B「AをBで覆う」

□ grass「草」　　□ clear「から邪魔なものを取り除く」

2 □ Robert Frost「ロバート・フロスト」米国の詩人（1874‐1963）。

□ recognize「に覚えがある，がそれだとわかる」　　□ situation「状況」

3 less traveled by は the one を修飾し，one は road の代用。travel by A で「Aを通って行く」という意味。

4 □ make all the difference「大きな違いを生じる，重要である」

— 第２段落 —

¹Most American school children are taught this poem, often with a lesson that's actually simpler than the poem itself. ²The lesson goes something like this: we can have an ordinary life by making the same choices others make or we can have a rich, more satisfying life by taking risks and choosing to be different. ³Or as the poem says, taking the less traveled road can make all the difference.

¹たいていのアメリカの小学生は，しばしばその詩自体よりも実は単純な教訓と共に，この詩を教えられる。²その教訓とはおよそ次のようなものである。人と同じ選択をすることで，平凡な生活を送ることもできるし，危険を冒して人と異なることを選ぶことで，豊かで満ち足りた生活を送ることもできる。³あるいは，その詩にあるように，人のあまり通っていない道を行くことで大きな違いが生まれることもあるのだ。

2 others make は the same choices を修飾する関係代名詞節。

　□ go something like A「およそAとなっている」　　　□ ordinary「平凡な」

　□ take risks「危険を冒す」

3 as the poem says の as は後続の節の内容を補足説明する関係代名詞。

. . . .

― 第3段落 ―

¹"To make the difference" is an expression that always has a positive meaning in English, whether you're talking about something big or small. ²If a man tells his wife, for example, that marrying her has made all the difference, he's saying that he's very happy he married her. ³Or in the case of something small, you might say that using honey instead of sugar in a cake recipe makes the difference. ⁴In other words, the honey is what makes the cake taste so good. ⁵In Frost's poem, of course, saying that the less traveled road has made all the difference suggests that the speaker has made the right choice.

¹「違いを生む」とは，話題にしていることが大きなことでも，小さなことでも，英語では常に積極的な意味を持つ表現である。²たとえば，もしもある人が妻に彼女と結婚したことで大きな違いが生じたと言えば，彼女と結婚してとても幸福であるということを言っている。³あるいは小さなことであれば，ケーキを作るのに砂糖の代わりに蜂蜜を使うことで違いが生まれると言うかもしれない。⁴すなわち，蜂蜜こそが，そのケーキをとてもおいしくするものなのである。⁵もちろん，フロストの詩では，あまり人の通っていない道が大きな違いを生むと言うことで，話し手は正しい選択をしたことを示唆しているのである。

1 that 以下は an expression を修飾する関係代名詞節。

　□ expression「表現」　　　□ positive「積極的な」

2 □ be happy（that）節「…して幸福である」

3 □ in the case of A「Aの場合」　　　□ instead of A「Aの代わりに」　　　□ recipe「調理法」

5 □ suggest that 節「…だと示唆する」

. . . .

― 第4段落 ―

¹I suppose this poem expresses part of the American Dream. ²That is, the idea that if you have the courage to be different and to follow your own path, life will be more rewarding. ³It's fairly common for teachers or parents to tell children, "If you believe in yourself, you can do anything: become a doctor, a successful musician, or even the

President of the United States. ⁴It's up to you."

---

　¹この詩はアメリカン・ドリームの一部を表現していると思う。²つまり，人と異なり，自分の道を進む勇気があれば，人生はもっと報いのあるものになるという考えである。³教師や親が子供に次のように言うことはとてもよくあることだ。「自分を信じれば，何だってできる。医者でも，成功したミュージシャンでも，アメリカの大統領になることだって。⁴それも自分次第なんだ。」

1 □ suppose that 節「…と思う」　　□ express「を表す」

2 that 以下は the idea と同格の名詞節。

　□ that is「つまり，すなわち」　　□ the courage to *do*「…する勇気」

　□ follow「に沿って行く」

3 It's fairly common for teachers or parents to tell children ... の It は形式主語で，真主語は to tell 以下。for teachers or parents は to tell 以下の意味上の主語。

　□ fairly「かなり」　　□ common「よくある」

　□ believe in A「Aを信頼する，正しいと信じる」

4 □ be up to A「A次第である，Aの責任である」

健全な競争

解 答

問1 優勝者を選ぶのに苦労するということ。(18字)

問2 ア. if

問3 優勝者を選ぶつもりがないのなら，なぜコンテストなどするのだろう。

問4 負けることは誰も直面すべきでない苦難であるということ。

問5 エ. our children are not strong enough to endure losing

問6 私が言いたいことは，健全な競争は子供たちに人生について多くのことを教えられるということである。

問7 ウ，エ

▶▶▶ 設問解説 ◀◀◀

問1 下線部(1)を含む文の主語は直前の文にある the judges を指している。「審査員は同じことを思ったに違いない」というのが下線部(1)を含む文の意味。よって，審査員以外の人が思ったことを本文中に求めればよい。直前の文に I thought that ... とあるので，この that 節の内容をまとめればよい。

問2 (2) his entry had won の部分は see の目的語となる節である。したがって，名詞節を導く接続詞を入れなければならないので，アが正解。

→ **Point** ⑯

問3 この文は筆者が心の中で思ったことを述べた1文である。you は一般の人を表し「人は(誰でも)」という意味。また，should は疑問詞を強めて「いったい」という意味。ここで用いられた if は副詞節を導いている。

□ pick a winner「優勝者を選ぶ」

問4 コロン(：)以下に具体的に述べられている。no one should face は a hardship を修飾する関係代名詞節。

問5 too ... to *do* は「あまりにも…なので～できない」という意味。したがって，下線部(5)は「子供はとても弱いので敗北に対処できない」という意味なので，エが正解。 → **Point** ⑲

ア.「競争はとても困難なので子供はそれに対処できない」

イ.「競争は子供が対処できるほど簡単ではない」

ウ.「子供はとても強いので敗北に耐えられない」

エ.「子供は敗北に耐えられるほど強くはない」

□ handle「を扱う」   □ defeat「敗北」

問6 全体の文構造は，What I want to say(S) is(V) that ... (C)である。What は関係代名詞。 ➡ **Point ⑨** that 節内の主語 healthy rivalries とは「健全な競争」のことで，動詞は teach O_1 O_2「O_1〈人〉に O_2〈こと〉を教える」という形。したがって，a lot が名詞として用いられていることに注意。

□ a lot「多くのこと」

問7 ア.「筆者の息子は自分の参加作品を誇りに思っていなかった」第1段落第2文の内容に不一致。

イ.「筆者の息子は誰もが黒と金色のリボンを与えられてとてもうれしく思った」第2～5段落第10文の内容に不一致。

ウ.「最近大人たちは学校の競技会でどの子供も敗者にならないように気をつけている」第2～5段落第12文および第6・7段落第2文の内容に一致。

エ.「人間は生まれつき競争好きである」第6・7段落第4文の内容に一致。

オ.「雪だるまを作った子供がカボチャコンテストで優勝した」第8～10段落の内容に不一致。

Point ⑯ if

if に導かれる節は，「もし…ならば」という意味の副詞節になる場合，「…かどうか」という意味の名詞節になる場合がある。

例1 I'll believe it **if** you show me some proof.
「君が証拠を示すなら信じるよ」

例2 She asked me **if** I liked Chinese food.
「彼女は私に中華料理は好きかと尋ねた」

▶▶ **構文・語句解説** ◀◀

— 第1段落 —

¹One recent Halloween my five-year-old son entered a pumpkin-decorating contest at his school. ²He proudly took his entry to his school. ³It was a wild combination of carvings, paint and feathers he had constructed himself. ⁴We placed it among the other creative pumpkins—witches, a snowman, and even a bubble-gum-blowing pumpkin wearing a baseball cap. ⁵I thought that the judges were going to have a tough time choosing a winner.

> ¹数年前のハロウィーンに私の当時5歳だった息子が学校のカボチャの飾り付けコンテストに参加した。²彼は誇らしげに自分の参加作品を学校に持って行った。³それは自由奔放に彫ったり色を付けたり羽根を付けたりして彼が自分で作ったものだった。⁴私たちはそれを魔女や，雪だるま，野球帽をかぶった風船ガムまでふくらましているカボチャといった他の独創的なカボチャの間に置いた。⁵審査員は優勝者を選ぶのに苦労するだろう，と私は思った。

1 One recent Halloween とは「去年のハロウィーン」ではなく，「2，3年前のハロウィーン」ということ。　□ recent「最近の」

　□ Halloween「ハロウィーン」万聖節の前夜祭。特にアメリカでは，この夜，子供たちはカボチャをくりぬいた「お化け提灯」を作ったり，お化けや悪魔などの扮装をして"Trick or treat!"と言って家々を回り，近所の人は子供たちに菓子や果物を与える。　□ enter「に参加する」

2 □ proudly「誇らしげに」　　□ entry「出品物，参加者」

3 he had constructed himself は a wild combination を修飾する関係代名詞節。wild combination とは，普通はカボチャをくりぬいて顔を彫るだけなのだが，色を付けたり羽根を付けたりと余分な飾り付けが施されたものを述べたもの。

　□ combination「組み合わせ」　　□ carving「彫刻」　　□ feather「羽根」

　□ construct「を造る」

4 wearing a baseball cap は a bubble-gum-blowing pumpkin を修飾する現在分詞句。

　□ place「を置く」　　□ creative「独創的な」　　□ witch「魔女」

5 □ judge「審査員」　　□ have a tough time *doing*「…するのに苦労する」

・・・

― 第2～5段落 ―

　¹They must have thought the same thing, because when we returned to the school that evening, we discovered all the pumpkins were awarded the same black-and-gold ribbon. ²My son, eagerly looking to see if his entry had won, kept asking me, "Which pumpkin won? ³Where's the winner?"

　⁴What could I say? ⁵"Well, it looks like everyone won. ⁶Look. ⁷You got a ribbon, son!"

　⁸Kids are smart. ⁹"Yeah, but who won?" he asked. ¹⁰I could sense his disappointment —and my own. ¹¹Why should you have a contest if you're not going to pick a winner?

　¹²I understand that the school was trying to convey that everyone had done a great job, but I worry that a different message was sent: that losing is a hardship no one should face.

¹審査員も同じことを思ったに違いない。というのはその日の夕方学校に戻ると，すべてのカボチャに同じ黒と金色のリボンが与えられていたことに気づいたからである。²息子は，自分の作品が優勝したかどうか確かめようと熱心に見ていたが，「どのカボチャが1等なの？³優勝したのはどこにあるの？」と何度も私に聞いた。

⁴私はなんと言ったらいいのか？⁵「あのね，みんなが優勝したみたいよ。⁶ほら。⁷お前もリボンをもらったじゃないの」

⁸子供は賢い。⁹「うん，でも誰が優勝したの？」と彼は聞いた。¹⁰私は彼の失望を感じた。そして自分自身の失望も。¹¹優勝者を選ぶつもりがないのなら，なぜコンテストなどするのだろう。

¹²学校側はみんながすばらしかったと伝えようとしているのは理解できるが，違うメッセージが伝えられたのでは，と心配である。つまり，敗北は誰も直面すべきでない苦難である，というメッセージだ。

1 □ must have *done*「…したにちがいない」　　□ return「戻る」
　□ award O₁ O₂「O₁〈人〉に(賞として)O₂を与える」
2 eagerly looking ... won は分詞構文。　　□ eagerly「熱心に」
　□ see if ...「…かどうか確かめる」　　□ keep *doing*「…し続ける」
5 □ It looks like S V ...「…するように見える」
8 □ smart「利口な」
10 □ my own＝my own disappointment　　□ sense「を感じる」　　□ disappointment「失望」
12 no one should face は hardship を修飾する関係代名詞節。　　□ convey that 節「…を伝える」
　□ worry that 節「…を心配する」　　□ hardship「苦難」　　□ face「に直面する」

─── 第6・7段落 ───

¹I've noticed this trend a lot lately. ²It's as if we adults believe our children are too weak to handle defeat. ³But without a winner, a game or contest loses its excitement. ⁴It's part of human nature to be competitive. ⁵A competitive spirit is key to our success as adults; why shouldn't we foster it in our children?

⁶I'm not suggesting we make our children compete against each other in all aspects of life. ⁷What I want to say is that healthy rivalries can teach our kids a lot about life.

---

¹私は最近この傾向に気づくことが多い。²まるで大人たちは子供がとても弱いので，負けることを受け入れられないと思っているようである。³しかし，優勝者がいなければ試合やコンテ

ストはわくわくすることがなくなってしまう。⁴競争好きは人間性の一部である。⁵競争精神は大人になって成功するのに重要である。いったいなぜ子供の競争心を育ててはいけないのだろうか？

⁶子供に生活のあらゆる側面においてお互いに競争させよう，と言っているのではない。⁷私が言いたいことは，健全な競争は子供たちに人生について多くのことを教えられるということである。

1 □ notice「に気づく」　　□ trend「傾向」　　□ lately「最近」

2 It's as if S V ...「まるで…するようだ」

4 □ nature「性質」　　□ competitive「競争好きな」

5 key to A「Aにとって重要な」本来 key は名詞であるが，形容詞的に用いられている。
　　□ foster「を育成する」

6 □ suggest (that) 節「…だと示唆する」　　□ make O do「Oに…させる」
　　□ compete against A「Aと競争する」　　□ each other「お互い」　　□ aspect「側面」

- -

── 第8〜10段落 ──

¹Kids can endure failure. ²My son understood that he might not win the pumpkin-decorating contest. ³The disappointment for him was that nobody won. ⁴The following morning he asked, "Mummy, who really won the contest?"

⁵"They didn't pick a winner," I explained again.

⁶"Well, I think the snowman won," he said with a nod. ⁷And then he was satisfied.

¹子供は失敗に耐えられるのだ。²私の息子はカボチャの飾り付けコンテストで優勝できないかもしれないことがわかっていた。³彼が失望したのは誰も優勝しなかったことである。⁴翌朝，彼は「お母さん，本当は誰が優勝したの？」と聞いてきた。

⁵「優勝者は選ばれなかったのよ」と私は再び説明した。

⁶「うーん，僕は雪だるまだったと思うな」と彼はうなずいた。⁷そしてそのとき彼は満足していた。

1 □ endure「に耐える」

4 □ following「次の」

6 □ with a nod「うなずいて」　　7 □ satisfied「満足している」

孤独感

問1 実際には1人でないときに孤独を感じることが多いから。（26字）

問2 自分以外の人は皆自信にあふれ，他の人たち全員と知り合いなのに，自分だけが無力で1人ぼっちであるという印象を受ける。

問3 イ. capable

問4 イ. depressed

問5 周りの人がどんなに近くにいても，1人きりであることがよくあるという事実に向き合わなければならない。

▶▶▶ 設問解説 ◀◀◀

問1 下線部(1)は「孤独とは奇妙な状況である」という意味。第1段落第3文に述べられた「実際は1人でないときに，孤独に打ちのめされることが多い」ということが，「奇妙な」と言える理由である。

　　□ loneliness「孤独」　　□ curious「奇妙な」　　□ situation「状況」

問2 the impression に続く that 節は同格の名詞節。 ➡ **Point ⑧** and は is confident と knows all the others を結んでいる。また，接続詞 while は主節の内容と対照的な事柄を述べるときに，主節に続けて用いられる。while 以下の「自分だけが無力で独りぼっちである」というのは，that 節内の「自分以外の人は皆自信にあふれ，他の人たち全員と知り合いである」という内容と対照的なことである。

　　例 Their country has plenty of oil, while ours has none.

　　　　「彼らの国は石油が豊富にあるが，わが国にはまったくない」

　　□ the impression that 節「…という印象」　　□ confident「自信がある」
　　□ helpless「無力な」　　□ alone「1人で」

問3 空所(3)の直後には of concealing ... と続いている。選択肢の中で，capable だけが be capable of *doing*「…することができる」という形で用いる。

　　ア.「できる」イ.「能力がある」ウ.「可能な」エ.「不可能な」

問4 「どのように見えたら，パーティーの席で誰も挨拶してくれないのか」を考える。直前では「明るい表情をするようにしなければならない」と述べている。

　　ア.「興奮している」イ.「落ち込んでいる」ウ.「うれしそうな」エ.「1人で」

問5 the fact に続く that 節は同格の名詞節。→ Point ⑧ また，that 節内で，譲歩を表す副詞節を導く no matter how が用いられている。
→ Point ⑰ are to people ... は be close to A「Aに近い」の close が how と結びついて，前に移動したもの。

□ face「に立ち向かう，を直視する」　　□ be close to A「Aに近い」

Point ⑰ no matter wh-節

no matter wh-節は「たとえ…しようとも」という意味の副詞節になる。wh-ever でも同じ意味を表すことができる。

例1 **No matter what** you say, I won't believe you.
「たとえあなたが何と言おうと，私はあなたの言うことは信じません」

例2 Phone me when you arrive, **however** late it is.
「どんなに遅くなっても，到着したら電話してください」

▶▶ 構文・語句解説 ◀◀

― 第1段落 ―

[1]Loneliness is a curious situation. [2]Almost everybody has experienced it at some time in their life. [3]It can often overcome you when in fact you are not alone; at a party, in the theater, or in any group where you are surrounded by people who give evidence of being supremely confident, friendly and capable of smooth, happy communication. [4]What should you do? [5]Lonely people are advised to go out and meet people. [6]But is this the answer?

---

[1]孤独とは奇妙な状況である。[2]ほとんど誰もがそれを人生の何らかの時に経験している。[3]実際は1人でないときに，孤独に打ちのめされることが多い。パーティーや劇場で，あるいはこのうえなく自信にあふれ，友好的で，円滑で楽しいコミュニケーションができそうな人が周りにいるどのような集団にいてもそうである。[4]どうしたらよいのだろうか。[5]孤独な人は出かけて人に会うように勧められる。[6]しかし，これが解決策なのだろうか。

2 □ experience「を経験する」

3 any group where you are surrounded by people who give evidence of being supremely confident, friendly and capable of smooth, happy communication の where 以下は any group を修飾する関係副詞節。また，who 以下は people を修飾する関係代名詞節。肯定文で用いられた any は「どんな」という意味。

□ overcome「を打ちのめす，圧倒する」　　□ in fact「実際には」

□ surround「を取り囲む」　　□ give evidence of A「Aの徴候を示す」

□ supremely「このうえなく」　　□ smooth「円滑な」

5 □ lonely「孤独な」　　□ advise O to *do*「Oに…するように勧める」

□ go out「外出する」

第2段落

[1]In a typical situation, such as your first day at a new school, you get the impression that everybody else is confident and knows all the others, while you are helpless and alone. [2]But in reality most people put on a show of confidence to hide their true feelings. [3]They may be as lonely as you. [4]There is no reason at all to assume that, in a big city for example, all the people around you are leading active, rich, fulfilling lives, while you alone are on the outside looking in. [5]You may be less capable of concealing your loneliness than others. [6]You must try to put on a cheerful face; nobody will greet you at a party if you look utterly depressed. [7]Another point to remember is that you should try to avoid joining groups where in fact you are a total stranger. [8]For many reasons established groups do dislike intrusions and to accept you requires considerable effort. [9]However, if you can offer something special any group may need, your entry may be quicker and less troublesome.

---

[1]新しい学校での初日のような典型的な状況では，自分以外の人は皆自信にあふれ，他の人たち全員と知り合いなのに，自分だけが無力で1人ぼっちであるという印象を受ける。[2]しかし，実際にはたいていの人は，本当の気持ちを隠すために，自信があるふりをしているのだ。[3]彼らは同じくらい孤独なのかもしれない。[4]たとえば大都市では，周りの人は皆活動的で，豊かで，充実した生活を送っているのに，自分だけが外にいて覗き込んでいるのだ，と思い込む理由はまったくない。[5]他の人と比べて，孤独であることを隠すのが下手なのかもしれない。[6]明るい表情をするように努めなければならない。すっかり落ち込んでいるように見えたら，パーティーの席で誰も挨拶してくれないだろう。[7]もう1つ覚えておくべき点は，実際に周りが皆知らない人ばかりの集団に加わるのは避けるように努めるべきである。[8]多くの理由で，すでに出来上がった集団は立ち入られることを嫌い，人を受け入れるにはかなりの努力を必要とする。[9]しかし，どのような集団でも必要とするような何か特別のものを提供できれば，より速く，問題もなく入っていけるだろう。

---

1 □ typical「典型的な」

2 to hide ... は目的を表す副詞用法の不定詞句。

□ in reality「実際には」　　□ put on a show of A「Aを装う，Aのふりをする」

□ confidence「自信」　　□ hide「を隠す」

4 you alone are on the outside looking in の looking in は分詞構文。また，主語の直後で用いられた alone は「…だけ」という意味。

□ no ... at all「少しも…でない」　　□ assume that 節「…と決めてかかる」

□ lead a ... life「…な生活を送る」　　□ active「活動的な」　　□ fulfilling「充実した」

□ outside「部外者の位置に」　　□ look in「覗く」

5 □ conceal「を隠す」

6 □ try to *do*「…しようとする」　　□ cheerful「元気のいい，陽気な」

□ greet「に挨拶する」　　□ utterly「すっかり，まったく」

7 Another point to remember is that ... の to remember は another point を修飾する形容詞用法の不定詞句。that 以下は補語になる名詞節。

where 以下は groups を修飾する関係副詞節。

□ avoid *doing*「…するのを避ける」　　□ join「に加わる」　　□ stranger「見知らぬ人」

8 to accept you は and 以下の文の主語になる名詞用法の不定詞句。

do dislike の do は動詞強調の助動詞。

□ established「既成の，確立された」　　□ intrusion「立ち入られること，侵入」

□ accept「を受け入れる」　　□ require「を必要とする」　　□ considerable「かなりの」

9 something special any group may need の special は something を修飾。any group may need も something を修飾する関係代名詞節。

□ offer「を提供する」　　□ entry「入ること，加入」

□ troublesome「面倒な，わずらわしい」

・・

── 第3段落 ──

¹It is best to get to know other people who share a common interest with you. ²Even if you don't like all of them, at least the shared experience is better than being alone. ³This may all seem rather grim, but we must face the fact that, no matter how close we are to people around us, we are often alone.

¹共通した関心を持つ人と知り合いになるのが最もよい。²たとえ全員が好きではなくても，少なくとも人と経験を共有することは，1人でいるよりはましである。³こうしたことはすべてかなり不快であると思えるかもしれないが，周りの人がどんなに近くにいても，1人きりであることがよくあるという事実に向き合わなければならない。

1 It is best to get ... の It は形式主語で，真主語は to get 以下。

who 以下は other people を修飾する関係代名詞節。

□ get to *do*「…するようになる」　　□ share A with B「AをBと共有する」

□ common「共通の」

2 □ at least「少なくとも」

恐竜の子孫

解 答

問1　descendants

問2　イ. as

問3　イ

問4　知られている化石の数がまだ少なすぎるためにその疑問を解明することができないでいるのだ。

問5　ウ

▶▶ 設問解説 ◀◀

問1　第1段落第2文の「現存している大型爬虫類の一部を恐竜の子孫と考えるのは魅力的なことだ」という内容を，空所(1)を含む第3文で「ところが実際には，これらの動物は遠い親戚ではあっても，（　1　）ではない」と否定している。また，第2段落第1・2文で「鳥が恐竜の子孫と考えられている」とある。したがって，空所には，第1文で用いられている descendants「子孫」を入れる。

問2　形容詞＋as S V ... で「…だけれども」という意味を表す譲歩の副詞節。

　➡ **Point ⑱**

問3　the resemblance とは，同じ文の if 節内に述べられている「約1億4000万年前に生きていた，最も古くから知られている鳥の骨格を恐竜の骨格と比べる」ときの「類似」である。したがって，正解はイ。

　□ resemblance「類似，類似性」

問4　too ... to *do* は「あまりに…なので～できない」という意味。➡ **Point ⑲**
　the question は前文の What happened ... disaster occurred? のことなので，「その疑問」と訳すとよい。

　□ known「知られている，既知の」　　□ few in number「数が少ない」

　□ allow O to *do*「Oが…するのを可能にする」　　□ resolve「を解決する，解明する」

問5　ア.「化石による証拠は，恐竜の時代には鳥の種がほんの少数しか存在しなかったことを示している」第3段落第1文の内容に不一致。

　イ.「恐竜を消滅させた大惨事はわずかな数の鳥の種に影響を及ぼしただけだった」第3段落第4文の内容に不一致。

ウ.「専門家は，羽根で覆われた恐竜が白亜紀に存在したことを示唆している」第2段落第5文の内容に一致。

エ.「第三紀には，すべての恐竜が絶滅し，最初の鳥が進化を開始した」第3段落第4文の内容に不一致。

Point ⑱ 譲歩の as

形容詞＋as S V ... で「…だけれども」という意味の譲歩の副詞節になる。形容詞の代わりに副詞や無冠詞の名詞がくることもある。なお，as の代わりに though も使われるが，although は使われないことに注意。

例1 Angry **as** he was, he couldn't help smiling.
「彼は怒っていたけれども，微笑まざるを得なかった」

例2 Much **as** I loved her, I decided to leave her.
「彼女をとても愛していたけれども，私は別れようと決心した」

▶▶ **構文・語句解説** ◀◀

― 第1段落 ―

¹Did all the dinosaurs disappear 65 million years ago? ²It is sometimes tempting to seek the distant descendants of dinosaurs in some of the larger reptiles alive today, such as crocodiles or Komodo dragons. ³In fact, these animals, although distant relations of dinosaurs, are not their descendants.

¹恐竜はすべて6500万年前に消えてしまったのだろうか？²ワニやコモドドラゴンのような，現存している大型爬虫類の一部に恐竜の遠い子孫を見いだそうとするのは，時には魅力的である。³だが実際は，これらの動物は，恐竜の遠い親戚ではあっても，その子孫ではないのである。

1 □ dinosaur「恐竜」　　□ disappear「消える，姿を消す」　　□ million「100万」

2 It は形式主語で，真主語は to seek 以下。alive today は the larger reptiles を修飾する形容詞句。　　□ tempting「魅力的な，誘惑する」　　□ seek「を捜す，得ようとする」
□ distant「遠い」　　□ reptile「爬虫類」　　□ alive「生きている」
□ A, such as B「たとえばBのようなA」　　□ crocodile「ワニ，クロコダイル」

3 although distant relations of dinosaurs ＝ although they are distant relations of dinosaurs
□ in fact「（ところが）実際は，実は」　　□ relation「親類，親戚」

91

[1]In order to find descendants of the dinosaurs in today's world, strange as it may seem, we need to turn to birds. [2]In fact, the majority of today's scientists think that birds are descended from certain small meat-eating dinosaurs. [3]If the skeleton of the oldest known bird, which lived about 140 million years ago, is compared to that of the dinosaurs, the resemblance is great. [4]This has been confirmed by numerous recent finds of primitive birds that had dinosaur features, and of dinosaurs that were close to birds. [5]Some Chinese remains from the beginning of the Cretaceous period, approximately 120 million years old, have even yielded the fossils of animals that may have been dinosaurs with feathers.

[1]今日の世界で恐竜の子孫を見つけるためには，奇妙に思えるかもしれないが，鳥に目を向けなければならない。[2]実際，今日の学者の大多数は，鳥はある小さな肉食の恐竜の子孫である，と考えている。[3]約1億4000万年前に生きていた，最も古くから知られている鳥の骨格を恐竜の骨格と比べてみると，類似点が非常に多い。[4]このことは，恐竜の特徴を備えていた原始時代の鳥，および鳥によく似ている恐竜に関する最近の数多くの発見によって裏付けられている。[5]およそ1億2000万年前の白亜紀初期の中国の遺跡からは，羽毛のある恐竜だった可能性のある動物の化石が出土することもある。

1 ☐ in order to *do*「…するために」　　☐ strange「奇妙な」　　☐ seem C「Cのように思える」
　☐ turn to A「Aに目を向ける」

2 ☐ the majority of A「大多数のA」　　☐ be descended from A「Aの子孫である」
　☐ certain A「あるA」　　☐ meat-eating「肉食の」

3 which lived ... years ago は the oldest known bird を補足説明する非制限用法の関係代名詞節。
　that of the dinosaurs の that は the skeleton の代用。
　☐ skeleton「骨格」　　☐ the oldest known「最も古くから知られている」
　☐ compare A to B「AをBと比較する」

4 of primitive birds ... dinosaur features と of dinosaurs ... to birds の2つの前置詞句が and で結ばれている。that had dinosaur features は primitive birds を修飾する関係代名詞節。that were close to birds は dinosaurs を修飾する関係代名詞節。
　☐ confirm「を裏付ける，確認する」　　☐ numerous「数多くの」　　☐ recent「最近の」
　☐ find「発見，発見物」　　☐ primitive「原始的な，原始時代の」　　☐ feature「特徴」
　☐ be close to A「Aに近い」

5 that may ... with feathers は animals を修飾する関係代名詞節。　　☐ remains「遺跡」

92

□ beginning「始まり，初期」　　□ approximately「およそ，約」

□ yield「を産み出す，もたらす」　　□ fossil「化石」

□ may have *done*「…したかもしれない」　　□ feather「羽毛」

第3段落

¹Fossils show us that at the time of the dinosaurs' disappearance, birds had already been in existence for a long time and had developed into many different species. ²What happened to them when the disaster occurred? ³Experts have different opinions on this question, and the known fossils are still too few in number to allow the question to be resolved. ⁴However, it is possible that a great extinction took place among birds as well and that the group's evolution, when it started again at the beginning of the Tertiary period, was based only on a few surviving species.

¹恐竜が姿を消した時には，鳥がすでに長期にわたって存在しており，非常にさまざまな種へと進化していた，ということが化石によってわかる。²恐竜の消滅という大惨事が起きたとき，鳥はどうしたのだろう？³専門家はこの問題に関してさまざまな意見を持っていて，知られている化石の数がまだ少なすぎるためにその疑問を解明することができないでいるのだ。⁴しかし，大規模な絶滅は鳥の間にも起きたのであり，その仲間の進化は，第三紀初期に再び始まった時には，ほんの数種の生き残った種に基づいていた，という可能性もある。

1 that 節内の主語は birds。また，and は had already ... long time と had developed ... different species の2つの動詞句を結んでいる。　　□ show O that 節「Oに…ということを示す」

□ at the time of A「Aの時に」　　□ disappearance「消滅，消えること」

□ be in existence「存在している」　　□ develop into A「進化してAになる」

□ species「(生物の)種」

2 the disaster は前文の the dinosaurs' disappearance のこと。them は前文の birds を指す。

□ happen to A「Aに起きる，生じる」　　□ disaster「大惨事」　　□ occur「起きる，生じる」

3 this question は前文の What happened ... ? という疑問文を指す。　　□ expert「専門家」

□ opinion「意見，見解」

4 it は形式主語。and は真主語となる that 節を2つ結んでいる。the group's evolution の the group's は birds' のこと。　　□ possible「可能な，起こりうる」

□ great extinction「大規模な絶滅」　　□ take place「起きる，生じる」

□ among A「Aの間で」　　□ ... as well「…も」　　□ evolution「進化」

□ be based on A「Aに基づいている」　　□ surviving「生き残っている」

巨大ダムが抱える問題

解　答

問1　are too high to yield a positive return

問2　イ. ineffective

問3　ほとんど例外なく起きることだが，現地通貨がドルに対して下落すると，そのような貸付金の負担が大きくなる。

問4　多くの国にとって，国家の経済はとても脆弱なので，たった１つの巨大ダムによる負債が，国家の経済に相当大きなマイナスの影響を与えることもある。

問5　エ

▶▶▶　設問解説　◀◀◀

問1　整序部分は直前の the actual construction costs of large dams「大型ダムの実際の建設費用」を主部とする文の述部である。また，第２段落第２文前半に「実際のダムの建設費用は平均して建設前の見積もりのほぼ２倍で」とあることから，整序部分も「（ダムの建設費用が）高すぎる」という内容になると考えられる。したがって，「あまりにも…なので～できない」という意味を表す too ＋形容詞＋to *do* を用いて，are too high to yield a positive return とすれば「高額すぎてプラスの利益を生み出すことができない」という意味になり，文意が成立する。➡ **Point** ⑲

□yield「を生じる，生む」　　□positive「プラスの／正の」　　□return「利益，収益」

問2　空所(2)を含むダッシュ以下の部分は，「とても…なので～」という意味を表す so ... that ～構文が用いられて，「研究者によれば，とても長く時間がかかるので，大型ダムは『切迫しているエネルギー危機を解決するのに（　２　）』のである」という意味になっている。➡ **Point** ⑲　時間がかかりすぎれば，切迫する危機を解決するのに「効果的でない」ので，正解はイ。

ア.「効果的である」イ.「効果的でない」ウ.「役に立つ」エ.「（人が）無力な，どうすることもできない」

問3　When local ... the dollar が副詞節，the burden of those loans grows が主節という文構造になっている。なお，as almost invariably happens は直前の節の内容を補足説明する非制限用法の関係代名詞節。

例　Every morning my grandpa takes a walk before breakfast, <u>as</u> is his habit these days.

　　「毎朝祖父は朝食の前に散歩をするが，それは祖父の近頃の習慣である」

☐ local「現地の，その地方の」　　☐ currency「通貨」

☐ fall against A「（通貨などが）Aに対して下落する」　　☐ almost「ほとんど，ほぼ」

☐ invariably「例外なく，いつも」　　☐ burden「負担，重荷」

☐ loan「貸付金，ローン」　　☐ grow「大きくなる，成長する」

問4　so fragile that ... は「とても脆弱なので…」という so ... that ～構文。

➡ **Point ⑲** have a ... effect on A は「Aに…な影響を与える」という意味。文末の it は the national economy を指す。

☐ national「国家の，国民の」　　☐ economy「経済」　　☐ fragile「脆弱な，もろい」

☐ mega-dam「巨大ダム」　　☐ significant「相当な，かなりの」

☐ negative「マイナスの，否定的な」

問5　下線部⑸の things that fit ... be easily transported は，直前の things that are more easily standardized の言い換えであり，下線部全体は「もっと簡単に規格化されるもの，つまり，コンテナの中にぴったり収まり，簡単に輸送できるものが私たちには必要なのだ」という意味。これは，第5段落第1・2文の「大型ダムのような巨大な建造物を建設する代わりに，風力，太陽光，ミニ水力のような『動かしやすい代替エネルギー』を用いるべきだ」という内容を言い換えていると考えられるので，正解はエ。

☐ standardize「を規格化する，標準化する」　　☐ fit「ぴったり収まる」

☐ container「コンテナ，容器」　　☐ transport「を輸送する」

Point ⑲ 程度を表す表現

1．too + 形容詞[副詞] +(for A) to do「あまりにも…なので（Aは）〜できない」

例　That camera was **too** expensive **for** me **to** buy.
　　「そのカメラはとても高かったので，私には買えなかった」

2．形容詞[副詞] + enough (for A) to do「（Aが）〜するほど…」

例　This book is short **enough to** read in a couple of hours.
　　「この本は2，3時間で読めるほど短い」

3．so + 形容詞[副詞] + that S V 〜「とても…なので〜する，〜するほど…」

例　She was **so** tired **that** she went to bed early.
　　「彼女はとても疲れていたので早めに寝た」

4．such（a)＋形容詞＋名詞＋that S V 〜「とても…なので〜，〜するほど…」

例　It was **such** a nice day **that** we went for a drive.
「とてもよい天気だったので，私たちはドライブに出かけた」

▶▶▶　構文・語句解説　◀◀◀

── 第1段落 ──

¹A study by Bent Flyvbjerg and his colleagues draws upon cost statistics for 245 large dams built between 1934 and 2007. ²It is by far the largest data set that any study of dam finances has collected. ³Without even taking into account social and environmental impacts, which are almost invariably negative and frequently vast, the study finds that "the actual construction costs of large dams are too high to yield a positive return."

¹ベント・フライフヨルグと彼の共同研究者による研究は，1934年から2007年の間に建設された245の大型ダムに要した費用の統計を利用している。²それはダムの財政状態に関する研究が収集したものとしては，飛び抜けて大きなデータセットである。³その研究によると，ほとんどいつも否定的でしばしば莫大なものとなる社会的，環境的な影響を考慮に入れなくても，「大型ダムの実際の建設費用は高額すぎてプラスの利益を生み出すことができない」ということがわかっている。

1 built 以下は 245 large dams を修飾する過去分詞句。
　□ study「研究，調査」　　□ colleague「共同研究者，同僚」
　□ draw upon A「Aを利用する，Aに頼る」　　□ statistics「統計」
2 □ by far「（最上級を修飾して）飛び抜けて，断然」　　□ data set「データセット」
　□ finance「財政，財源」　　□ collect「を収集する，集める」
3 which are ... frequently vast は，social and environmental impacts を補足説明する非制限用法の関係代名詞節。なお，social and environmental impacts は，take A into account の A が後ろに移動したもので，and は social と environmental を結んでいる。
　□ take A into account「Aを考慮に入れる」　　□ social「社会的な」
　□ environmental「環境の」　　□ impact「影響，衝撃」
　□ frequently「しばしば，頻繁に」　　□ vast「莫大な」　　□ actual「実際の」
　□ construction「建設」

....

── 第2段落 ──

¹The researchers say planners are biased toward excessive optimism, which dam

promoters exploit with deception or corruption. [2]The study finds that actual dam expenses were on average nearly double pre-building estimates, and these additional costs were several times greater than those of other kinds of infrastructure construction, including roads, railroads, bridges and tunnels. [3]In addition, dam construction on average took 8.6 years, more than a third longer than predicted — so much time, the researchers say, that large dams are "ineffective in resolving urgent energy crises."

[1]立案者が過度の楽観主義に偏向していて，そこをダムの推進者たちが詐欺や汚職を用いて利用している，と研究者は述べている。[2]実際のダムの建設費用は平均して建設前の見積もりのほぼ2倍で，この費用の超過が，道路，鉄道，橋，トンネルを含む他の種類のインフラの建設費用の超過の数倍になっていたことがその研究でわかっている。[3]さらに，ダムの建設は平均して8.6年かかっていて，これは予測より3分の1以上長く，研究者によれば，とても長く時間がかかるので，大型ダムは「切迫しているエネルギー危機を解決するのに効果的ではない」のである。

1 which 以下は planners are biased toward excessive optimism という内容を補足説明する非制限用法の関係代名詞節。

☐ researcher「研究者」　　☐ planner「立案者，計画者」

☐ be biased toward A「Aの方に偏向している」　　☐ excessive「過度の，度を越えた」

☐ optimism「楽観主義」　　☐ promoter「推進者」　　☐ exploit「を利用する，搾取する」

☐ deception「詐欺，ごまかし」

2 1つめの and は actual dam expenses were ... pre-building estimates と these additional costs were ... and tunnels の2つの節を結んでいる。2つめの and は roads, railroads, bridges, tunnels の4つの名詞を結んでいる。those は the additional costs の代用。

☐ expense「費用，出費」　　☐ on average「平均して」　　☐ double A「2倍のAで」

☐ pre-building「建設前の」　　☐ estimate「見積もり，概算」

☐ additional「超過の，追加の」　　☐ infrastructure「インフラ，社会の基礎設備」

☐ including A「Aを含めて」　　☐ tunnel「トンネル」

3 ☐ in addition「さらに，そのうえ」　　☐ take O「O（時間）がかかる」

☐ more than A「A以上，Aより多く」　　☐ than predicted「予測よりも」

☐ resolve「を解決する」　　☐ urgent「切迫した，緊急の」

☐ crises＜crisis「危機」の複数形

[1]Dams typically consume large amounts of developing countries' financial resources. [2]Many of the funds that support large dams arrive as loans to the host countries and must eventually be paid off. [3]But most dam revenue comes from electricity sales in local currencies. [4]When local currencies fall against the dollar, as almost invariably happens, the burden of those loans grows.

---

[1]ダムは一般に，発展途上国の財源を多額に消費する。[2]大型ダムを支える資金の多くは，ダムを建設する国に貸付金として届き，最終的には完済しなければならない。[3]しかし，ダムの歳入の大半は現地通貨による電気の売り上げから来ている。ほとんど例外なく起きることだが，現地通貨がドルに対して下落すると，そのような貸付金の負担が大きくなる。

1 □ typically「一般に，典型的に」　　□ consume「を消費する」　　□ amount「金額，量」
　 □ developing country「発展途上国」　　□ financial resources「財源」
2 and は arrive as loans to the host countries と must eventually be paid off の 2 つの動詞句を
　結んでいる。
　 □ fund「資金」　　□ support「を支える，を支援する」　　□ as A「A として」
　 □ host country「主催国」ここでは「ダムを建設する国」のこと。
　 □ eventually「最終的には」　　□ pay A off「A（借金・負債など）を全額返済する」
3 □ revenue「歳入，収入」

· ·

[1]The economic impact on host countries was often destructive. [2]Dam projects are so huge that since the 1980s, dam expenses have become major components of debt crises in Turkey, Brazil, and Mexico. [3]"For many countries, the national economy is so fragile that the debt from just one mega-dam can have a significant negative effect on it," stated Mr. Flyvbjerg.

---

[1]ダムを建設する国に対する経済的な影響はしばしば破壊的である。[2]ダム建設のプロジェクトはあまりに巨大なので，1980 年代以来，ダムの費用は，トルコ，ブラジル，メキシコにおいては，債務危機の大きな要素となった。[3]「多くの国にとって，国家の経済はとても脆弱なので，たった 1 つの巨大ダムによる負債が，国家の経済に相当大きなマイナスの影響を与えることもある」とフライフヨルグ氏は語った。

1 □ destructive「破壊的な，壊滅的な」

2 and は Turkey，Brazil，Mexico の3つの名詞を結んでいる。

　□ huge「莫大な，巨大な」　　　□ component「構成要素」　　　□ Turkey「トルコ」

3 □ state「を述べる」

- -

— 第5段落 —

[1]Instead of building massive, one-of-a-kind edifices like large dams, the researchers recommend "agile energy alternatives" like wind, solar and mini-hydro power. [2]"We're stuck in a 1950s mode where everything was done in a very customized, manual way," Mr. Flyvbjerg added. [3]"We need things that are more easily standardized, things that fit inside a container and can be easily transported."

---

　[1]大型ダムのような巨大で他に類を見ない大建造物を建設する代わりに，風力，太陽光，ミニ水力による電力のような「動かしやすい代替エネルギー」を研究者は推奨している。[2]「私たちは，すべてが注文通りに手作業で行われていた1950年代の様式から抜け出せないでいる」とフライフヨルグ氏は付け加えて言った。[3]「もっと簡単に規格化されるもの，つまり，コンテナの中にぴったり収まり，簡単に輸送できるものが私たちには必要なのだ」

1 and は wind，solar，mini-hydro を結んでいる。

　□ instead of *doing*「…する代わりに」　　　□ massive「巨大な」

　□ one-of-a-kind「他に類を見ない，特別な」　　　□ A like B「BのようなA」

　□ recommend「を推奨する，推薦する」　　　□ alternative「代替物，代用品」

　□ solar「太陽光線の」　　　□ mini-hydro「ミニ水力の」　　　□ power「電力」

2 where everything ... manual way は a 1950s mode を修飾する関係副詞節。

　□ be stuck in A「Aにはまって抜け出せない」　　　□ mode「方法，様式」

　□ customized「注文通りの」　　　□ manual「手作業の，肉体労働の」

　□ add「を付け加えて言う」

20 気候変動

解　答

問1　エ．while

問2　このような予期せぬ気象パターンは，予想される気温と降雨量がもはや当てにならないので，農業に頼っている地域では作物の維持や栽培を困難にすることがある。

問3　極地では，気候変動と関連のある地球規模の気温の上昇により，氷床の融解が季節ごとに加速していることが，地球上の様々な地域での海面の上昇の原因となり，その結果，海岸線が後退し低地の島が一部水に浸かっている。

問4　releases what are called greenhouse gases

問5　ア．human-influenced

▶▶▶　**設問解説**　◀◀◀

問1　空所の直前には「気候は長期間にわたって測定される」ことが述べられいて，後ろには「天候は日ごと，あるいは年ごとに変化する」と述べられていることから，空所には「対比・対照」を表す接続詞が必要である。したがって，正解はエ。

　　　ア．「ひとたび…すると」イ．「…以来」ウ．「今や…なので」エ．「だが一方…」

問2　全体の文構造は，形式目的語を用いた S make it C to *do*「Sは…するのをCにする」という形である。➡ **Point ⑦** and が maintain と grow を結び，crops が共通の目的語。that rely on farming は regions を先行詞とする関係代名詞節。because 以下は関係詞節でなく主節を修飾している。また，1つめの can は可能性を表し「…することがある」という意味。

　　　□ unexpected「予期しない」　　□ maintain「を維持する」　　□ grow「栽培する」
　　　□ crop「作物」　　□ region「地域」　　□ rely on A「Aに頼る」　　□ farming「農業」
　　　□ temperature「温度，気温」　　□ rainfall level「降雨量」
　　　□ no longer「もはや…ない」

問3　This は直前の文全体の内容を指している。sea levels は動名詞 rising の意味上の主語。so that は「結果」を表す。➡ **Point ⑳** and は coastlines retreat と low-lying islands are partially underwater の2つの節を結んでいる。

□ contribute to A「Aの一因となる」　　□ sea level「海面」

□ different＋複数名詞(A)「様々なA」　　□ coastline「海岸線」　　□ retreat「後退する」

□ low-lying「低地の」　　□ partially「部分的に」　　□ underwater「水面下にある」

問 4 第4段落では「化石燃料の燃焼によって，温室効果ガスが発生し気温が上昇するメカニズム」について述べられており，「これらの物質を燃やすことが，温室効果ガスを地球の大気中に放出する」という意味になるようにする。what be called C は「いわゆるC」という意味。

□ release A into B「AをBに放出する」　　□ greenhouse gas「温室効果ガス」

問 5 空所(5)を含む文は「現在の（　5　）気候変動ははるかに速い速度で起こっている」と述べている。第4段落第1文に述べられているように「現在の気候変動の原因は人間の活動によるものが多い」ので，正解はア。

ア.「人間の影響による」イ.「自然の」ウ.「地域の」エ.「長期間の」

Point ⑳ 目的・結果を表す表現

1 ．so that S will [can / may] do ...「Sが…するように，するために」

例1　The lecturer spoke slowly **so that** everyone **could** understand him.
「講師は全員にわかってもらえるようにゆっくりと話した」

例2　Leave as soon as possible **so that** you **won't** miss the train.
「列車に乗り遅れないように，できるだけ早く出なさい」

2 ．in order to do ... / so as to do ...「…するために」

例1　Kenji practices every day **in order to** improve his soccer skills.
「ケンジはサッカーの技術を上達させるために毎日練習をしている」

例2　They spoke as quietly as possible **so as** not **to** awaken the baby.
「赤ん坊を起こさないように彼らはできるだけ静かに話をした」

3 ．, so that S V ...「その結果…，それで…」

例　The tunnel was only three feet high, **so that** I had to crawl through on hands and knees.
「トンネルはたった3フィートの高ささかなかった，それで僕は這って通らなければならなかった」

▶▶ **構文・語句解説** ◀◀

― 第1段落 ―

¹Climate is sometimes mistaken for weather. ²But climate is different from weather

because it is measured over a long period of time, while weather can change from day to day, or from year to year. ³The climate of an area includes seasonal temperature, rainfall averages, and wind patterns. ⁴Different places have different climates. ⁵A desert, for example, has an arid climate because little water falls, as rain or snow, during the year. ⁶Other types of climate include tropical climates, which are hot and humid, and temperate climates, which have warm summers and cooler winters.

¹気候は天候と間違えられることがある。²しかし，気候が天候と異なるのは，気候は長期間にわたって測定されるが，一方，天候は日ごと，あるいは年ごとに変化しうるからである。³ある地域の気候には，季節ごとの気温，降水量の平均値，風のパターンが含まれる。⁴場所が異なれば気候も異なる。⁵たとえば，砂漠は1年を通して雨や雪としての降水がほとんどないため，乾燥気候である。⁶他にも，高温多湿の熱帯気候や，夏は暖かく冬は比較的涼しい温帯気候などがある。

1 □ climate「気候」　　□ mistake A for B「AをBと間違える」　　□ weather「天気，天候」
2 □ measure「を測定する」　　□ period「期間」　　□ from day to day「日ごとに」
　 □ from year to year「年ごとに」
3 □ area「地域」　　□ include「を含む」　　□ seasonal「季節ごとの」
　 □ average「平均(値)」
5 □ desert「砂漠」　　□ for example「たとえば」　　□ fall「＜雨などが＞降る」
6 which are hot and humid は tropical climates を補足説明し，which have warm summers and cooler winters は temperate climates を補足説明する非制限用法の関係代名詞節。
　 □ tropical「熱帯の」　　□ humid「湿気の多い」　　□ temperate「温帯性の，温暖な」

― 第2段落 ―

¹Climate change is the long-term alteration of temperature and typical weather patterns in a place. ²Climate change could refer to a particular location or the planet as a whole. ³Climate change may cause weather patterns to be less predictable. ⁴These unexpected weather patterns can make it difficult to maintain and grow crops in regions that rely on farming because expected temperature and rainfall levels can no longer be relied on. ⁵Climate change has also been connected with other damaging weather events, such as more frequent and more intense hurricanes, floods, downpours, and winter storms.

¹気候変動とは，ある場所の気温や典型的な気象パターンが長期的に変化することである。²気候変動は特定の場所について言うこともあれば地球全体について言うこともある。³気候変動は気象パターンの予測を難しくすることがある。⁴このような予期せぬ気象パターンは，予想される気温と降雨量がもはや当てにならないので，農業に頼っている地域では作物の維持や栽培を困難にすることがある。⁵気候変動はまたハリケーン，洪水，豪雨，冬の嵐が頻繁に発生し，強くなるなど，他の損害を与える気象現象にも関係するようになっている。

1 and は temperature と weather patterns を結んでいる。

　□ alteration「変化」　　□ typical「典型的な」

2 could は可能性を表し「…こともある」という意味。or は a particular location と the planet as a whole を結んでいる。

　□ refer to A「Aについて言う，関連する」　　□ particular「特定の」　　□ location「場所」

　□ the planet「地球」　　□ as a whole「全体として(の)」

3 □ cause O to *do*「Oに…させる(原因となる)」　　□ predictable「予測できる」

5 □ be connected with A「Aと関係している」　　□ damaging「損害を与える」

　□ weather event「気象現象」　　□ A such as B「たとえばBのようなA」

　□ frequent「頻繁な」　　□ intense「激しい」　　□ hurricane「ハリケーン」

　□ flood「洪水」　　□ downpour「豪雨」　　□ storm「嵐」

- -

── 第3段落 ──

　¹In polar regions, the warming global temperatures associated with climate change have meant ice sheets are melting at an accelerated rate from season to season. ²This contributes to sea levels rising in different regions of the planet, so that coastlines retreat and low-lying islands are partially underwater.

　¹極地では，気候変動と関連のある地球規模の気温の上昇により，氷床の融解が季節ごとに加速している。²このことが地球上の様々な地域での海面の上昇の原因となり，その結果，海岸線が後退し低地の島が一部水に浸かっている。

1 associated with climate change は the warming global temperatures を修飾する過去分詞句。

　□ polar「極地の」　　□ global「地球規模の」　　□ associate A with B「AをBと結びつける」

　□ mean (that)節「…を意味する」　　□ ice sheet「氷床」　　□ melt「溶ける」

　□ accelerated「加速した」　　□ rate「速度」

¹The cause of the climate change we're experiencing now is largely human activity, such as burning fossil fuels, like oil, coal, and natural gas. ²Burning these materials releases what are called greenhouse gases into Earth's atmosphere. ³There, these gases trap heat from the sun's rays inside the atmosphere, causing Earth's average temperature to rise. ⁴This rise in the planet's temperature, which is called global warming, impacts local and regional climates. ⁵Throughout Earth's history, the climate has continually changed. ⁶When occurring naturally, this is a slow process that has taken place over hundreds and thousands of years. ⁷The present human-influenced climate change is occurring at a much faster rate.

---

¹我々が今体験している気候変動の原因は，石油，石炭，天然ガスのような化石燃料の燃焼といった人間の活動によるものが多い。²これらの物質を燃やすことが，いわゆる温室効果ガスを地球の大気中に放出する。³そこでは，これらのガスが太陽光線による熱を大気中に閉じ込め，地球の平均気温を上昇させる。⁴地球温暖化と呼ばれている，このような地球の温度上昇はその土地や地方の気候にも影響を与える。⁵地球の歴史を通して，気候は絶えず変化してきた。⁶自然に起こる場合には，何百，何千年かけて起こってきたゆっくりとした過程である。⁷現在起こっている人間の影響による気候変動ははるかに速い速度で起こっている。

---

1 we're experiencing now は the climate change を修飾する関係代名詞節。

□ cause「原因」　　□ experience「を経験する」　　□ largely「主に」

□ human activity「人間の活動」　　□ burn「を燃やす」　　□ fossil fuel「化石燃料」

□ A like B「たとえばBのようなA」　　□ coal「石炭」　　□ natural gas「天然ガス」

2 □ material「物質」　　□ atmosphere「大気」

3 causing 以下は分詞構文。

□ trap「を閉じ込める」　　□ heat「熱」　　□ ray「光線」　　□ inside A「Aの中に」

□ average「平均の」　　□ rise「上昇する」

4 □ global warming「地球温暖化」　　□ impact「に影響を与える」　　□ local「地方の」

□ regional「地域の」

5 □ throughout A「Aを通して」　　□ continually「絶えず」

6 When occurring は副詞節中の主語と be 動詞の省略で When it is occurring ということ。この it は前文に述べられている the climate change を指している。that 以下は a slow process を修飾する関係代名詞節。

□ occur「起こる」　　□ naturally「自然に」　　□ process「過程」　　□ take place「起こる」

□ over A「Aにわたって」　　□ hundreds and thousands of A「何百，何千ものA」

7「自然に起こる場合と比べて」という比較対象が省略されている。

□ present「現在の」　　□ rate「速度」

ロボットと雇用

解 答

問1 オートメーション化によって仕事を失い，ロボットに生計の手段を奪われるという心配は，肉体労働で雇用されている人に関連があるだけではなく，多くの事務職の仕事も影響を受ける。

問2 イ. Don't worry

問3 ウ

問4 人間の労働者はほとんどの場合一緒に働くロボットを生物と見なすということを示している研究をハントは引き合いに出す。

問5 ウ

問6 イ. The Future of Work

▶▶ **設問解説** ◀◀

問1 This worry は直前の文の fear losing their jobs to automation and having robots "steal" their livelihoods を指す。and は losing their jobs to automation と having robots "steal" their livelihoods の2つの動名詞句を結んでいる。have O *do* は「Oに…される／Oが…することを経験する」の意味。

例 He had his cat die on him.

「彼は飼っていた猫に死なれてしまった」

not only X but Y too は「XだけでなくYも」という意味。➡ **Point ㉑**

☐ fear *doing*「…することを恐れている」　　☐ lose A to B「BでAを失う」

☐ automation「オートメーション化」　　☐ steal「を盗む」　　☐ livelihood「生計の手段」

☐ worry「心配」　　☐ be relevant to A「Aに関連がある」

☐ blue-collar「肉体労働の，ブルーカラーの」　　☐ employee「雇用されている人，従業員」

☐ white-collar「事務職の，ホワイトカラーの」

☐ vulnerable「影響を受ける，傷つきやすい」

問2 空所(2)を含む文は But で始まっているので，直前の第1段落第6文「それほど多くの労働者がそれほど不安になるのも不思議ではない」と逆接的な内容になる。したがって，イが正解。

ア.「わかりません」イ.「心配することはありません」ウ.「行動を起こしましょう」エ.「気をつけてください」

問3 主語の Doing that は直前の文の if 節の内容を指す。depend on A「Aにかかっている，Aで決まる」の A に，意味上の主語を伴った動名詞句がきている。したがって，下線部(3)は，「デジタル化を適切に行うことは，主に企業が考え方を変えられるかどうかにかかっている」という意味になるので，ウが正解。

□ mainly「主に」　　　□ mindset「考え方」

問4 全体の構造は Hunt(S)　cites(V)　research(O) である。1つめの that は関係代名詞で，文末までが research を修飾する関係代名詞節，2つめの that は接続詞で，shows の目的語になる名詞節を導いている。they　work　with は robots を修飾する関係代名詞節。

□ cite「を引き合いに出す」　　□ research「研究」

□ treat A as B「AをBとして扱う」　　□ living things「生物」

問5 Martin　Feldstein の見解は第2段落に述べられている。第1～4文では「歴史的に見て，科学技術の進歩によって仕事が奪われる心配がない」こと，第6文では「労働者は科学技術の変化に柔軟に適応できる」ことが述べられているので，ウが正解。

ア.「多くの人が将来仕事を失うかもしれない」

イ.「労働者が機械のように仕事をすることを企業は期待するのをやめるべきだ」

ウ.「人間は科学技術の変化に順応することができることを歴史は証明している」

エ.「ロボットは生きていないので，状況にうまく適応できる」

問6 「AI とロボットによって仕事が奪われる不安」に関して，専門家の見解を紹介している。したがって，イが正解。

ア.「ロボット工学の歴史」

イ.「労働の将来」

ウ.「ロボット：最高の労働者」

エ.「機械のような労働」

Point ㉑ not only X but also Y

1. not only X but (also) Y「XだけでなくYも」 only の代わりに just / merely / simply が，also の代わりに Y の後ろに too / as well が用いられることもある。

例1 She **not only** wrote the text **but also** selected the illustrations.
「彼女は本文を書いただけでなく，挿絵を選ぶこともした」

例2 People laugh **not only** when they feel good **but** in uncomfortable situations **as well**.
「人は気分がいいときだけではなく，不快な状況でも笑う」

2．not X but Y「XではなくY」Y, (and) not X という語順になることもある。

例 Hilda helped Tony **not** because he was injured **but** because she was bored.
「ヒルダはトニーが怪我をしていたからではなく，自分が退屈だったので助けてあげた」

▶▶ 構文・語句解説 ◀◀

── 第1段落 ──

[1]Understandably, many workers today suffer from job anxiety. [2]They fear losing their jobs to automation and having robots "steal" their livelihoods. [3]This worry is not only relevant to blue-collar employees, but many white-collar jobs are vulnerable, too. [4]Let's face it: AI and robots can do many routine jobs more efficiently and more cheaply than human workers. [5]This makes massive layoffs a real possibility. [6]No wonder so many workers are so uneasy.

[1]もっともなことだが，今日多くの労働者が仕事に関する不安を抱えている。[2]こういう人は，オートメーション化によって仕事を失い，ロボットに生計の手段を「奪われる」ことを恐れている。[3]このような心配は，肉体労働で雇用されている人に関連があるだけではなく，多くの事務職の仕事も影響を受ける。[4]現実に向き合おう。AIとロボットは，人間の労働者よりも効率的にそして安価に多くの決まりきった仕事を行うことができる。[5]これによって大量解雇が現実に起こり得ることとなる。[6]それほど多くの労働者がそれほど不安になるのも不思議ではない。

1 □ understandably「もっともなことだが」　□ suffer from A「Aで苦しむ」
　 □ anxiety「不安」
4 □ Let's face it「現実に向き合おう」　□ routine「決まりきった，日常的な」
　 □ efficiently「効率的に」　□ cheaply「安価に，安く」　□ human「人間の」
5 □ massive「大量の，大規模な」　□ layoff「解雇」
　 □ possibility「起こり得ること，可能性」

6 □ no wonder S V ...「…は不思議ではない」　　□ uneasy「不安な」

━━ 第2段落 ━━━━━━━━━━━━━━━━━━━━━━━━━━━━━━━━━━━━
[1]But Martin Feldstein, an economics professor at Harvard, says, "Don't worry." [2]Why? [3]"Simply put: history. [4]For many years, we have been experiencing rapid technological change that substitutes machines and computers for individual workers." [5]But this only means that new, more interesting "human" jobs are being created. [6]At any rate, Feldstein believes that workers have the flexibility it takes to "adjust positively to any changing technology."

　　[1]しかし，ハーバード大学の経済学の教授，マーティン・フェルドスタインは「心配すること
はありません」と言う。[2]なぜなのだろう。[3]「簡単に言えば，歴史です。[4]長年にわたり，私た
ちは個々の労働者を機械やコンピュータに置き換える急速な科学技術の変化を経験してきまし
た」[5]しかし，このことが意味するのは，新たなより興味深い「人間の」仕事が創られてるとい
うことに過ぎない。[6]ともかく，フェルドスタインの考えでは，「変化するいかなる科学技術に
もうまく適応する」のに必要な柔軟性を労働者は持っているのだ。

1 □ economics「経済学」　　□ professor「教授」　　□ Harvard「ハーバード大学」
3 □ simply put「簡単に言えば／要するに」
4 □ experience「を経験する」　　□ rapid「急速な」　　□ technological「科学技術の」
　 □ substitute A for B「BをAに置き換える，Bの代わりにAを用いる」
　 □ individual「個々の，個人の」
5 □ create「を創る」
6 it takes 以下は the flexibility を修飾する関係代名詞節。
　 □ at any rate「ともかく，いずれにせよ」　　□ flexibility「柔軟性」
　 □ it takes O to *do*「…するのにOを要する」　　□ adjust to A「Aに適応する」
　 □ positively「うまく，前向きに」

━━ 第3段落 ━━━━━━━━━━━━━━━━━━━━━━━━━━━━━━━━━━━━
[1]Business experts don't expect large-scale unemployment to happen either. [2]They predict that most workers won't actually be replaced by robots. [3]Instead, more and more, they will be teamed up with them. [4]What will that be like? [5]How will human workers get along with their machine partners? [6]Dr. Steve Hunt, a business psychologist and systems designer, believes that "digitization" can, paradoxically, create a more human,

more productive workplace. [7]But this can only happen if digitization is applied correctly. [8]Doing that depends mainly on companies changing their mindset. [9]Most managers, Hunt says, tend to expect workers to perform like machines. [10]They judge employee performance by "concrete, immediate outcomes that measure the kind of output a machine would produce."

[1]ビジネスの専門家もまた，大規模な失業が起こるとは予想していない。[2]彼らの予測では，ほとんどの労働者がロボットに取って代わられるようなことは実際にはないとしている。[3]そうではなく，労働者はますますロボットとチームを組むことになるだろう。[4]それはどのような感じだろうか。[5]人間の労働者は機械のパートナーとどうつきあっていくのだろう。[6]経営心理学者でありシステム設計者のスティーブ・ハント博士は，逆説的ではあるが，「デジタル化」によってより人間的で生産的な職場が生まれる可能性があると考えている。[7]しかし，そのようなことが起きるとしたら，デジタル化が適切に行われる場合のみである。[8]それは，主に企業が考え方を変えられるかどうかにかかっている。[9]たいていの経営者は，労働者が機械のように仕事をするように期待しがちである，とハントは述べる。[10]彼らは，機械でも生み出せるようなものを測る具体的ですぐに出る結果によって従業員の業績を判断するのだ。

1 □ expert「専門家」　　□ expect O to *do*「Oが…すると予想する」
　□ large-scale「大規模な」　　□ unemployment「失業」
　□ either「（否定文で）また…でない」
2 □ predict that 節「…すると予測する」　　□ actually「実際には」
　□ be replaced by A「Aに取って代わられる」
3 □ instead「そうではなくて」　　□ more and more「ますます」
　□ team A up with B「AをBとチームにまとめる」
4 □ What will S be like?「Sはどのようなものになるだろうか」
5 □ get along with A「Aとうまくやっていく」
6 □ business psychologist「経営心理学者」　　□ systems designer「システム設計者」
　□ digitization「デジタル化」　　□ paradoxically「逆説的ではあるが」
　□ productive「生産的な」　　□ workplace「職場」
7 □ apply「を適用する」　　□ correctly「正しく」
9 Hunt says は S say that 節の S say が that を省略して節内に挿入された形。
　□ manager「経営者／管理職」　　□ tend to *do*「…しがちである／…する傾向がある」
　□ perform「遂行する」　　□ like A「Aのように」
10 that 以下は concrete, immediate outcomes を修飾する関係代名詞節。

□ judge「を判断する」　　□ performance「業績，成績」　　□ concrete「具体的な」

□ immediate「直接の，即座の」　　□ outcome「結果，成り行き」　　□ measure「を測る」

□ output「産出，生産」　　□ produce「を生産する」

━━ 第 4 段落 ━━

¹This must stop, says Hunt. ²"We are going to need more and more workers to do the things robots can't do well. ³Humans excel at making emotional connections, scanning environments, and recognizing patterns. ⁴They can then adapt their behavior to fit the situation." ⁵Hunt cites research that shows that human workers almost always treat the robots they work with as living things. ⁶Companies must recognize this and incorporate this information into their management policies. ⁷They must prepare for the inevitable social and psychological interactions that will take place between man and machine.

¹こんなことはやめなければならない，とハントは言う。²「私たちは，ロボットにはうまくできないことをますます多くの労働者にやってもらう必要がありそうです。³人間は，感情的なつながりを築くことや，周囲の状況に目を走らせたりすること，パターンを認識することに秀でています。⁴したがって，人間は状況に合うように自分の行動を適合させられます」⁵人間の労働者はほとんどの場合一緒に働くロボットを生物と見なすということを示している研究をハントは引き合いに出す。⁶企業はこのことを認めて，この情報を経営方針に組み入れなければならない。⁷人間と機械の間で起こる避けられない社会的心理的相互作用に備えなければならないのである。

1 says Hunt は S say that 節の S say が that を省略し，say S の語順で節の後に挿入された形。

2 robots can't do well は the things を修飾する関係代名詞節。

　　□ need O to *do*「Oに…してもらう必要がある」

3 and は making emotional connections, scanning environments, recognizing patterns の 3 つの動名詞句を結んでいる。

　　□ excel at *doing*「…するのに秀でている」　　□ emotional「感情の」

　　□ connection「つながり」　　□ scan「に目を走らせる，を調べる」

　　□ environment「周囲の状況，環境」　　□ recognize「を認識する，認める」

4 □ adapt「を適合させる」　　□ fit「に合う」　　□ situation「状況」

6 and は recognize this と incorporate ... policies を結んでいる。

　　□ incorporate A into B「AをBに組み入れる」　　□ information「情報」

111

□ management「経営，管理」　　□ policy「方針，政策」

7 that 以下は the inevitable social and psychological interactions を修飾する関係代名詞節。

□ prepare for A「Aに備える」　　□ inevitable「避けられない」　　□ social「社会の」

□ psychological「心理的な」　　□ interaction「相互作用」　　□ take place「起こる」

マニュアル思考の限界

▶▶▶ **設問解説** ◀◀◀

問1　第1段落第2文には「帽子を脱いであいさつをする」とは書かれていない。

□ extensive「詳しい，広範囲に渡る」　　□ manual「マニュアル，指導書」

問2　第2段落第1文の her baby grabbed と第2文の内容をまとめる。なお，下線部(2)の and は could not ... saying と had to ... twice の2つの動詞句を結んでいる。

□ concentrate on A「Aに集中する」

□ ask O to do「Oに…するように頼む」　　□ repeat「を繰り返す」

□ twice「2回，2度」

問3　直前の文から，この従業員は何をしたらよいのかわからないでいることが読み取れるので，正解はイ。

ア.「泣きながら」イ.「無力で」ウ.「希望を持って」エ.「くつろいで」

問4　Simply put は「簡単に言えば／要するに」という意味。主語 the manual と述語動詞 fails の間に detailed as it may be が挿入されているがこれは形容詞＋as S V ... の譲歩を表す表現。 ➡ **Point** ⑱ cover の目的語は what to do in a situation。where 以下は a situation を修飾する関係副詞節。

➡ **Point** ⑪

□ detailed「詳しく書かれた」　　□ fail to do「…できない，しない」

□ cover「を扱う」　　□ situation「状況」　　□ steal「を盗む，奪う」

問5 空所(5)を含む文は「(　5　)ができないことが日本の深刻な問題だ」と述べている。この文の後に続く第4段落では，その第2文以降で「客を相手にする仕事で重要なもの」として「従業員自身が自分の頭を使って現実の状況に対処すること」を挙げている。したがって，正解はエ。

ア.「礼儀正しく振る舞う」イ.「冷静でいる」ウ.「適切な謝罪をする」エ.「自分で主導権を握る」

問6 (6a) it は，強調構文の it。 ➡ **Point ㉒**

(6b) it は形式主語で，真主語は to think 以下。 ➡ **Point ⑦**

ア.「私は春が大好きだ。1年で一番いい季節だ」（指示代名詞）

イ.「1カ月で外国語をマスターするのは不可能だ」（形式主語）

ウ.「冬はとても早い時間に暗くなる」（天候の it）

エ.「スミス氏に初めて会ったのはフランスだった」（強調構文の it）

問7 not only allow but actively encourage が not only X but (also) Y の表現になっている。したがって，文の始まりの A company <u>must not</u> を「会社は…してはいけない」と読んではいけないことに注意。 ➡ **Point ㉑** its employees to use their heads は allow と encourage に共通して続く語句であり，in order 以下は not only ... their heads を修飾している。

➡ **Point ⑳**

□ allow O to *do*「Oが…するのを許す」　□ actively「積極的に」

□ encourage O to *do*「Oが…するのを奨励する」　□ employee「従業員」

□ in order to *do*「…するために」

□ deal with A「Aに対処する」　□ real-life「現実の，実生活の」　□ situation「状況」

Point ㉒ 強調構文

　名詞や副詞の働きをするものを It is ... that ～ の ... の部分に置くことで強調することができる。これを強調構文と呼ぶ。「～するのは…である」と意味を取ればよい。

例1　**It is** Japanese pop music **that** my sister enjoys listening to.
　　　「私の妹が聞くのを楽しんでいるのはJポップです」

例2　**It was** three years ago **that** we got married.
　　　「私たちが結婚したのは3年前です。」

─ 第1段落 ─

[1]One fast-food company is well known in Japan for its extensive worker manual and the sales talk it covers. [2]From the book, workers learn how to greet a customer, how to bow, how to take an order, pack a bag and give correct change. [3]Customers find the same nice service in all the franchised outlets, which contributes to both customer satisfaction and corporate profits.

[1]日本では，あるファーストフードの会社が広範囲にわたる従業員用マニュアルとそこで扱われている接客の際の口のきき方で有名である。[2]その本から，従業員は客へのあいさつの仕方，おじぎの仕方，注文をとり，袋に入れ，きちんとおつりを渡す方法を知る。[3]客はそのフランチャイズのすべての店で同じ心地のよいサービスを受けられるが，このことは客の満足と会社の利益の双方に貢献している。

1 its extensive worker manual と the sales talk it covers の2つの名詞句が and で結ばれている。it covers は the sales talk を修飾する関係代名詞節。

　☐ fast-food「ファーストフード（の）」　　☐ be well known for A「Aで有名である」
　☐ sales talk「営業用のしゃべり方」

2 pack a bag と give correct change の前には how to を補うことができる。

　☐ greet「にあいさつする」　　☐ customer「客」　　☐ bow「おじぎをする」
　☐ take an order「注文を取る」　　☐ pack「に物を詰める」　　☐ bag「袋」
　☐ correct「正しい」　　☐ change「おつり」

3 which は直前の節の内容を補足説明する非制限用法の関係代名詞。

　☐ franchised outlet「フランチャイズの店」　　☐ contribute to A「Aに貢献する，役立つ」
　☐ customer satisfaction「客の満足」　　☐ profit「利益」

─ 第2段落 ─

[1]One day, a mother came into one of these restaurants, and while she was ordering at the counter, her baby grabbed an employee's hat and began to play with it. [2]He was surprised and embarrassed. [3]He could not concentrate on what the customer was saying and had to ask her to repeat her order twice. [4]He knew he was losing his dignity as a company representative by having an infant tearing up part of his uniform, and he wanted to take it back, but at the same time he didn't know what to say or do. [5]He stood there helpless until the mother retrieved the hat and gave it back to him. [6]He put it on again,

resumed his normal calm attitude, and took her order efficiently as if nothing had happened. ⁷But everyone in the restaurant could see that a one-year-old child had the power to bring the operation to a halt and must have wondered about it.

---

¹ある日，一人の母親がこうしたレストランの１つに入ってきた。そして，彼女がカウンターで注文をしている間，彼女の赤ちゃんは従業員の帽子をひったくって，それで遊び始めた。²従業員は驚き，戸惑った。³彼は客が言っていることに集中できなくなり，彼女に２回も注文を繰り返すように頼まなければならなかった。⁴彼は，乳児に自分の制服の一部をむりやりもぎ取られるままにして会社の一員としての威厳を失いつつあることを知っていた。それで，彼は帽子を取り戻したいと思ったが，それでも何を言い，何をすべきかわからなかった。⁵彼がそこに何もできないまま立っていると，母親が帽子を取り戻して返してくれた。⁶彼は再び帽子をかぶって，普段の落ち着いた態度に戻り，まるで何事もなかったかのように母親の注文をてきぱきと取った。⁷しかし，店の中の人はみな，１歳の子どもが仕事を止めるだけの力を持っていることを見てとれたし，それについてあれこれ思いを巡らしたにちがいない。

1 while ... the counter は her baby 以下の節に対する副詞節になっている。
   □ while S V ...「…している間に」　　□ order「注文する」　　□ grab「をひったくる」
2 □ embarrassed「戸惑った，気恥ずかしい」
4 □ lose *one's* dignity「威厳を失う」　　□ company representative「会社の一員」
   □ have O *doing*「Oに…させておく」　　□ infant「乳児，幼児」
   □ tear A up「Aをもぎ取る」　　□ uniform「制服」　　□ take A back「Aを取り返す」
   □ at the same time「同時に／それにもかかわらず」
5 retrieved the hat と gave it back to him の２つの動詞句が and で結ばれている。
   □ until S V ...「…するまで」　　□ give A back to B「AをBに返す」
6 put it on again と resumed his normal calm attitude と took her order efficiently の３つの動詞句が and で結ばれている。as if 以下は took her order efficiently を修飾している。
   □ put A on「Aを身につける」　　□ resume「を再開する」　　□ normal「普段の，通常の」
   □ calm「冷静な，落ち着いた」　　□ attitude「態度，姿勢」
   □ efficiently「能率よく，てきぱきと」　　□ as if S V ...「まるで…のように」
7 □ see that 節「…ということがわかる」　　□ have the power to *do*「…する力がある」
   □ bring A to a halt「Aを停止する，止める」　　□ operation「作業」
   □ must have *done*「…したにちがいない」
   □ wonder about A「Aについてあれこれと考える」

¹What was the problem here? ²Simply put, the manual, detailed as it may be, fails to cover what to do in a situation where a young child steals part of your uniform. ³And without the manual to guide his behavior, the employee was lost. ⁴This is a trivial example of a very serious problem in Japan: the inability to take personal initiative.

¹ここでの問題は何なのだろう？²簡単に言えば，マニュアルは，たとえ詳細にわたっていても，幼児が制服の一部を取るという状況で何をすべきかを扱ってはいない。³そして，行動を導いてくれるマニュアルがないので，従業員は途方に暮れてしまったのである。⁴これは，日本におけるとても深刻な問題，つまり自分から主導権を握ることができないという問題の，ありふれた例なのである。

3 to guide his behavior は the manual を修飾する形容詞用法の不定詞句。
  □ without A「Aがないので」　　□ guide「を導く，指導する／指針」
  □ behavior「行動，振る舞い」　　□ be lost「途方に暮れる，困る」
4 □ trivial「ありふれた，取るに足らない」　　□ inability to do「…できないこと」

¹Training employees is important, especially employees who come into contact with customers on a regular basis. ²But in the end it is a worker's own creativity and initiative that constitute true salesmanship. ³A company must not only allow but actively encourage its employees to use their heads in order to deal with real-life situations. ⁴Corporate training is nothing more than a guide. ⁵When it comes to doing real business with real customers, it is up to each individual employee to think on his or her feet and do what is best.

¹従業員の訓練は重要であり，常に客と接する従業員に関しては特にそうである。²しかし，結局は真の販売手腕となるのは従業員自身の創造力と主導権なのである。³会社は，従業員が現実の状況に対処するために自分の頭を使うことを認めるばかりではなく，それを積極的に奨励することもしなければならない。⁴会社での訓練など，指針にすぎない。⁵実際の客と実際に仕事をするということになると，独自に考えて最善のことをするかどうかはそれぞれの従業員次第なのである。

1 Training employees は動名詞句で主語。

☐ train「を訓練する」 　 ☐ especially「特に」 　 ☐ come into contact with A「Aと接する」

☐ on a regular basis「常に」

2 ☐ in the end「結局は，最終的には」 　 ☐ *one's* own A「自分自身のA」

☐ creativity「創造力，創造性」 　 ☐ constitute「を構成する」 　 ☐ salesmanship「販売手腕」

4 ☐ training「訓練」 　 ☐ nothing more than A「Aにすぎない，A以外の何ものでもない」

5 what is best は関係代名詞 what が導く名詞節。

☐ when it comes to A「Aに関しては，Aということになると」

☐ be up to A「A次第である，Aの責任である」 　 ☐ individual「個々の」

☐ think on *one's* own feet「自分で考える」

23 心臓発作

問1　ガンが合衆国の第1位の死因ではない。

問2　(2a)エ. result in　　(2b)ウ. caused　　(2c)イ. decreasing

問3　(3a)エ　　(3b)ア

問4　幸いなことに，血圧を下げる様々な方法，血圧を押し上げる行動とまった
　　く同じくらい多様な方法がある。

問5　エ

▶▶ 設問解説 ◀◀

問1　it は cancer を指す。not の後ろには the number one killer in the United
　　States が省略されている。 ➡ **Point ㉓**

　　□ cancer「ガン」　　□ killer「死因，殺すもの」

問2　(2a) account for A は「Aを説明する，Aの原因である／Aの割合を占める」
　　という意味の熟語。ここでは，「Aの原因である」という意味で使われていて，
　　「心臓発作が1年で50万を超える死亡の原因である」ということは「心臓発作が
　　死亡という結果になる」と読み換えられる。

　　ア.「に依存する」イ.「の世話をする」ウ.「を延期する」エ.「という結果になる」

　　(2b) bring A on は「Aを引き起こす」という意味の熟語。

　　ア.「を上げる」イ.「を下げる」ウ.「を引き起こす」エ.「を治療する」

　　(2c) decline は「減少する，衰退する／(を)断わる」という意味。ここでは，
　　「減少する」という意味で使われている。

　　ア.「増加する」イ.「減少する」ウ.「を断わる」エ.「を受け入れる」

問3　(3a)「そのような遅れ」とは，直前の文の「胸の痛みを覚えても，心臓発作を
　　起こしているとは気づかずに，病院に行く前にあまりに長く待つ」というこ
　　と。

　　□ delay「遅れ」　　□ can「…することがありえる，…する可能性がある」

　　□ fatal「致命的な」

　　(3b) accompany は「を伴う」という意味。

　　□ sweat「発汗する」

問4　ways to lower blood pressure を，ways that 以下が補足説明している。ま

た，that are ... は直前の ways を，that drive blood pressure up は the behaviors を修飾する関係代名詞節。

☐ fortunately「幸いなことに，幸運にも」　　☐ way to *do*「…する方法」

☐ lower「を下げる」　　☐ blood pressure「血圧」　　☐ varied「多様な」

☐ behavior「行動」　　☐ drive A up「Aを押し上げる」

問5　ア．「心臓病は毎年合衆国における死亡のおよそ25％を引き起こしている」第1段落第4文の内容に一致。

　　　イ．「心臓発作を警告する徴候には2分以上続く胸の中心部の痛みがある」第3段落第2文の内容に一致。

　　　ウ．「高血圧は心臓発作の危険性を高める要因の1つである」第4段落第1文の内容に一致。

　　　エ．「コーヒーを飲むことや，犬や猫に優しく触れることで血圧を下げることができる」第4段落第4文および第5段落第3文の内容に不一致。

Point ㉓ 省略

前に出てきた語句の反復を避けるために繰り返しとなる部分が省略されることがある。

例1　His daughter is studying physics and **his son history**.
　　　「彼の娘は物理を研究しているが，息子は歴史を研究している」

his son の後ろに is studying が省略されている。

例2　Some people believe that societies which resemble American society are democratic, and societies which **do not are not**.
　　　「アメリカ社会に似ている社会は民主的で，似ていない社会は民主的ではないと考える人もいる」

which do not の後ろに resemble American society が，are not の後ろに democratic が省略されている。

▶▶ **構文・語句解説** ◀◀

―― 第1段落 ――

¹A lot of people think cancer is the number one killer in the United States, but it's not. ²The leading killer is heart disease. ³Cancer is number two. ⁴Heart disease is responsible for about one-quarter of the deaths in the U.S. each year.

^{1}合衆国ではガンが第 1 の死因であると思っている人が多いが，そうではない。^{2}最大の死因は心臓病である。^{3}ガンは第 2 位なのだ。^{4}毎年，合衆国における死亡のおよそ 4 分の 1 は心臓病によるものである。

2 □ leading「1 位の」　　□ heart disease「心臓病」
4 □ be responsible for A「A の原因である」　　□ quarter「4 分の 1」

─── 第 2 段落 ───

^{1}Heart attacks account for over 500,000 deaths a year.　^{2}One reason the number of deaths from heart attacks is so high is that when people experience chest pain, they don't realize they may be having a heart attack and wait too long before going to the hospital. ^{3}Such a delay can be fatal.　^{4}In fact, more than half of all heart attack victims die before they reach the hospital.

^{1}心臓発作が 1 年で50万を超える死亡の原因である。^{2}心臓発作による死亡数がそれほど多い理由の 1 つは，胸の痛みを覚えても，心臓発作を起こしているとは気づかずに，病院に行く前にあまりに長く待つということである。^{3}そのような遅れが命を奪うことになりかねない。^{4}実際，心臓発作を起こした人の半数以上が，病院に到着する前に亡くなっている。

1 □ heart attack「心臓発作」
2 One reason the number of deaths from heart attacks is so high is that ... において reason の後ろに why が省略されている。that 以下は補語となる名詞節。
　□ experience「を経験する」　　□ chest「胸」　　□ pain「痛み」
　□ realize that 節「…と気づく」
4 □ in fact「実際に」　　□ victim「患者，被害者」

─── 第 3 段落 ───

^{1}What are the warning signs of a heart attack?　^{2}According to the American Heart Association, the signs include uncomfortable pressure or pain in the middle of the chest for two minutes or longer; movement of pain to the shoulder, arm, neck, or jaw; sweating may accompany the pain; nausea and vomiting may also occur; and shortness of breath, dizziness, or fainting may be experienced with the other signs.

¹心臓発作を警告する徴候は何であろう。²米国心臓病協会によると，そのような徴候には，2分以上続く胸の中心部の不快な圧迫や痛み，肩，腕，首，あごへの痛みの転移，痛みに伴う発汗などがあり，吐き気と嘔吐が起きることもあり，他の徴候とともに息切れ，めまい，失神を経験することもある。

1 □ warning sign「警告する徴候，危険信号」

2 □ according to A「Aによると」　　□ American Heart Association「米国心臓病協会」

□ include「を含む」　　□ uncomfortable「不快な」　　□ pressure「圧迫」

□ jaw「あご」　　□ occur「起きる」　　□ shortness of breath「息切れ」

□ dizziness「めまい」　　□ faint「失神する」

── 第4段落 ──

¹One of the factors that increase the risk of heart attack is high blood pressure. ²Today, with the stresses of everyday life, nearly one out of every three adults suffers from high blood pressure. ³High blood pressure can be brought on by a fight with one's spouse, problems at work, speaking in public, or even telling a lie. ⁴But it can also be brought on by something you enjoy, like the caffeine in a cup of coffee, cigarettes, or alcohol.

¹心臓発作の危険性を高める要因の1つに高血圧がある。²今日では，日常生活のストレスで，成人のほぼ3人に1人が高血圧を患っている。³夫婦喧嘩，仕事の上での問題，公の場で話をすること，さらにはうそをつくことで，高血圧は起きる。⁴しかし，一杯のコーヒーに含まれるカフェインやタバコ，アルコールのような，嗜好品が原因になることもある。

1 that increase ... heart attack 以下は the factors を修飾する関係代名詞節。

□ factor「要因」　　□ increase「を高める」

2 □ nearly「ほとんど」　　□ A out of (every) B「BのうちA」

□ suffer from A「Aを患う，Aで苦しむ」

3 □ fight「けんか」　　□ in public「公の場で，人前で」

4 you enjoy は something を修飾する関係代名詞節。

□ caffeine「カフェイン」　　□ alcohol「アルコール」

¹There are, fortunately, ways to lower blood pressure — ways that are just as varied as the behaviors that drive blood pressure up. ²They include maintaining a healthy diet, attaining one's recommended weight, and doing regular aerobic exercise. ³And there are unexpectedly simple ways of lowering blood pressure, such as laughing or petting a dog or cat.

¹幸いなことに，血圧を下げる様々な方法，血圧を押し上げる行動とまったく同じくらい多様な方法がある。²健康的な食事を続けること，理想体重に達すること，定期的に有酸素運動することが含まれる。³また，笑ったり，犬や猫を可愛がったりといった，血圧を下げる意外に単純な方法もある。

2 ☐ maintain「を維持する」　　☐ diet「食事，日常の飲食物」　　☐ attain「に到達する」
　☐ recommended weight「理想体重，推奨される体重」　　☐ aerobic exercise「有酸素運動」
3 ☐ unexpectedly「意外に」　　☐ A such as B「たとえばBのようなA」
　☐ pet「を可愛がる，なでる」

¹So while the bad news is that heart disease is the number one killer, the good news is that the death rate from heart disease has been declining since the 1950s as people adopt healthier lifestyles and the medical world develops improved drugs and surgical techniques.

¹ということで，心臓病が死因の第1位であるということは悪い知らせではあるが，人々がより健康的な生活様式を取り入れ，医学界が改良された薬や手術方法を開発しているため，1950年代以降心臓病による死亡率が下がっているというよい知らせもある。

1 as people adopt 以下は the death rate from heart disease has been declining ... に対して理由を述べている副詞節。
　☐ while S V ...「…する一方で」　　☐ the bad news is that 節「悪い知らせは…ということだ」
　☐ death rate「死亡率」　　☐ adopt「を取り入れる」　　☐ medical「医学の」
　☐ develop「を開発する」　　☐ improved「改良された」　　☐ surgical「手術の，外科の」

24 不眠症

解　答

問1　ウ. In short

問2　イ. not all

問3　実験によれば，睡眠を奪われると人は数学的作業や言語作業において鈍くなり，注意力の持続時間や記憶力が低下するということだ。

問4　イ. with

問5　3週間にわたって就寝前に45分間音楽を聴いた学生は睡眠の効率に好ましい効果が見られたが，同様の効果は高齢者でも見られたという証拠。

▶▶▶　設問解説　◀◀◀

問1　空所(1)を含む文は「よい睡眠は人間の健康の基盤なのだ」という意味であり，これは空所の前の第1段落第1～3文で述べた内容をまとめたものである。したがって，ウが正解。

　　　ア.「対照的に」イ.「たとえば」ウ.「要するに」エ.「そのうえ」

問2　空所(2)を含む文に続く第2段落第2文に「成人のおよそ30%が人生の中で一時期慢性的な不眠症—1か月以上にわたって睡眠が乱される経験をしたことがある」とあるので，イが正解。not all は「すべてが…というわけではない」という部分否定の表現。

問3　reveal の目的語である that 節内の when deprived of sleep は when の後ろに they are が省略されている。➡ **Point ㉔** their attention span and memory decline は people are less sharp at mathematical and verbal tasks と and で結ばれている。

　　　□ experiment「実験」　　□ reveal that 節「…を明らかにする」

　　　□ deprive A of B「AからBを奪う」　　□ sharp「頭の切れる，利口な」

　　　□ mathematical「数学の」　　□ verbal「言語の」　　□ task「作業」

　　　□ attention span「注意力持続時間」　　□ memory「記憶力」

　　　□ decline「低下する，衰える」

問4　空所の直後には，「アメリカだけでも1年に7万2千件を超える交通事故が睡眠不足に関連する」というように主語＋述語という意味関係が成立する名詞＋*done* が続いているので付帯状況の with が入る。➡ **Point ⑤**

問5 this evidence「こうした証拠」とは,「不眠症を予防する手段として就寝前に静かな音楽を聴くことを勧める」根拠になる証拠である。直前の文で「就寝前に音楽を聴くことで睡眠の効率が上がった」という研究結果が述べられている。

Point ㉔ 副詞節内の省略

　時・条件・譲歩を表す副詞節に S be があり, 主語が文脈から明らかなときに, S be が省略されることがある。

例 Though **(I am)** tired, I will go to the meeting, if **(it is)** necessary.
「疲れてますけど, 必要であれば私が会議に出ます」

▶▶ 構文・語句解説 ◀◀

第1段落

¹In our hectic world, a good night's sleep is worth its weight in gold when it comes to improving physical and mental well-being. ²Much more than a basic method of energy conservation, sleep is a state during which muscle and bone are generated and repaired, and memories and learning systems are updated. ³Sleep also allows the body and brain to clear out the toxic byproducts of the day's waking activity that might cause harm if we didn't sleep. ⁴In short, good sleep is a foundation of human health.

---

¹我々のせかせかした世の中では, ぐっすり一晩眠ることは, 身体的にも精神的にも健康状態を改善するということでは, 同じ重さの金と同じくらいの価値がある。²エネルギー保存のための基本的な方法にとどまらず, 睡眠は, その間に筋肉と骨が作られ修復され, 記憶や学習システムが更新される状態である。³睡眠はまた, 身体と脳が, もし睡眠をとらないと害を与えるかもしれない, 日中起きている間にたまる有毒な副産物を一掃することができるようにする。⁴要するに, よい睡眠は人間の健康の基盤なのだ。

---

1 □ be worth its weight in gold「金の重さの価値がある, 非常に重要な」
　□ when it comes to A「Aということになると」　　□ improve「を改善する」
　□ physical「肉体的な」　　□ mental「精神的な」　　□ well-being「健康, 幸福」

2 during which 以下は a state を修飾する関係代名詞節。
　□ much more than A「Aにとどまらず」　　□ method「方法」　　□ conservation「保存」
　□ state「状態」　　□ muscle「筋肉」　　□ bone「骨」　　□ generate「を生み出す」
　□ update「を更新する」

3 that 以下は the toxic byproducts of the day's waking activity を修飾する関係代名詞節。節内は

仮定法過去になっている。

□ allow O to *do*「Oが…するのを可能にする」　　□ clear A out「Aを一掃する」

□ toxic「有毒な」　　□ byproduct「副産物」　　□ waking activity「覚醒中の活動」

4 □ foundation「基盤」

━━ 第2段落 ━━

[1]Sadly, not all of us are blessed with the benefit of a good night's sleep after a long and often tiring day. [2]Around 30% of adults experience chronic insomnia at some point in their life — where sleep is disrupted for more than a month. [3]Estimates are even higher in older populations and those who experience regular stress.

[1]残念なことに，すべての人が長くてくたびれることも多い一日の後でぐっすり一晩眠る恩恵を受けているわけではない。[2]成人のおよそ30%が人生の中で一時期慢性的な不眠症―1か月以上にわたって睡眠が乱される―経験をしたことがある。[3]推定では，高齢者や定期的なストレスがある人の場合さらに高くなる。

1 □ sadly「残念なことに」　　□ be blessed with A「Aに恵まれている」　　□ benefit「恩恵」
　 □ tiring「くたびれる，疲れさせる」

2 □ around＋数詞「およそ…」　　□ experience「を経験する」　　□ chronic「慢性の」
　 □ insomnia「不眠症」　　□ disrupt「を混乱させる」

3 □ estimate「推定，見積り」　　□ even「(比較級を強調して)さらに，いっそう」
　 □ population「住民／人口」　　□ those who ...「…する人々」

━━ 第3段落 ━━

[1]Insomnia can be devastating, and it has been linked to cognitive deficiencies. [2]Experiments reveal that when deprived of sleep, people are less sharp at mathematical and verbal tasks, and their attention span and memory decline. [3]Severe cases of chronic insomnia can cause psychological problems, including mood and anxiety disorders, and long-term health concerns, including obesity and dementia.

[1]不眠症はひどいことになりかねないし，認知機能の低下と関連づけられてきた。[2]実験によれば，睡眠を奪われると人は数学的作業や言語作業において鈍くなり，注意力の持続時間や記憶力が低下するということだ。[3]慢性の不眠症がひどくなると，気分や不安障害を含む心理的な

問題，そして肥満や認知症を含む長期的な健康に関する不安が生じることがある。

1 ☐ devastating「ひどい，壊滅的な」　　☐ be linked to A「Aと関連がある」

　☐ cognitive「認知の」　　☐ deficiency「低下，欠陥」

3 and は psychological problems, including mood and anxiety disorders と long-term health concerns, including obesity and dementia の2つの名詞句を結んでいる。

　☐ severe「ひどい，厳しい」　　☐ case「症例」　　☐ cause「を引き起こす」

　☐ psychological「心理的な」　　☐ including A「Aを含む」　　☐ mood「気分」

　☐ anxiety「不安」　　☐ disorder「障害，不調」　　☐ long-term「長期的な」

　☐ concern「心配事」　　☐ obesity「肥満」　　☐ dementia「認知症」

―――― 第4段落 ――――

　[1]The cost of insomnia goes well beyond just health.　[2]According to the National Sleep Foundation, insomniacs are two to four times more likely to have an accident — with over 72,000 traffic accidents a year in the US alone linked to sleep deprivation.　[3]Insomnia also costs US companies an estimated $150 billion in reduced productivity every year.

　[1]不眠症の代償は単に健康にとどまるものではない。[2]国立睡眠財団によると，不眠症患者は事故にあう可能性が2倍から4倍高い―アメリカだけでも1年に7万2千件を超える交通事故が睡眠不足に関連するものである。[3]また不眠症によって，アメリカの企業では生産性が年間推定で1千5百億ドル低下している。

1 ☐ cost「代償／費用」　　☐ go well beyond A「Aにとどまらない，Aの範囲を超える」

2 ☐ according to A「Aによると」　　☐ insomniac「不眠症患者」

　☐ be likely to do「…する可能性が高い」　　☐ ... times＋比較級「…倍」

　☐ have an accident「事故にあう，事故を起こす」　　☐ a year「1年につき」

　☐ A alone「Aだけで」　　☐ (be) linked to A「Aと関連している」

　☐ sleep deprivation「睡眠不足」

3 ☐ cost O_1 O_2「O_1にO_2を払わせる」　　☐ an estimated＋数詞「推定で…，およそ…」

　☐ billion「10億」　　☐ reduced「減少した」　　☐ productivity「生産性」

―――― 第5段落 ――――

　[1]Research has shown that listening to self-selected music, or music of your choice, can actually shorten stage two sleep cycles.　[2]This means people reach REM sleep, which is

the restorative part of our sleep, more quickly.

¹研究によって，自選の音楽，あるいは自分の好みの音楽を聴くことで睡眠サイクルの第2段階を実際に短くすることができることが示されている。²これは，睡眠の中でも回復に役立つ部分であるレム睡眠に人々がより早く到達するということである。

1 □ research「研究」   □ self-selected「自選の」   □ of *one's* choice「自分の好みの」
  □ actually「実際に」   □ shorten「を短くする」
  □ stage two sleep cycles「睡眠サイクルの第2段階」
2 □ mean that 節「…ということを意味する」   □ reach「に到達する」
  □ restorative「回復させる」

─── 第6段落 ───

¹In one study, students who listened to 45 minutes of music before bedtime for three weeks saw a positive effect on sleep efficiency, and another study found a similar effect on older citizens. ²Following this evidence, the NHS now recommends listening to soft music before bedtime as a method to prevent insomnia.

¹ある研究では，3週間にわたって就寝前に45分間音楽を聴いた学生は睡眠の効率に好ましい効果が見られたが，別の研究でも同様の効果が高齢者でも見られた。²こうした証拠に基づき，国民保健サービスでは現在，不眠症を予防する手段として就寝前に静かな音楽を聴くことを勧めている。

1 □ study「研究，調査」   □ positive「好ましい」   □ effect on A「Aに対する効果」
  □ efficiency「効率」   □ similar「同様の」   □ older citizen「高齢者」
2 Following this evidence は分詞構文。
  □ follow「に基づく，従う」   □ evidence「証拠」
  □ recommend *doing*「…することを勧める」   □ soft「静かな，穏やかな」
  □ method to *do*「…する方法」   □ prevent「を予防する」

25 日本人の礼儀正しさ

問1　日本語に敬語の体系があること。(15字)
問2　日本人が常に礼儀正しいという神話は，その観察を行っているのが誰であるかと大いに関係がある。
問3　do Japanese speakers drop the expected level of politeness
問4　状況に応じて，これらの集団の1つが他の集団より重要視される。
問5　ウ. less

▶▶▶　設問解説　◀◀◀

問1　this を含む文全体を見ると，「日本語には多数の適切な丁寧さの水準を必要とする敬語の体系があるが，これは日本人が常に礼儀正しいということにはならない」という意味である。したがって，this は Although 節内の内容を指す。that 以下の関係詞節は答えに含まれなくても可。

問2　that the Japanese are always polite は The myth と同格の名詞節である。
　　→ **Point ⑧** have much to do with A「Aと大いに関係がある」のAに相当するのは who is ... の疑問詞節である。
　　□myth「神話」　　□do the observing「観察をする」

問3　only が副詞(句・節)を伴って文頭にくると，必ず倒置が起きることに注意。
　　→ **Point ㉕** 第1段落第4文に「『内』グループの外にいる観察者にとって，日本人の不作法な面はほとんど表に出てこない」と述べられている。ただし，「当事者が実際に議論している場合に限り，日本人の話し手は『外』の人に対して礼儀と堅苦しさの期待される水準を下げる」という文脈を押さえること。

問4　depending on A は，前置詞句で「Aに応じて，A次第で」という意味。one of 以下は emphasize A over B「BよりAを重要視する」が受動態になった形。問いの指示にある the others は the other groups のことである。なお，these groups は第2段落第1文の several social groups を指している。

問5　前に述べられた「礼儀正しさがたいてい避けられる」という内容に矛盾しないものを選ぶ。したがって，「親密な，あまり形式張らない表現」という意味になるウが正解。

通常，文頭にこない否定の副詞表現が文頭に置かれると，倒置文（疑問文の語順と考えればよい）になる。また，only＋副詞(句・節)が文頭にきた場合も倒置文になることに注意。なお，only＋副詞(句・節)は「…してはじめて，…してようやく」と意味を取るとよい場合が多い。

例1　Little **did I dream** that I would never see Thomas again.
「トーマスに二度と会えないとは，まったく思わなかった」

例2　Only yesterday **did I receive** the manuscript from Joe.
「昨日になってようやくジョーからその原稿を受け取った」

例3　Only if he wins **is the lawyer paid**.
「弁護士は勝った場合にはじめて報酬を得る」

▶▶ 構文・語句解説 ◀◀

第1段落

[1]Japanese people are usually characterized as polite. [2]Although the Japanese language has a system of politeness that requires a pack of appropriate politeness levels, this does not mean that the Japanese are always polite. [3]As a casual look into a karaoke bar or a similar place for dining and drinking reveals, Japanese people, given the right place and the right time, talk casually in a way that may seem to a foreigner quite impolite or even rude. [4]The myth that the Japanese are always polite has much to do with who is doing the observing; to an observer who is outside the *uchi* group, the impolite side of the Japanese is hardly ever expressed. [5]Only if participants are actually arguing do Japanese speakers drop the expected level of politeness and formality toward the *soto* person.

[1]日本人はたいてい礼儀正しいと言われている。[2]日本語には多数の適切な丁寧さの水準を必要とする敬語の体系があるが，これは日本人が常に礼儀正しいということにはならない。[3]カラオケバーや飲食をする類似の場所をちょっとのぞいてみればわかることだが，日本人はふさわしい場所と時間が与えられれば，外国人にはかなり不作法で，また無礼とすら思われるかもしれないやり方でうちとけて話す。[4]日本人が常に礼儀正しいという神話は，その観察を行っているのが誰であるかと大いに関係がある。「内」グループの外にいる観察者にとって，日本人の不作法な面はほとんど表に出てこない。[5]当事者が実際に議論している場合に限り，日本人の話し手は「外」の人に対して礼儀と堅苦しさの期待される水準を下げる。

1 □characterize O as C「OをCとみなす，述べる」　　　□ polite「礼儀正しい」

2 that requires ... levels は a system of politeness を修飾する関係代名詞節。

　□ system「体系」　　　□ require「を必要とする」　　　□ a pack of A「多数のA」

　□ appropriate「適切な」　　　□ level「水準」

3 As a casual ... reveals の As は関係代名詞で，後続の主節の内容を補足説明している。that may seem ... even rude は a way を修飾する関係代名詞節。

　□ casual「何気ない」　　　□ similar「類似の」　　　□ reveal「を明らかにする，示す」

　□ given A「Aが与えられると」　　　□ right「適切な」　　　□ casually「うちとけて」

　□ impolite「不作法な」　　　□ rude「無礼な」

4 □ hardly「ほとんど…ない」　　　□ express「を表現する」

5 □ participant「当事者，関係者」　　　□ actually「実際に」　　　□ argue「議論する」

　□ formality「堅苦しさ」

── 第2段落 ──

[1]Each individual is a member of several social groups — family, university, workplace, and so on. [2]Depending on the situation, one of these groups is emphasized over the others. [3]Within two contrasting and yet constantly changing social areas, *uchi* and *soto*, different social behaviors are observed. [4]In *uchi* relations, where there is less psychological distance among the participants, politeness is usually avoided, and intimate and less formal expressions are used. [5]In *soto* relations, where the psychological and social distance is emphasized, appropriate levels of politeness must be maintained.

---

[1]人はそれぞれ，家族，大学，職場などのいくつかの社会的集団の構成員である。[2]状況に応じて，これらの集団の1つが他の集団より重要視される。[3]「内」と「外」という2つの対照的であるが絶えず変化している社会的な領域の中では，様々な社会行動が観察される。[4]当事者の間に心理的距離が小さい「内」の関係では，礼儀正しさがたいてい避けられ，親密な，より形式張らない表現が使われる。[5]心理的，社会的距離が重要視される「外」の関係では，適切な水準の礼儀が維持されなければならない。

1 □ individual「個人」　　　□ several「いくつかの」　　　□ social「社会的な」

　□ workplace「職場」　　　□ and so on「…など」

3 □ contrasting「対照的な」　　　□ and yet「しかし」　　　□ constantly「絶えず」

　□ area「領域」

4 In *uchi* relations, where ... の where は関係副詞。第5文の where も同じ。

□ psychological「心理的な」　　□ distance「距離」　　□ avoid「を避ける」

□ intimate「親密な」　　□ formal「形式張った」

5 □ maintain「を維持する」

26 人の話を聞くこと

問1　成功の秘訣は，話し上手になることであるが，それ以上に聞き上手になる
　　ことである，という忠告。(45字)

問2　よい聞き手になれば，相手は安心し，心を開いてくれるだろう。

問3　(3)イ. invaluable　　　(4)ウ. irresponsible　　　(6)ア. grateful

問4　(b) (d) (e) (f)

問5　もし彼らがそんなに多く話すのをやめてお互いの話に耳を傾け始めるな
　　ら，彼らは対話を始めることができるだろう。

問6　イ. Being a Responsible Listener

▶▶▶　設問解説　◀◀◀

問1　some advice の内容は次の文に具体的に述べられている。a good speaker とい
　　う原級表現と，a better listener という比較級の表現の違いに着目して，制限
　　字数に注意してまとめること。引用符の中の文構造は，The key to success が
　　主語，is が述語動詞，being a good ... 以下が動名詞句で補語となっている。

問2　and が結んでいるのは，will feel ... you と will open their hearts である。
　　feel at ease は「気持ちが落ち着く，くつろぐ」という意味。

問3　(3)主語である these wise words の wise に着目する。また最終段落の内容か
　　ら，筆者にとって父の忠告の言葉が「非常に価値のある」ものであったことが
　　わかる。
　　(4)直後の because 節の内容，また空所(4)に続く第5段落第2文以降の内容か
　　ら「聞くのが下手な人は社会的に無責任な人である」ことがわかる。
　　(6)本文全体から，「よい忠告をもらったことで筆者は父と教授に感謝している」
　　ことがわかる。
　　ア.「感謝している」イ.「非常に価値のある」ウ.「無責任な」エ.「非現実的な」

問4　第4段落第1文に，「筆者が教授の発言に驚いた」と述べられている。教授の発
　　言とは，第3段落に述べられた「聞くことが社会的な責任である」というも
　　の。したがって，筆者としては「聞くことをあまり重要視していなかった」こ
　　とが読み取れる。また，第4段落第4文には，「教授の説明のおかげで，
　　（　e　）は意思疎通を作り出し，ゆがめ，破壊することができる強力な社会的

な道具だということを知った」とあるので，筆者は「話すことは能動的で，聞くことは受動的だ」という理由から「話すことが聞くことよりも重要であると考えていた」とわかる。よって，(a) (c)には speaking が，(b) (d)には listening が入ることになる。さらに，「筆者は聞くことが重要であるとわかったのだが，残念なことに多くの人はそれに気づいていない」という第4段落第5・6文の内容から(e) (f)には listening が入ることになる。

問5 文全体が仮定法過去であることを見抜くことがポイント。また，and が結んでいるのは，stopped talking so much と started listening to each other である。 **➡ Point** ㉖

  □ stop *doing*「…するのをやめる」　　□ each other「お互い」

問6 「聞くこと」に関して，筆者の父と大学院の教授がした同じ忠告を通じて，「社会的にも責任を伴う重要な技術である」ことが述べられている。したがって，イが正解。

  ア.「自信のある話し手になること」
  イ.「責任ある聞き手になること」
  ウ.「大学における意思疎通」
  エ.「目上の人の話を聞くこと」

Point ㉖ **仮定法**

1．仮定法過去 If S *did* ... , S would [could / might] *do* 〜
  現在の事実に反する事柄，および現実に起こる可能性がないことを表す場合，仮定法過去を用いる。

例 If he **had** time, he **might** come to see me.
  「もし彼に時間があれば，私に会いに来るかもしれないだろう」

2．仮定法過去完了 If S had *done* ... , S would [could / might] have *done* 〜
  過去の事実に反する事柄を表す場合，仮定法過去完了を用いる。

例 If you **had worked** harder, you **would have passed** the exam.
  「もしもっと勉強していたら，君は試験に合格しただろう」

▶▶ **構文・語句解説** ◀◀

── 第1段落 ──

¹My father had a special way with people. ²His warm smile and relaxed manner immediately made them feel comfortable. ³He always said the right word at the right moment. ⁴For years, I was convinced that his success with people was due to his speaking skills.

¹父は人と接するときある特別な方法を心得ていた。²彼の温かい微笑みとくつろいだ態度はすぐに人をなごませた。³彼は常に適切なときに適切な言葉を言った。⁴何年もの間，父が人間関係でうまくいったのはその話術によるものだと，私は思っていた。

2 His warm smile ... feel comfortable は使役動詞 make を用いた表現。第3文に用いられた make も同じく使役動詞である。　　□ relaxed「くつろいだ」　　□ manner「態度」
　□ immediately「すぐに」　　□ comfortable「心地よい」
3 □ right「適切な」　　□ moment「時，場合」
4 □ be convinced that 節「…だと確信している」　　□ be due to A「Aのせいである」
　□ skill「技術」

- -

── 第2段落 ──

¹Before I went off to college, my father gave me some advice that surprised me. ²"The key to success," he told me, "is being a good speaker and a better listener." ³Then he explained why. ⁴You learn more from listening than from talking. ⁵If you are a good listener, people will feel at ease with you, and will open their hearts. ⁶For me, these wise words have been invaluable.

¹私が大学に行く前に，父は私を驚かせる忠告をしてくれた。²「成功の秘訣は」と，彼は言った。「よい話し手になること，そしてそれ以上によい聞き手になることだよ」と。³それから彼はその理由を説明した。⁴人は話すことより聞くことから多くを学ぶ。⁵よい聞き手になれば，相手は安心し，心を開いてくれるだろう。⁶私にとって，これらの賢明な言葉はかけがえのないものであった。

1 that surprised me は some advice を修飾する関係代名詞節。
2 □ key to A「Aの鍵，秘訣」
4 You learn more と現在時制になっているのは，筆者の父の発話の内容だからである。第5文の現在時制も同様である。

- -

¹In graduate school, I was given the same advice from a professor who was one of the world's most famous linguistic scholars. ²He defined listening as a social responsibility which promotes communication. ³When you listen, he told me, you receive and then process the other person's spoken message. ⁴Your willingness to open a dialogue creates the miracle of communication.

¹大学院で，私は世界的に最も著名な言語学者の一人である教授から同じ忠告をもらった。²彼は聞くことを意思疎通を促す社会的な責任と定義していた。³人の話を聞くとき，相手の話すメッセージを受け取りそれから処理するのだと彼は私に言った。⁴対話の道を開こうとする意欲が意思疎通の奇跡を生み出すのである。

1 □ graduate school「大学院」　　□ professor「教授」　　□ linguistic scholar「言語学の学者」

2 □ define O as C「OをCと定義する」　　□ social「社会的な」　　□ responsibility「責任」
　□ promote「を促進する」

3 When you listen, he told me, you receive and ... spoken message は S tell O that 節「S は O〈人〉に…だと言う」の表現の that を省略して，S tell O を挿入的に用いたもの。
　□ process「を処理する」

4 □ willingness to *do*「…しようとする意欲」　　□ dialogue「対話」　　□ miracle「奇跡」

¹At first, I was surprised by my professor's comment. ²I had always thought that in communication, speaking was more important than listening. ³Perhaps I had reached this conclusion, because speaking is active while listening is passive. ⁴Thanks to my professor's explanation, however, I learned that listening is a powerful social tool which can create, distort, or destroy communication. ⁵Unfortunately most women and men do not learn this skill. ⁶Only a few realize that listening is a social responsibility.

¹最初，私は教授の話に驚いた。²私は，意思疎通では話すことが聞くことよりも大切だといつも思っていた。³話すことは能動的だが，聞くことは受動的だから，たぶん私はこのような結論に達したのであろう。⁴しかし，教授の説明のおかげで，聞くことは意思疎通を作り出し，ゆがめ，破壊することができる強力な社会的な道具だということを知った。⁵不幸なことに，ほとんどの人はこの技能を身につけていない。⁶聞くことが社会的な責任であるとわかっている人は

ほんのわずかである。

1 □ at first「最初は」　　□ comment「発言」
3 □ conclusion「結論」　　□ active「能動的な」　　□ while S V ...「ところが一方…」
　□ passive「受動的な」
4 which can create, distort, or destroy communication は a powerful social tool を修飾する関係
　代名詞節。or が結んでいるのは 3 つの他動詞 create, distort, destroy で，communication が共通
　の目的語である。　　□ thanks to A「Aのおかげで」　　□ tool「道具」
　□ distort「をゆがめる」
5 □ unfortunately「不幸なことに」
6 □ a few「わずかな人々」

── 第 5 段落 ──

¹Poor listeners are socially irresponsible, because they stop or block communication. ²You probably know people who do not listen. ³They never stop talking. ⁴If you try to say a word, they do not listen, or they interrupt you in a loud voice. ⁵They are not interested in communication. ⁶They just want to be the center of attention. ⁷Quite simply, poor listeners are self-centered.

---

　¹聞くのが下手な人は社会的に無責任な人である。なぜなら意思の疎通を止めたり邪魔したりするからである。²あなたはおそらく人の話を聞かない人たちを知っているだろう。³彼らは決して話すのをやめない。⁴あなたがひとこと言おうとしても，彼らは耳を貸さないか大声で遮る。⁵彼らは意思疎通には興味がない。⁶ただ注目の的になりたいだけなのである。⁷きわめて簡単に言えば，聞き下手な人たちは自己中心的なのである。

1 □ block「を邪魔する，妨害する」
4 □ interrupt「の邪魔をする」
6 □ attention「注目，関心」
7 □ quite simply「きわめて簡単に言えば」　　□ self-centered「自己中心的な」

── 第 6・7 段落 ──

¹Many social problems stem from the behavior of women and men who are poor listeners. ²If they stopped talking so much and started listening to each other, they could open a dialogue. ³It is amazing how many problems can be solved when people

communicate.

[4]I am grateful to both my father and my professor for teaching me why it is important to be a responsible listener. [5]I hope that this lesson will help you too.

[1]多くの社会的な問題は聞き下手な人の行動から生じる。[2]もし彼らがそんなに多く話すのをやめてお互いの話に耳を傾け始めるなら，彼らは対話を始めることができるだろう。[3]人が意思疎通すれば，どれほど多くの問題が解決できるかということは驚くほどである。

[4]私は責任ある聞き手になることがなぜ大切であるのかを教えてくれた父と教授の両方に感謝している。[5]この教訓があなたにも役立つことを望んでいる。

1 □ stem from A「Aに起因する，Aから起こる」　　□ behavior「行動，振る舞い」

2 If they stopped ... , they could～は仮定法過去の文。

3 It is amazing how many ... の It は形式主語で，真主語は how many ... 以下。
　　□ amazing「驚くべき」

4 teaching me why it is important to ... は teach O_1 O_2「O_1〈人〉に O_2〈こと〉を教える」の表現を用いたもので，ここでは O_2 に疑問詞節がきている。なお，it は形式主語で，真主語は to be 以下。　　□ be grateful to A for B「A〈人〉にBのことで感謝している」

5 □ lesson「教訓」

138

グローバル化時代のニュース

解 答

問1　ウ

問2　特に日本は，世界の他の国々から孤立してしまったら，一年でさえ生き延びることはできないだろう。

問3　海外の大手の通信社から記事や写真を買って，自社の記事や番組を作り上げること。(38字)

問4　・アメリカからの好ましい政治ニュース
　　　・ペルー沖の悪天候のニュース
　　　・アラブの石油価格に関するニュース

問5　ウ. borderless

▶▶▶ **設問解説** ◀◀◀

問1　下線部(1)を含む第1段落第1文は「『地球村』とは，すべての人間は地球という惑星で平和に暮らしている一つの大きな村の成員のようなものだ，ということを意味する理想主義的なフレーズである」という意味だが，その実情は，続く第2文に The fact is that 節を用いて書かれている。したがって，ウが正解。
　　　ア.「『地球村』という考えは，地球上のすべての人間に受け入れられている」
　　　イ.「世界中の人々が，1つの大きなコミュニティの成員として平和に暮らしている」
　　　ウ.「地球は目に見えない境界線によって，何百もの国々に分けられている」
　　　エ.「他の国とのビジネスは，国境に沿ってうまく行われている」

問2　下線部(2)は，仮定法過去の条件節が if を用いずに倒置の語順で書かれている。

→ **Point** ㉗

　　　□ in particular「特に，とりわけ」　　　□ survive「生き延びる」
　　　□ be isolated from A「Aから孤立している」
　　　□ the rest of A「Aの残り」the rest of the world は「当該国を除いた世界の残り＝世界の他の国々や地域」を意味する。

問3　日本の新聞やテレビ局に関しては，第4段落第1文後半に「日本の新聞やテレビ局は，報道記事や写真を海外の大手の通信社から買い，それらをまとめて自社のニュース記事やニュース番組を作り上げていることが非常に多い」と述べ

られているので，この内容をまとめる。

問4 下線部(4)の具体例は，第5段落の3つの文の主語の部分で述べられている。

　　□ fresh「新しい，新鮮な」　　□ from abroad「海外から（の）」

問5 空所(5)を含む第6段落第4文は，同じ段落の3つの文の内容を受けて「したがって」と述べられているので，その3文の内容を検討すればよい。第1文は「インターネットは，衛星やパラボラアンテナに繋がっていて，私たちが世界との接触を保つことを可能にしてくれている」，第2文は「生のニュースが世界中を飛び回り国境を壊していく」，第3文は「どの国も自国内の出来事を世界の他の国々や地域に知られないように隠しておいたり，好ましくない国際的なニュースを自国民に知られないようにしておいたりすることはできない」という内容で，「私たちは国境のない世界に暮らしている」という意味になっている。したがって，ウが正解。

ア.「工業の」イ.「安定した」ウ.「国境のない」エ.「平和な」

Point ㉗ 仮定法の条件節の倒置

　仮定法の条件節が，if を用いずに倒置の語順にすることで表現されることがある。

例1　**Were I** in his circumstances, I would do the same thing.
　　＝**If I were** in his circumstances, I would do the same thing.
　　「彼の状況に置かれたら，私も同じことをするだろう」

例2　A lot of murderers would have remained innocent **had they** not possessed a knife or a gun.
　　＝A lot of murderers would have remained innocent **if they had** not possessed a knife or a gun.
　　「多くの殺人犯はナイフや銃を所持していなければ，罪を犯すことはなかったであろう」

▶▶ **構文・語句解説** ◀◀

── 第1段落 ──

¹The "global village" is an idealistic phrase meaning that all human beings are like members of one big village living peacefully on planet Earth. ²The fact is, however, that the surface of Earth is divided into some 200 nations by mostly unseen borders. ³Business activities between nations can be either difficult or easy depending on these borders.

¹「地球村」とは，すべての人間は地球という惑星で平和に暮らしている一つの大きな村の成員のようなものだ，ということを意味する理想主義的なフレーズである。²ところが実情は，地球の表面は，たいていは目に見えない境界線によって，200ほどの国々に分けられている。³国と国との間の経済活動は，そういった境界線によって，困難であるか容易であるかのいずれかになりかねない。

1 meaning 以下は，an idealistic phrase を修飾する現在分詞句。また，living 以下は members of one big village を修飾する現在分詞句。

　□ idealistic「理想主義的な」　　□ phrase「フレーズ，語句」

　□ mean that 節「…ということを意味する」　　□ human beings「人間」

　□ be like A「Aに似ている，Aのようである」　　□ peacefully「平和に，平穏に」

　□ planet Earth「地球という惑星」

2 □ The fact is that 節「実情は…である」　　□ surface「表面」

　□ divide A into B「AをBに分割する」　　□ some＋数詞「およそ…，約…」

　□ nation「国家，国」　　□ mostly「たいていは，通常」　　□ unseen「目に見えない」

　□ border「境界（線）」

3 □ business activity「経済活動，事業活動」　　□ either X or Y「XかYのいずれか」

　□ depending on A「Aによって，A次第で」

— 第2段落 —

¹Only a few countries could survive without trading with other countries. ²Most countries depend on each other. ³Japan, in particular, could not survive even one year were it isolated from the rest of the world. ⁴Japan's large economy is totally supported by many other nations. ⁵To maintain their healthy economy, Japanese people should always be alert to what is going on in the world.

¹他の国々との交易をせずに生き延びることのできる国はほんの少数しかないだろう。²ほとんどの国々がお互いに依存し合っている。³特に日本は，世界の他の国々から孤立してしまったら，一年でさえ生き延びることはできないだろう。⁴日本の大規模な経済は他の多くの国々によって完全に支えられている。⁵その健全な経済を維持するためには，日本の人々は常に世界で何が起きているかに注意しているべきである。

1 □ only a few A「ほんの少数のA」　　□ trade with A「Aと交易する，貿易を行う」

2 □ depend on A「Aに依存する」　　□ each other「お互い」

4 □ economy「(国や自治体などの)経済」　　□ support「を支える」

5 To maintain their healthy economy は目的を表す副詞用法の不定詞句。

　□ maintain「を維持する」　　□ healthy「健全な，健康な」

　□ be alert to A「Aに注意している，敏感である」　　□ go on「起きる，生じる」

———— 第3段落 ————

[1]News articles are sent from every corner of the world by worldwide news agencies.　[2]These big news agencies send hundreds of reporters and photographers all over the world, and they send back reports and pictures day and night.

　[1]ニュース記事は，全世界をカバーする通信社によって，世界の隅々から送られている。[2]これらの大きな通信社は世界中に何百もの報道記者とカメラマンを送っており，彼らは報道記事や写真を日夜送り返している。

1 □ article「記事」　　□ every corner of the world「世界の隅々，世界のあらゆる場所」

　□ worldwide「世界中に及ぶ，全世界に広がる」　　□ news agency「通信社」

2 □ hundreds of A「何百ものA，数百のA」　　□ reporter「報道記者」

　□ photographer「カメラマン，写真家」　　□ all over the world「世界中に」

　□ send A back「Aを送り返す」　　□ report「報道記事」

　□ day and night「日夜，昼も夜も」

———— 第4段落 ————

[1]Japanese news crews are also active in many places, but quite often Japanese newspapers and TV stations buy reports and pictures from major news agencies abroad to put together their news articles and programs.　[2]If you are able to read or listen to English news, you may be able to get news directly from international news sources.　[3]Fresh news from abroad can affect the Japanese economy.

　[1]日本のニュース取材班も多くの場所で活動しているが，日本の新聞やテレビ局は報道記事や写真を海外の大手の通信社から買い，それらをまとめて自社のニュース記事やニュース番組を作り上げていることが非常に多い。[2]英語のニュースを読んだり聴いたりすることができるなら，国際的なニュースソースから直接ニュースを手に入れることができるだろう。[3]海外から届

いたばかりのニュースは日本の経済に影響を与えることがある。

1 to put together their news articles and programs は目的を表す副詞用法の不定詞句。

☐ news crew「取材班」　　☐ active「活動的な」　　☐ major「大手の，主要な」

☐ put A together「(いろいろなものをまとめて)Aを作る」　　☐ program「番組」

2 ☐ directly「直接，じかに」　　☐ international「国際的な」

☐ news source「ニュースソース，取材源」

3 ☐ affect「に影響を与える」

─── 第5段落 ───

[1]A piece of good political news from the United States may lift the Japanese stock market. [2]News of bad weather off the coast of Peru may have unfavorable effects on the Japanese fish market. [3]News about Arab oil prices can have a particularly big impact on the Japanese economy.

[1]アメリカからの好ましい政治ニュースが日本の株式市場の値をつり上げるかもしれない。
[2]ペルー沿岸沖の悪天候のニュースが日本の魚市場に好ましくない影響を与えるかもしれない。
[3]アラブの石油価格に関するニュースが日本の経済に特に大きな衝撃を及ぼすことがある。

1 ☐ a piece of A「1つのA」　　☐ political「政治の，政治的な」

☐ lift「を上げる」　　☐ stock market「株式市場」

2 ☐ weather「天気，天候」　　☐ off the coast of A「A沖の，Aの沖合で」

☐ have a ... effect on A「Aに…な影響を与える」

☐ unfavorable「好ましくない，都合の悪い」　　☐ fish market「魚市場」

3 ☐ Arab「アラブの」　　☐ oil price「石油価格」

☐ have a ... impact on A「Aに…な衝撃を与える」　　☐ particularly「特に」

─── 第6段落 ───

[1]The Internet, linked by satellites and parabolic antennas, enables us to keep in touch with the world. [2]Raw news flies all over the world and breaks down national borders. [3]No nation can hide its own domestic events from the rest of the world or keep unfavorable international news from its people. [4]Therefore, we should learn to adapt to the present borderless century.

¹インターネットは，衛星やパラボラアンテナに繋がっていて，私たちが世界との接触を保つことを可能にしてくれている。²生のニュースが世界中を飛び回り国境を壊していく。³どの国も自国内の出来事を世界の他の国々や地域に知られないように隠しておいたり，好ましくない国際的なニュースを自国民に知られないようにしておいたりすることはできない。⁴したがって，私たちは現在の国境のない世紀に適応できるようになるべきである。

1 linked by satellites and parabolic antennas は，主語の The Internet を補足説明する過去分詞句。

　□ link「を繋げる」　　　□ satellite「衛星」　　　□ parabolic antenna「パラボラアンテナ」

　□ enable O to *do*「Oが…するのを可能にする」

　□ keep in touch with A「Aとの接触を保つ，Aと連絡を取り続ける」

2 and は，flies all over the world と breaks down national borders の2つの動詞句を結んでいる。

　□ raw「生の，未処理の」　　　□ break A down「Aを壊す，打ち破る」　　　□ national「国家の」

3 or は，hide its own domestic events from the rest of the world と keep unfavorable international news from its people の2つの動詞句を結んでいる。

　□ hide A from B「AをBから隠す」　　　□ domestic「国内の」　　　□ event「出来事」

　□ keep A from B「AをBから隠しておく」　　　□ people「国民」

4 □ therefore「したがって」　　　□ learn to *do*「…できるようになる」

　□ adapt to A「Aに適応する，順応する」　　　□ present「現在の」　　　□ century「世紀」

読みとつづりの学習

問1　読むことは書かれた言語を認識して解釈するということで，書くことは読まれる目的で言語を計画して作り出すことである。

問2　イ. given

問3　イ

問4　ウ. Nor

問5　読むことには苦労しないが，つづりでは大きな困難を抱えている人がたくさんいる。

問6　ウ. were

問7　ア. reverse

▶▶▶　**設問解説**　◀◀◀

問1　セミコロン（；）は意味的につながりが強い2つの独立した文を接続詞の代わりにつなぐことができる。ここでは，セミコロンの前後がともに to do(S) be(V) to do(C) という構造の文である。前半の and は recognize と interpret を結んでいて，language 以下が共通する目的語であり，that 以下は language を修飾する関係代名詞節である。後半の and は plan と produce を結び，language 以下が共通する目的語。▶ **Point** ㉘　so that 以下は目的を表す副詞節である。▶ **Point** ⑳
　　　□ recognize「を認識する」　　□ interpret「を解釈する」　　□ produce「を作り出す」

問2　it is felt 以下に「つづり方は自然な，あるいは自発的な過程の中で習得されると考えられている」とあるので，空所(2)を含む部分が「子供は読み方を教えられても，つづり方の正式な授業を受けることはない」となるように，イ. given を入れる。直前の but は，children are に続く taught to read と given no formal lessons ... を結んでいる。▶ **Point** ㉘

問3　counterpart は「対応するもの」という意味。its は the　attitude を指し，the attitude は前の文の「読み方を教えれば自然につづり方を習得する」という考え方のことである。したがって，「それに対応するもの」は，when 以下の「つづりを教えれば，自然に読めるようになるという考え方」である。

問4　空所の直後が is there any necessary link ... と倒置の語順になっていること

に着目する。nor「また…でない」は否定文に続いて用いられ，後ろに S V …
がくると必ず倒置が起きる。

　例　Yesterday Bob was not at the meeting, nor was he at work.
　　「昨日ボブは会議には出席していなかったし，仕事にも出ていなかった」

問5　there be S「Sがある」の構文の主語 many people を修飾する2つの関係代
　　名詞節を but が結んでいる。**➡ Point ㉘**

　　□ have no difficulty in *doing*「…するのに苦労しない」　　□ major「大きな」
　　□ handicap「困難／不利な条件」　　□ spell「正しく字をつづる」

問6　主節の述部が would be となっていることから，仮定法過去の文である。ま
　　た，次の文に but this is not so「しかし，このようにはなっていない」とあ
　　ることからも，空所(6)を含む文では，事実に反する内容を述べていると考えら
　　れる。よって，仮定法過去の条件節の形が入る。**➡ Point ㉖**

問7　前の文には「つづることに比べてずっとうまく読むことができる子供に出会う
　　ことはよくあることだ」とある。後ろには「数人の子供は，実際に，正しく読
　　むことができる単語よりも，正しくつづることができる単語のほうが多かった」
　　とあるので，アが正解。

　　ア.「逆」　イ.「間違い」　ウ.「同じこと」　エ.「事故」

Point ㉘ 共通関係

　and/but/or は文の中で対等の働きをするものを結びつける。文構造を把握す
るためには，and/but/or が何と何を結んでいるのかを，構造と文脈をふまえて
正解に読み取る必要がある。

　例1　Good cooking can disguise **but** cannot improve the quality of the
　　ingredients.
　　「優れた調理は材料の質を隠すことはできても，高めることはできない」

　but は can disguise と cannot improve を結び，the quality of the ingredients
が disguise と improve とに共通する目的語である。

　例2　Even today, only a tiny minority of the world's population has the
　　money, the time **or** the opportunity to travel far beyond the borders
　　of its own village.
　　「今日でも，自分の村の境界を越えて旅するお金と時間，機会に恵まれて
　　いる人は世界の中でもごくわずかである」

　or は the money と the time と the opportunity を結び to travel 以下は
the money と the time と the opportunity を共通して修飾している。

▶▶▶ 構文・語句解説 ◀◀◀

第1段落

¹Reading and writing have long been thought of as skills supporting each other: to read is to recognize and interpret language that has been written; to write is to plan and produce language so that it can be read. ²It is therefore assumed that being able to read implies being able to write — or, at least, being able to spell. ³Often, children are taught to read but given no formal lessons in spelling; it is felt that spelling will be learned in a natural or spontaneous process. ⁴The attitude has its counterpart in the methods of 200 years ago, when teachers carefully taught spelling, and assumed that reading would follow automatically.

¹読むことと書くことはお互いを補完する技能であると久しく見なされてきた。読むことは書かれた言語を認識して解釈するということで，書くことは読まれる目的で言語を計画して作り出すことである。²したがって，読むことができるということは，書くことができるということ，正確に言うと，正しくつづることができるということを伴うとされている。³しばしば，子供は読み方を教えられても，つづり方の正式な授業を受けることはない。つづり方は自然な，あるいは自発的な過程のなかで習得されると考えられているのである。⁴そのような考え方に対応する考え方が200年前の教え方にある。当時，教師は注意してつづり方を教えていたが，読むことは後から自然にできるようになると考えていた。

1 supporting each other は skills を修飾する現在分詞句。

　□ think of O as C「OをCとみなす」　　□ skill「技能」

2 It is therefore assumed that ... の it は形式主語で，真主語は that 以下。

　□ therefore「したがって」　　□ assume that 節「…と想定する」

　□ imply「を暗に意味する」

　□ or, at least,「正確に言うと」前に述べたことを言い換えるときに用いる。

3 it is felt that ... の it は形式主語で，真主語は that 以下。

　□ formal「正式の」　　□ spontaneous「自発的な」

4 when teachers carefully taught ... は 200 years ago を修飾する関係副詞節。

　□ attitude「考え方，姿勢」　　□ method「方法」　　□ carefully「注意して」

　□ follow「続いて起こる」　　□ automatically「自然に，自動的に」

¹Recent research into spelling errors has begun to show that things are not so simple as you might think. ²There is no necessary link between reading and writing: good readers do not always make good writers. ³Nor is there any necessary link between reading and spelling. ⁴There are many people who have no difficulty in reading, but who have a major handicap in spelling — some researchers have estimated that this may be as many as 2 percent of the population.

¹つづりの間違いに関する最近の調査によって，事態は思われているほど単純ではないことが明らかになってきた。²読むことと書くこととの間には必然的な関連はなく，うまく読める人が，必ずしもうまく書けるわけではない。³また，読むこととつづり方の間にも必然的な関連はないのである。⁴読むことには苦労しないが，つづりでは大きな困難を抱えている人がたくさんいる。こうした人は人口の2パーセントにも及ぶと推定する研究者もいる。

1 □ recent「最近の」　　□ research「調査」
　 □ not so [as] + 原級 + as S（might）think「思っているほど…でない」
2 □ link between A and B「AとBの間の関連」　　□ not always「必ずしも…でない」
4 □ researcher「研究者」　　□ estimate that 節「…と推定する」
　 □ as many as + 数詞「…も」　　□ population「人口」

¹With children, too, there is evidence that knowledge of reading does not automatically transfer to spelling. ²If there were a close relationship, children would be able to read and spell the same words: but this is not so. ³It is common to find children who can read far better than they can spell. ⁴More surprisingly, the reverse happens with some children in the early stages of reading. ⁵One study gave children the same list of words to read and to spell: several actually spelled more words correctly than they were able to read correctly.

¹また，子供に関しては，読むことに関する知識が自動的につづり方に移行するのではないという証拠もある。²もしも密接な関係があるのであれば，子供は同じ単語を読み，つづることができるであろう。しかし，このようにはなっていない。³つづることに比べてずっとうまく読むことができる子供に出会うことはよくあることだ。⁴さらに驚くべきことに，読むことを習得す

る初期段階では逆のことが起きる子供もいる。⁵ある研究では，読む単語とつづりを書く単語の同じリストを子供に渡した。数人の子供は，実際に，正しく読むことができる単語よりも，正しくつづることができる単語のほうが多かったのである。

1 With children の with は「…に関しては」という意味。that 以下は evidence と同格の名詞節。

　□ evidence「証拠」　　□ transfer to A「Aに移行する」

2 □ close「密接な」　　□ relationship「関係」

3 It is common to find ... の it は形式主語で，真主語は to find 以下。

　□ common「ありふれた，普通の」　　□ far＋比較級「ずっと…，はるかに…」

4 □ more surprisingly「さらに驚くべきことに」　　□ stage「段階」

5 to read and to spell は words を修飾する形容詞用法の不定詞句。

　□ several「数人」　　□ correctly「正しく」

動植物に対する人間の姿勢

問1　ウ

問2　(2a) ウ. what　　　(2b) エ. which　　　(2c) ア. where

問3　エ. similar to

問4　実は，サメや草を絶滅させてしまうのはよくないことである。

問5　エ. affect

問6　全世界でゴリラ以上に私たちに似ている種はいない。

▶▶ **設問解説** ◀◀

問1　play favorites は「えこひいきする」という意味の決まり文句であるが，「人間にとって有用かどうかで動植物を評価する」という第1段落全体の内容からも答えは推測できる。

問2　(2a) （　2a　）we do で is の補語となる名詞節を作ること，及び do の目的語が欠けていることから関係代名詞 what が入る。➡ Point ⑨

(2b) in （　2b　）they live で the ecosystem を修飾する関係詞節を作る。前置詞に続く関係代名詞として which が入る。

(2c) 場所を表す名詞直前に Cameroon があり，空所以下 protected までが完全な文であることから，関係副詞の where が入る。➡ Point ⑪

問3　第2段落第2・3文の内容から「人間は自分たちにより近い種をより高く評価する」ことが推測できる。したがって，正解はエ。

ア.「より優れている」イ.「より劣っている」ウ.「とは異なっている」エ.「に似ている」

問4　them は第3段落第2文後半の them を指しており，その them は同じ文の前半の sharks と grass を指している。it が形式主語で，真主語は to allow 以下。➡ Point ⑦

□ The reality is, S V ...「実は…である」　　　□ allow O to *do*「Oに…させておく」

□ become extinct「絶滅する」

問5　第4段落第4・5文の内容「サメが絶滅すると生態系のバランスが崩れて他の動物も危険にさらされる」から，動物をたくさん殺した場合，どのようなことが人間に起きるのかを考える。なお，ウの damage は人間を目的語に取らない

ことに注意。

ア.「を満足させる」イ.「の利益になる」ウ.「に損害を与える」エ.「に影響を及ぼす」

問6　否定語＋比較級＋than A で「A以上に…なものはない」という最上級相当表現になる。➡ **Point ㉙**　that 以下は species を修飾する関係代名詞節。

　□ entire「全体の，すべての」　□ be like A「Aに似ている」

Point ㉙ 最上級相当表現

　形容詞・副詞の原級や比較級を用いた構文で，最上級を用いた構文と同等の意味を表すことができる。

1．**否定語 + as [so] + 原級 + as ...「…ほど～なものはない」**

例　**No** other city in the United States is **as exciting as** New York.
　「ニューヨークほどエキサイティングな都市はアメリカには他にない」

2．**否定語 + 比較級 + than ...「…以上に～なものはない」**

例　**No** other city in the United States is **more exciting than** New York.
　「ニューヨーク以上にエキサイティングな都市はアメリカには他にない」

3．**比較級 + than any other ...「他のどの…よりも～」**

例　New York is **more exciting than any other** city in the United States.
　「ニューヨークはアメリカの他のどの都市よりもエキサイティングだ」

▶▶ **構文・語句解説** ◀◀

― 第1段落 ―

　[1]It is no secret that humans play favorites when it comes to the life or death of a species. [2]We rate animals and plants based on our use for them. [3]If they are more valuable to us dead than alive, we kill them. [4]We, as a species, see animals or plants as valuable if they give us food or medicine, or if they are beautiful or cute. [5]We often measure these values on the basis of money. [6]Perhaps it is not right to put a price on animals or plants, but that is what we do.

---

　[1]生物種の生死に関して人間がえこひいきをするということは，秘密でも何でもない。[2]私たちは，動物や植物を用途に基づいて評価する。[3]生きているよりも死んでいる方が私たちにとって価値がある場合には，私たちは殺す。[4]生物種の1つとして人間は，食物や薬を提供してくれたり，あるいは美しかったり可愛かったりすると動物や植物を価値があると見なす。[5]私たちは

しばしばお金に基づいてこういった価値を測る。⁶ひょっとすると動物や植物に値段をつけるのは正しいことではないのかもしれないが，それが私たちのやっていることなのである。

1 It is no secret that ... の It は形式主語で，真主語は that 以下。　□ humans「人間」

　□ when it comes to A「Aに関して言えば，Aということになると」　□ life「生」

　□ death「死」　□ species「(生物の)種」

2 based on 以下は「…に基づいて」という意味の分詞構文。　□ rate「を評価する」

　□ plant「植物」　□ use「用途，利用法」

3 □ more valuable to us dead than alive「生きているよりも死んでいる方が私たちにとって価値がある」

4 if they give us food or medicine と if they are beautiful or cute の2つの if 節が or で結ばれている。　□ as A「Aとして」　□ see O as C「OをCと見なす」　□ medicine「薬」

　□ cute「可愛らしい」

5 □ measure「を測る」　□ value「価値」　□ on the basis of A「Aに基づいて」

6 it is not right to put ... plants は it が形式主語で，真主語は to put 以下。what we do は関係代名詞 what が導く名詞節で「私たちがやっていること」という意味。

　□ perhaps「たぶん，ひょっとすると」　□ right「正しい」　□ put a price on A「Aに値段をつける」

────── 第2段落 ──────

¹Humans also value species if they are similar to us. ²In terms of animals, we value mammals over birds, birds over fish, fish over reptiles, and reptiles over insects. ³In addition, we value animals more than plants.

¹人間はまた，私たちに似ている場合に生物種を高く評価する。²動物に関して言えば，私たちは鳥よりも哺乳動物を，魚よりも鳥を，爬虫類よりも魚を，昆虫よりも爬虫類を高く評価する。³さらに私たちは，植物よりも動物を高く評価する。

1 □ value「を高く評価する」

2 mammals over birds 以下，A over B のパターンが4つ繰り返されて and で結ばれている。

　□ in terms of A「Aに関しては」　□ mammal「哺乳動物」　□ reptile「爬虫類」

　□ insect「昆虫」

3 □ in addition「さらに，そのうえ」

─ 第3段落 ─

¹It is very difficult to find support to save a species of shark or a kind of grass. ²People do not like sharks, and grass does not walk around or show feelings, so we think it's okay to let them become extinct.

¹サメの一種や草の一種を救おうとするために支援を得るのはとても難しい。²人はサメが好きではないし，草が歩き回ったり感情を表したりはしないので，私たちはそれらを絶滅させても構わないと思うのだ。

1 It is very difficult to find ... の It は形式主語で，真主語は to find 以下。to save 以下は目的を表す副詞用法の不定詞句。　　□ support「支持，後援」　　□ save「を救う」
□ shark「サメ」　　□ a kind of A「一種の A，A の一種」　　□ grass「草」

2 it's okay 以下は think の目的語となる名詞節。it は形式主語で，真主語は to let 以下。
□ feeling「感情，気持ち」　　□ okay「正しい，結構な」
□ let O do「O に…させる，O を…するがままにする」

- -

─ 第4段落 ─

¹The reality is, it's not okay to allow them to become extinct. ²Although sharks are not really important to humans, they are important to other animals and plants. ³They are important to the ecosystem in which they live. ⁴If they die out, the ecosystem will become unbalanced. ⁵An unbalanced ecosystem puts other animals at risk. ⁶If we kill enough animals, it will eventually affect humans as well.

¹実は，それらを絶滅させてしまうのはよくないことである。²サメは人間にはそれほど大切ではないかもしれないが，他の動物や植物にとっては大切なのだ。³サメはサメが暮らしている生態系にとっては大切なのである。⁴もしサメが絶滅したら，その生態系はバランスが崩れるであろう。⁵バランスの崩れた生態系は他の動物を危険にさらす。⁶もし私たちが十分な数の動物を殺すなら，それはいずれ人間にも影響を及ぼすであろう。

2 □ not really ...「あまり…でない」　　3 □ ecosystem「生態系，エコシステム」
4 □ die out「絶滅する」（= become extinct）　　□ unbalanced「バランスの崩れた，均衡を失った」
5 □ put O at risk「O を危険にさらす」
6 □ eventually「最終的に，やがては」　　□ ... as well「…も」

¹The gorilla is a perfect example of how humans play favorites with popular animals. ²In the entire world there is no species that is more like us than the gorilla. ³For many years, however, they were hunted for sport and for food. ⁴The gorilla was used for human entertainment, turned into a monster in movies like *King Kong*. ⁵People take their land away. ⁶Even today in Cameroon, where they are protected, people see gorillas as more valuable dead than alive.

¹ゴリラは，人気のある動物に関して人間がいかにえこひいきをしているかを表す完璧な例である。²全世界でゴリラ以上に私たちに似ている種はいない。³しかし，長年の間，ゴリラは楽しみのために，および食べるために狩猟の対象となっていた。⁴ゴリラは人間の娯楽のために利用され，「キングコング」のような映画では怪物にされた。⁵人はゴリラの土地を奪っている。⁶ゴリラが保護されているカメルーンでは今日でも，生きているよりも死んでいる方がゴリラにはより価値がある，と人々は見なしている。

1 how 以下は「いかに…か」という意味の名詞節。
　□ perfect「完璧な」　　□ example of A「Aの例」　　□ with A「Aに関して」
　□ popular「人気のある」
3 □ hunt「を狩る，狩猟する」　　□ for sport「楽しみのために」
4 turned 以下は連続・結果を表す受身の分詞構文。
　□ entertainment「娯楽」　　□ turn A into B「AをBに変える」　　□ monster「怪物」
5 □ take A away「Aを奪う」
6 □ Cameroon「＜国名＞カメルーン」　　□ protect「を保護する，守る」

語い力と成功の関係

解 答

問1　ウ. vocabulary and success

問2　asked to explain the results of this study

問3　指導者に欠かせないのは，説明したり理解したりするこの能力なのだ。

問4　ウ. higher

問5　the better your chances for success

問6　必要なのは，勉強と復習に毎日数分費やすことだけだ。

▶▶ 設問解説 ◀◀

問1　空所(1)の直後に「successful people には a strong vocabulary という共通点がある」と述べられていること，また第3段落に Another example of the connection between a strong vocabulary and success と書かれていることから，ウが正解。

　　ア.「語い力と職業」イ.「語い力と意思疎通」ウ.「語い力と成功」エ.「語い力と大学での勉強」

問2　時を表す副詞節を導く when の後ろで，S be が省略されることがある。ここでは When he was asked が When asked となっている。➡ **Point 24**

　　□ ask O to do「Oに…するように頼む」　　□ explain「を説明する」　　□ result「結果」

問3　It is ... that ～で「～するのは…だ」という意味の強調構文。ここでは makes の主語の this ability to explain and understand が強調されている。

　　➡ **Point 22**　　なお，ここの make は「を完成させる，成功させる」という意味。

　　□ ability to do「…する能力」　　□ leader「指導者，リーダー」

問4　空所(4)を含む段落は，第1文に書かれているように，「語い力と成功の関係を示すもう一つの例」を示している。したがって，語いを増強する勉強を行った学生は「より高い成績」をおさめたはずである。

問5　The＋比較級 ..., the＋比較級 ～は「…すればするほど，ますます～」という意味を表す構文。➡ **Point 30**

　　□ chance for A「Aの見込み」

問6　All S need to do is (to) do は All S V ... is ～「Sが…するのは～だけであ

る」を用いた表現で，「Ｓが…する必要があるのは～だけである」という意味。

□ spend O *doing*「Ｏ＜時間＞を…して過ごす」　　□ each day「毎日」

□ review「復習する」

Point ㉚ the ＋ 比較級

１．The ＋ 比較級 ... , the ＋ 比較級～「…すればするほど，ますます～」

例　**The more popular** he became, **the more money** he earned.

「彼は人気が出れば出るほど，多くの金を稼いだ」

２．all the ＋ 比較級（＋理由を表す表現）「(…のため)ますます～」

例　I'm **all the more inclined** to help him because he works so hard.

「彼がそんなに一生懸命がんばっているので，ますます手を貸してやりたくなる」

▶▶▶ 構文・語句解説 ◀◀◀

── 第１段落 ──

¹There is a very close relationship between vocabulary and success. ²One study showed that successful people in the United States of America always had one thing in common—a strong vocabulary. ³The study tested the vocabularies of thousands of people from all age groups and backgrounds. ⁴It was discovered that the people who had the highest salaries also had the highest vocabularies.

¹語い力と成功の間にはとても密接な関係がある。²ある調査によって明らかになったのは，アメリカ合衆国で成功をおさめた人はある１つのもの，すなわちすぐれた語い力を必ず共通して持っている，ということである。³その調査では，あらゆる年齢層のあらゆる経歴の数千人が語い力を調べられた。⁴その結果，最高の給与を得ている人は語い力も最も高い，ということがわかった。

1 □ close「密接な，親密な」　　□ relationship between A and B「ＡとＢとの間の関係」

2 □ study「調査，研究」　　□ show that 節「…ということを示す」

　□ successful「成功した」　　□ have A in common「Ａを共通点として持つ，Ａを共有する」

3 □ test「を検査する，テストする」　　□ thousands of A「数千のＡ，何千ものＡ」

　□ age group「年齢層」　　□ background「経歴」

4 It was discovered ... の It は形式主語，真主語は that 以下。　　□ salary「給料」

[1]When asked to explain the results of this study, the director of the study group said, "Words are the tools of thought. [2]We think with words, we communicate our ideas to others with words and we understand the ideas of others with words. [3]The more words we know, the better we can explain and understand. [4]It is this ability to explain and understand that makes leaders."

[1]この調査の結果を説明するよう求められたとき，調査チームの責任者はこう言った。「言葉は思考の道具である。[2]私たちは言葉を使って考え，言葉を使って他人に自分の考えを伝え，言葉を使って他人の考えを理解する。[3]より多くの言葉を知っていれば知っているほど，より上手に説明したり理解したりすることができる。[4]指導者に欠かせないのは，説明したり理解したりするこの能力なのだ」

1 □ director「責任者」　　□ tool「道具」　　□ thought「思考」
2 □ with A「Aを使って」　　□ communicate A to B「AをBに伝える」
3 The + 比較級 ... , the + 比較級〜の構文。

[1]Another example of the connection between a strong vocabulary and success can be seen in a study of university students. [2]Half of the students were put into special classes where they studied only to improve their vocabulary. [3]The other students were put into regular classes. [4]The group of students who studied only to improve their vocabulary got higher grades in their 2nd, 3rd and 4th years at the university than did the students who had been placed in the regular classes.

[1]すぐれた語いと成功との間に関係があることを示すもう一つの例は，大学生の調査に見られる。[2]学生の半分は語いを増強するための勉強しかしない特別授業に入れられた。[3]残りの学生は通常の授業に入れられた。[4]語いを増強するための勉強しかしなかった学生のグループは，大学の2，3，4年次において，通常授業に入れられた学生よりも好成績をおさめた。

2 where 以下は special classes を修飾する関係副詞節。only to do は「…するためだけに」という目的を表す副詞用法の不定詞句。
　　□ put A into B「AをBに入れる」　　□ improve「を改善する」

3 □ the other A「残りのA，その他のA」　　□ regular「通常の」

4 did the students who ... classes は倒置の語順となっている。who 以下は the students を修飾する関係代名詞節。

　　□ grade「成績」　　□ place「を置く」

- -

┌─ 第 4 段落 ─────────────────────────────────┐

　[1]The bigger your vocabulary is, the better your chances for success are at school, in your profession or your business. [2]And the best part is that you can increase your vocabulary quickly and easily, much more easily than you thought you could. [3]All you need to do is spend a few minutes each day studying and reviewing. [4]Within two or three months, you will notice a big improvement in your vocabulary power.

└───┘

　[1]語いが多ければ多いほど，学校において，職場において，あるいは事業において，成功する見込みが高くなる。[2]そして，何よりもすばらしいことに，語いはすばやく簡単に，しかも思ったよりもはるかに簡単に増強することができる，ということである。[3]必要なのは，勉強と復習に毎日数分費やすことだけだ。[4]2，3ヶ月のうちに，自分の語い力がずいぶん高まっているのに気づくであろう。

1 □ profession「職業」　　□ business「事業」

2 that you can ... は is の補語となる名詞節。

　　□ increase「を増強する」　　□ quickly「すばやく」

　　□ much＋比較級「ずっと…，はるかに…」

　　□ 比較級＋than S thought「Sが思ったよりも…」

4 □ within A「Aのうちに，A以内に」　　□ improvement「改善，向上」

158